UNDERSTANDING
Foreign Correspondence

This books is part of the Peter Lang Media and Communication list.
Every volume is peer reviewed and meets
the highest quality standards for content and production.

PETER LANG
New York • Washington, D.C./Baltimore • Bern
Frankfurt • Berlin • Brussels • Vienna • Oxford

UNDERSTANDING
Foreign Correspondence

A Euro-American Perspective of Concepts,
Methodologies, and Theories

EDITED BY Peter Gross AND Gerd G. Kopper

PETER LANG
New York • Washington, D.C./Baltimore • Bern
Frankfurt • Berlin • Brussels • Vienna • Oxford

Library of Congress Cataloging-in-Publication Data
Understanding foreign correspondence:
a Euro-American perspective of concepts, methodologies, and theories /
edited by Peter Gross, Gerd G. Kopper.
p. cm.
Includes bibliographical references and index.
1. Foreign news. 2. Foreign correspondents. 3. Journalism—
Handbooks, manuals, etc. 4. Reporters and reporting—
Handbooks, manuals, etc. I. Gross, Peter. II. Kopper, Gerd G.
PN4784.F6U53   070.4'33—dc22   2010040632
ISBN 978-1-4331-1045-0

Bibliographic information published by **Die Deutsche Nationalbibliothek**.
Die Deutsche Nationalbibliothek lists this publication in the "Deutsche
Nationalbibliografie"; detailed bibliographic data is available
on the Internet at http://dnb.d-nb.de/.

The paper in this book meets the guidelines for permanence and durability
of the Committee on Production Guidelines for Book Longevity
of the Council of Library Resources.

© 2011 Peter Lang Publishing, Inc., New York
29 Broadway, 18th floor, New York, NY 10006
www.peterlang.com

Printed in the United States of America

Table of Contents

Preface

Foreign correspondents "swoop into our imaginations with flash and gravitas," writes John Maxwell Hamilton in the introduction to his superb 2009 history of America's globetrotting reporters; "Here, in white tie, they dine with European royalty, trading *bon mots* and information. There, with sinister native guides, they slip through battle lines to find and interview rebel leaders." Fifty years hence, the next historians of the craft will no doubt have a less romantic and James Bond-like description of the new generations of foreign correspondents, no doubt be adorned with diminished sartorial splendor, and be the products of the rapid changes in the concept of foreign correspondence, technologies that feed into it, audiences and their needs, and societal and professional cultures. The gravitas, however, should not be lost given the centrality of foreign correspondence to the global economy, politics, and the general and specific relations among nations and peoples. The future of the traditional foreign correspondent is often described as glum but as métier it is not facing extinction. New varieties of foreign correspondents are already making their presence felt: The foreign correspondent, the local reporter sent abroad or using the Internet to collect foreign information of local interest, and the do-it-yourself correspondent making use of the Web disseminate information and views to anyone interested in accessing them. They are only some of the new reporters who are altering the traditional elite practice of foreign reporting. Who accesses the information disseminated by these new types of foreign correspondents, what the quality of their reports may be, what their effects might be, and how the reporters' information sources are adjusting to the faster, more complex and demanding pace of foreign correspondence is something that remains to be studies.

This collection of chapters should serve as the jump-off point for these studies, particularly those concerned with European media coverage of the United States, because they provide the historical contexts for anyone interested in knowing more about the topic of foreign correspondence and correspondents, both in the more traditional mode. It focuses on varied academic sources dealing with the nature of the work these reporters carry out, their effects and importance, and the theories that have arisen pertaining to their work. Foreign correspondence is a calling with a long recorded history, analyzed from different perspectives and considered by media scholars, political scientists and other in their respective works, many of them outlined in this book. Modern-era European media coverage of the United States, and vice versa, has the longest and most extensive history when compared to coverage of other continents by either European or American foreign correspondents.

In the last quarter of a century, changes in technology, media economics, geopolitics and rapid globalization have altered the working conditions and institutional frameworks of the foreign correspondence, and the exigencies of their profession. It was not long ago that reporting from areas out of direct reach of the Western world depended entirely on the postal service or access to a telephone landline. Clipped sentences based on sketchy notes were dictated to an editorial secretariat, and still photography and video images on tapes were faxed and mailed to their desired destinations.

Today, technology provides instant, live, multimedia access from anywhere in the world and the individual in Germany and the United States, no more so than the one in Ghana or Colombia, has come to expect a real-time front-seat view to worldwide events and information, just as if they were sitting in a lawn chair following the happenings in the backyard of their next-door neighbor. The interested public is also turning to new sources of international information, in many cases relying on photos, video materials and reports by amateurs, military personnel right out of action, and others present (or not) at an event, and the thousands of blogs and websites that allow for the disseminate of such often unedited fare. The cell phone has added yet another dimension to such reports, with its ability to have an individual send mini-notes describing observations, feelings, and fates witnessed, as well as photographs shot at the scene of events and incidents. Foreign correspondence can no longer ignore this new universe of international information that provides unprecedented and ill-understood competition. Any new analyses of the work of the foreign correspondents, begins with an understanding of their past work so that we may understand where there is continuity or discontinuity, and how and what a comparison of past, present and future may explain the success or failure of the functions that foreign correspondence has in the world.

The seed of our project was planted at a conference on European correspondents covering the United States that was held at the University of Oklahoma in Norman (followed by another conference that focused on Middle Eastern correspondents covering the United States). In subsequent years, the discussions about available sources, theories and methodologies related to foreign correspondence and its practitioners continued, culminating as it were in the decision to document these to provide some cohesive guidance to present and future scholars engaged in the subject. The invitees to the University of Oklahoma conference included European correspondents and scholars of the subject from Belgium, France, Germany, Great Britain, the Netherlands, Switzerland, and Turkey. We regret the absence of Eastern European correspondents and scholars, because the intellectual origins of the project are tied to the end of the Cold War when many of the institutionalized aspects of national politics, geopolitics, economics, cultures, and information gathering and dissemination were altered. Journalism in and from the countries liberated from the yoke of Communism had to be transformed in view of the need to understand new forms of democratic rule and the new nature of the European political, economic and cultural landscape. It was a new challenge for foreign correspondents reporting on the "new" and "old" Europe and, in fact, it was so for all foreign correspondents covering the almost 200 nations states in the world now freed of the bipolar U.S.-Soviet worlds.

The post-Communist world was more than just a new challenge for foreign correspondence and its practitioners, it was also the source of a new kind of foreign correspondence in the much revered and venerable prototype developed by Ryszard Kapuscinski, for example, created during the years of severe media censorship under Communist rule. His reports from Africa and South America described daily political and social life with a fresh and detailed acuteness that had no equal in the journalism from that continent practiced by Western foreign correspondents. It was a special approach to observing and, therefore, to describing seemingly "exotic" environments, one that was built on trust and empathy and created a different world of understanding by comparison to the event-driven classic foreign correspondence that most of us have grown up with in the Western world. This may indeed be the prescription for 21st-century foreign correspondence in a co-dependent world.

It also bears reminding the readers that technological innovations in the wake of the Cold War, even from very small countries like Estonia, changed the swiftness of international communication immensely. Thanks to Skype, for instance, the contemporary foreign correspondents can expect a direct call from his or her readers and viewers, because global calls cost next to nothing. Distances and even technological impediments have evaporated.

Our strong interest in the two formative elements of understanding foreign correspondence, i.e., the production of news and information, and the theoretical aspects of understanding foreign environments and their cultures that constitutes the core of this book, has evolved out of the overall evaluation of transatlantic research carried out to date on this topic. There is a clear and most often direct relationship between the praxis and theory of foreign correspondence, as the coverage of the Orange Revolution in the Ukraine demonstrates. After the attention-getting events at Kiev's Majdan Nezalezhnosti (Independence Square), a number of Western correspondents came together to reflect on the reporting during those tumultuous days and concluded that the impression their reports had created were responsible for the conviction in the West that the Ukrainians were almost completely united behind the "orange" leader of the opposition. Not having observed events throughout the rest of the country and, perhaps, not distancing themselves emotionally from the enthusiasm of the crowds in Independence Square, they under-reported the massive support for the incumbent and failed to report on the larger state of Ukraine's political culture. Knowing more beforehand about basic emotional aspects of foreign reporting, i.e., theoretical insight might have saved practice from pitfalls of this kind.

Another aspect of foreign correspondence that shows the merging of theoretical insight and the production practices in which foreign correspondents engage is again demonstrated in the work of Kapuscinski. In his last years, he was often referred to as "the world reporter." At a conference in Scandinavia, Kapuscinski's insights on the new dimensions of a now multipolar world, on the increased self-confidence among people in Asia, Africa and Latin America, and the fact that Europe and the United States are no longer the only points of reference, were officially cited on high-ranking diplomatic level as proof for the necessity of a multilateral change of perspectives in world diplomacy.

The marriage of theory and practice in academic research on foreign correspondents has become a necessity. It is in this spirit and with this objective that our volume is offered to readers. We believe that in this shrinking world of ours, there is no more important topic in journalism and intercultural communication that should hold the attention of scholars than foreign correspondence and the people who practice it.

We ordered the chapters of this book to provide what we considered to be a logical continuum for both the novice and experienced researcher seeking to understand foreign correspondence and their practitioners in the largest possible context. Thus, Chapter 1 endeavors to provide an inventory of the available sources on the subject and categorizes them. Chapter 2 is an overview of the theoretical perspectives employed in the study of foreign correspondence and the research methodologies employed. The political economy of foreign correspondence is considered in Chapter 3 and the research practices, methods and text in the ethnography of foreign correspondents is analyzed in Chapter 4. Chapter 5 takes a concerted look at gate keeping, agenda setting, and framing in international news and mythmaking in foreign correspondence is considered in Chapter 6. Chapter 7 explores how and when foreign correspondents are mediators and translators between cultures. The professional values, ethics and norms held (and put into practice) by foreign correspondents are examined in Chapter 8. Finally, with Chapter 9, this collection ends with a topic that does not yet offer a rich collection of data upon which to base conclusions, but is most certainly intrinsic to the present and future of foreign correspondence: the impact of the Internet on the work routines of foreign correspondents.

We thank all the contributors to this volume and the Peter Lang Publishing Group. We extend a special thank you to Natalie Manaeva and Dzmitry Yuran, graduate students in the College of Communication and Information at the University of Tennessee, for their extraordinary efforts in formatting the manuscript and readying it for publications, indexing and designing the cover; Sophie Appel, Production Editor at Peter Lang Publishing, for her guidance and help in finalizing the manuscript; and Mary Savigar, Senior Acquisitions Editor (Media and Communication Studies), for taking up this project and shepherding it to completion.

Peter Gross and Gerd G. Kopper
April 2010

The Starting Point: Studies on European Foreign Correspondents and Correspondence

Peter Gross[1]

The importance of the foreign correspondents corps stationed in the United States of America and of their work has increased commensurate with the world preeminence gained by the North American nation after World War II. Significantly, the number of foreign correspondents covering the U.S.A. had more than tripled by the mid-1970s, from a low of 300 in 1952 to over 900 in 1974; by 1985 Bonafede (Feb. 23, 1985), writing about foreign correspondents covering Washington, D.C. alone, claimed there were 550 foreign journalists in residence in the nation's capital and another 1,300 who came on short-term assignments. The Foreign Press Centers of the U.S. Department of State estimate there were as many as 3,400 foreign correspondents covering the United States in 2005, some for extended periods of time and

---

1 This chapter is based on the reports made on the state-of-the-art research available in Belgium (Els de Bens, Annelore Depres, Karin Raeymaeckers), France (Olivier Baisnée, Nicolas Harvey), Germany (Gerd Kopper, Oliver Hahn, Julia Loenendonker, Roland Schroeder), Great Britain (Rob Campbell), Spain (Laura del Rio Leopoldo), and Sweden (Frederik Miegel) on European foreign correspondents and correspondence at the "Europe's America" Conference held at the Gaylord College of Journalism and Mass Communication, The University of Oklahoma, in February 2005. My European colleagues are the true authors of this chapter. I have only facilitated their presentations here and I am indebted to them for their thorough examination of the topic in their respective countries. The American team that researched the studies on foreign correspondence and correspondents included Ralph Beliveau, Meta Carstarphen, Matt Cecil, Joe Foote, Peter Gade, Peter Gross, Jennifer Tiernan, Katerina Tsetsura, and Doyle Yoon. A comprehensive working bibliography is included at the end of this chapter; it does not pretend to be an all-exclusive bibliography.

others on short assignments.[2] Among them, 500 to 600 were European correspondents.

Today's U.S.A. appears to be a special posting for the foreign journalists.[3] Whether entirely true or not for most correspondents, and for the media
for whom they work and their audiences, as Martin Kettle of the leftist British newspaper *The Guardian* wrote after a four-year stint as the bureau chief
in Washington, D.C.,

> ...in journalistic terms America has to be treated differently from other foreign
> countries. America is incessant, relentless, and omnipresent...the defining nation of
> the modern world...America is the new Rome, and all around the globe we con-
> stantly define ourselves in its shadow. We are dazzled by it. We are in awe of it. We
> live in its shadow. We are besieged by it. We love it and hate it. (Kettle, Aug. 23,
> 2001)

The print, broadcast and news agency correspondents transmit and interpret American news events, as well as the United States' cultural, economic,
foreign affairs, legal, military, political and social profiles, to European audiences. Yet, these men and women, and their output that for better or worse
makes major contributions to the formulation of America's image abroad,
remain two of the most neglected subjects of scholarly investigation on both
sides of the Atlantic.

This is ironic given the growth of European and American media studies
in the last 30 years, the heightened importance of international cultural, economic and political relations, and the still central issues of war and peace in a
world made immeasurably more dangerous by the proliferation of weapons
of mass destruction, and new and old ideologies that are a threat to peace,
liberty and the pursuit of happiness. Few scholars, it seems, have taken seri-
ously the observation, perhaps somewhat exaggerated but nevertheless im-

---

2 This number included correspondents assigned full time to cover the U.S., those that were
send for short periods of time to cover particular stories, and American and foreign freelancers working for foreign media. According to Hess (2005, 132–33), there were 1,922
foreign correspondents in the U.S. in 2000; Western European media have the most correspondents by far in the U.S., Asian Media have the second highest number, followed by
Latin American, Middle Eastern, Eastern European, and African media.

3 The United States and Western Europe have the largest contingents of foreign correspondents assigned to them by the media of all regions, according to Cohen (Sept. 1995) who
identifies elitism and proximity—expressed in geographical, political, economic or cultural
terms—as the major determinants of foreign news reporting.

portant, made more than 60 years ago by the British political theorist Harold Laski that the problem of international news "lies at the heart of the major problems of the modern state." (Hamilton and Jenner, September/October 2003, 131–38).

Laski is not the only scholar to have posited a symbiotic relationship between the coverage of a country or of the world and the context within which national governments and peoples will accurately or inaccurately form attitudes about another country. Donald Roy Allen (1979, XV) suggested that even as far back as the 1930s, before the media became ubiquitous and instantaneous purveyors of information, news, and opinions, that the history of international relations

> ...depends at least in part on the feelings and the movement of ideas between peoples, and if we are to have a clear understanding between two nations, we must also comprehend the origins of distrusts, misunderstandings, and fears between them.

Foreign correspondence, therefore, is rightly or wrongly seen by foreign policy makers and implementers, non-governmental agencies, the public at large, scholars, and the media to play a key role in helping to minimize, even eliminate "distrusts, misunderstandings, and fears" between nations, or heightening these. To better understand the processes involved in foreign correspondence and its importance, the exigencies, pressures, problems, mentalities, perceptions, and cultural factors that underline the work of correspondents, as well as their output, should be the focus of continuous examination.

In Europe, the familial, extensive, multi-lateral ties between the United States and the Old Continent, and the strange love-hate relationship that persists, have failed to mobilize scholarly interest in the European correspondents stationed in American cities or in their work, its effects and consequences. There is nothing comparable, for instance, to the superb history of American reporting authored by Hamilton (2009). German academics, echoing their colleagues across Europe, point out that foreign correspondents are "unknown characters" whose work is virgin territory for researchers, because "The topic of foreign correspondence...is not a favorable research subject in the communications sciences" (Marten, 1989, 1; see also Dorsch, 1974/75).

In the United States, Rubin's (1979, 9) now almost 30-year-old lament that, "it is virtually impossible...to find any systematic study of how the press of any given country or region portrays the United States," is sadly still largely valid today. This despite the heightened concern with America's image abroad that is repeatedly expressed by Americans and their elected officials, pundits and academics, particularly after the Sept. 11, 2001 terrorist strikes in New York and Washington, D.C. and the response to these. The 2001 Council of Foreign Relations report, for example, concluded that the U.S. must "cultivate and improve access to foreign journalists because they are the main transmission belts for what the U.S. is doing and why."

Hess (2005, 129) reminds us that foreign correspondents and their work need to be considered in the wider context of each country's large image-making machinery; he also emphasizes that what must be acknowledge is that, "most journalistic images of the United States are produced by people who are not in the United States: editorialists, columnists, commentators, talk show hosts, headline writers, photo editors, and cartoonists in other countries." To this array of image-makers we might also add politicians, intellectuals, tourists and sundry other travelers, individuals temporarily assigned to work in the U.S., college students and so on.

The very definition of who and what a foreign correspondent is has no universal agreement and as Hamilton and Jenner (2004) remind us, a new typology of foreign correspondents is already taking shape: "The traditional elite foreign correspondent is a yardstick that no longer measures well." What this new typology of foreign correspondents may be, how their work will evolve and with what affects is still unknown and remains to be studied by scholars.

What concern us is the present. Since Sept. 11, 2001, few major American and European studies on foreign correspondents covering the United States and their work have been published; those available provide but an adumbrated view of these reporters and their special journalism.

This chapter provides and introductory overview to the major American and Western European scholarly publications that deal with the foreign correspondents covering the United States and with their work; in some cases the topic is broached as part of global examinations of foreign correspondence and correspondents.

The available literature can be placed under three related headings: (1) Roles, functions and affects of foreign correspondence, the news agencies and television coverage; (2) The foreign correspondents in the U.S.; and (3) The coverage and image of the U.S. in foreign media.

News Agencies, Television Coverage and Roles and Functions of Foreign

The general functions, roles, effects, and perspectives on European foreign correspondence are rarely examined. Three works are notable for their layered approach to the topic: the American Institute for Contemporary Germany Studies' (2004) *The Media and German-American Relations: Politics, Perspectives and Presentations in Conflict,* Strack-Zimmermann's (1987) study of the coverage of the U.S. in the Zud-Deutsche Funk, and Weigelt's edited (1986) work of the image of Germany and the U.S. in the media. A more general approach to the topic that does not single out coverage of the U.S. is Klaus' 1998 work, "Nachrichtengeographie. Themen, Strukturen und Prasentation internationaler Ereignisse: ein Vergleich."

Wilke (1986) examined the changing foreign coverage and international news flow, which has also changed over the last two decades, and Levo-Henriksson (1987) analysis compared the *New York Times* and some Scandinavian newspapers in regard to the factors influencing their foreign news coverage. For theoretical sustenance, three of the rare European works are Hafez's (2002) *Die politische Dimension der Auslandsberichterstattung,* Meier's 1984 study of the structure of foreign news coverage, and Schmidt and Wilke's (1998) content analysis of the German media's presentation of the world.

A greater number of studies on the subject of the political and policy dimensions of foreign correspondence is found in American works on the roles, functions and affects of foreign reporting on American foreign policy. For instance, Serfaty (1990), O'Heffernana (1991), Strobel (1997), Taylor (1997), Maled and Kavoori (1999), Robinson (2002), Seib (1997), Baum (2003), Levo-Henriksson (1987), Entman (2003), and Gilboa (2003 a and b), Perry (1987 and 1990), and Nye (2004) focus on media and foreign reporting as it relates to foreign policy making and the molding of domestic public opinion on international issues. In Europe, two rare studies focus on foreign news coverage: Wilke (1986) examined the changing foreign coverage and international news flow and Levo-Henriksson's (1987) analysis compared the *New York Times* and some Scandinavian newspapers in regard to the factors influencing their foreign news coverage.

Little is know about the workhorses of Europe's coverage of the U.S., the news agencies; this despite that in Germany, for example, 80 percent of international news is collected and disseminated by news agencies, and even

6 UNDERSTANDING FOREIGN CORRESPONDENCE

foreign correspondents rely heavily on information supplied by them (Zschunke, 2000, 86). According to Donsbach (2004, 140), "in Germany, as many as 90 percent of the news journalists mention news agencies as sources of orientation, between 50 and 64 percent [mention] 'leading national media.'" News agencies dominate the delivery of foreign news, more so in Europe than in the U.S., and are "the only news organizations approaching a global dimension" (Moisy, 1996, 4). This fact appears not to have sufficiently impressed European scholars and they remain largely disinterested in studying how European correspondents are covering the U.S.A. Despite the preponderant role that European news agencies play on the Old Continent, "we still know little about the dissemination of foreign news by agencies operating worldwide" (Wilke and Rosenberger, 1994, 421).

A general view of the European news agencies' foreign reporting is available in Anthony's (2000) contribution in Malek and Kavoori's edited volume, *The Global Dynamics of News: Studies in International News Coverage and News Agendas*. Unfortunately, it does not, however, specifically address the coverage of the United States. M. Kirat and D. Weaver's (1985) study of the AP, UPI and the nonaligned news agencies' coverage of foreign news is one of the few studies that focuses on the subject, partly encompassing the coverage of the U.S. The topic is also included in an in-depth study on international reporting in 29 countries that was completed for UNESCO in 1985 (Sreberny-Johammadi et al.). For those who are interested in a thorough description of news agencies, Oliver Boyd-Barrett's 1980 book is a good starting point. And in Europe, Thorein's (1972) now 34-year-old study examined the "Variations in the flow of foreign news to news agencies and newspapers in Sweden." These studies may now be nothing more than histories; foreign correspondence in general and the coverage of the U.S. by European correspondents in the 21st century may be an entirely different story, with different ramifications that in the last century.

Equally few and dated studies are available on European television news coverage of the U.S. In Germany, such works are general in scope, for example, Kunczik's 1998 description of television's coverage of the world's crisis region and Meckel's (1998) "Internationales als Restgrosse? Zur Auslandsberichterstattung in Fernsehnachrichten." In France, Marchetti's (2004) article examines the changing treatment of the "politique etrangère" on French television. Once again American studies (Adams, 1982; Larson, 1984; Ammon, 2001; Elasmar, 2003) appear to serve as models and a theoretical jump-off point for European scholars.

Other aspects related to foreign correspondents are broached in other chapters in this collection, including the ethics and ethos of foreign correspondents for which there is international interest, as evidenced in the consultative meetings from 1978 to 1983 under the auspices of UNESCO that culminated in a statement of "International Principles of Professional Ethics in Journalism."

A 1993 work (Christians, Ferre, and Fackler, 1993) raises a concern about professional values, arguing that foreign correspondence has traditionally been the province of reporters who are individualistic and wary of the ties of community. This ethos of independence may also influence how journalists explore and portray the cultures in which they work (Hafez, 2002; Herrscher, 2002; Kruckeberg and Tsetsura, 2004; John Calhoun Merrill, *The Imperative of Freedom: A Philosophy of Journalistic Autonomy,* 1979). If reporters are indeed aloof from these cultures, they may be able to report more critically, but they may also miss important elements of stories or fail to cover some stories, as indeed is suggested by Ryszard Kapuczinski, the famous Polish foreign correspondent, who suggested that, "Journalists must deepen their anthropological and cultural knowledge and explain the context of events" (Ryle, July 27, 2001). In this way too, then, the ethics of foreign correspondents are an important topic for focused study.

Europe's Foreign Correspondents in the U.S.

European scholars have neglected the study of the corps of foreign correspondents, whether their own or those of other nations, to a greater degree that their American counterparts. The pool of European and American sources on the subject can be divided into three categories: (A) biographical, autobiographical or the *memoires* of foreign correspondents, (B) sociological, and (C) anthropological and anecdotal.

A. Biographical, autobiographical, and memoires. These genres of writing on foreign correspondents have a long history. There is not enough space here to review all of the available works and, therefore, this subsection only offers a cursory introduction to a richly informative and entertaining resource pool.

Alexis de Tocqueville is arguably the first European "foreign correspondent" who covered the barely established U.S.A. and his work is without a doubt the most famous and lasting among those of his colleagues that followed in his footsteps. France's liberal and conservative press covered the American Civil War extensively, the former taking sides with the North and supporting the notions of liberty and democracy, and the latter siding with the South and hoping for the collapse of the United States (Blackburn, 1997). A latter-day de Tocqueville, Duvergier de Hauranne (1990; 1974), a young French journalist who visited the United States for eight months during the civil war, wrote two books about his visit and a couple of articles for *La Revue des Deux Mondes*.

John Graham Brooks (1909) opines that French observers of the United States after the Civil War appeared heavily influenced by stereotypes and prejudices, did not speak English well enough to communicate with Americans and followed identical itineraries: they slept in New York's Waldorf-Astoria Hotel, ate in French restaurants, visited Niagara Falls, Chicago, and "the cowboys." Furthermore, Brooks writes that these French writers were ethnocentric and made no attempt to understand the United States.

Whether other European journalists did a better job understanding and reporting the U.S. to their audiences remains open to examination. Tocqueville-like writers who, like Umberto Eco, for example, cast a critical eye on the American culture and people joined journalists such as the Italian Luigi Barzini, a graduate of the Columbia School of Journalism in the U.S., in dissecting the U.S.A. for their European audiences.[4] It was certainly the case that some of the best-known British writers, including Charles Dickens, Oscar Wilde, and Winston Churchill, offered their views of the Americans to the newspaper reading public back home. And before their visits, William Howard Russell (1863), C. Mackay (1887), and G.A. Sala (1865) reported the American Civil War to British readers, among a handful of other European correspondents. British journalist Alistair Cooke was perhaps the dean of European correspondents who for half a century told BBC listeners about the U.S. in his *Letter from America*. A small number of German journalists and early visitors to America's shores have also endeavored to record their thoughts and experiences.[5]

---

4 Umberto Eco's book, *Travels in Hyperreality* (1986), caused some ripples on both sides of the Atlantic; Luigi Barzini's long journalistic career was punctuated by two books that focused on the U.S.: *Americans are alone in the world* (1972) and *O America: When You and I Were Young* (1985).

5 See, for example, Bruce E. Burgoyne, ed., *Georg Pausch's Journals and Report of the Campaign in America*—As translated from the German Manuscript in the Lidgerwood Collection in Morristown. Heritage Books, Inc., 1996.

A few major, relatively contemporary works offer a historical perspective on the worldwide corps foreign correspondents, including those who have covered the United States, and are helpful in judging the nature and continuity or discontinuity of European foreign correspondence from the New World (Hohenberg, 1995, 1964; Knightly, 2000; Kruglak, 1974). They also provide a ready-made bibliography of the majority of biographical works by foreign correspondents and their memoirs.

B. Sociological works. Lonnendonker, Nitz, and Stamm's (2006) study on the work routines and self-perceptions of U.S. and German foreign correspondents is the most comprehensive and recent study of its kind. It is based on interviews and reviews of the limited empirical works available.

The latest published study of the foreign correspondents corps stationed in the United States is Stephen Hess's *Through Their Eyes. Foreign Correspondents in the United States* (2005).

What this survey-based work has in common with those of its predecessors is the small, 25 percent response rate (439 of 2,000) to its questionnaires that were distributed. In fact, as Hess (2005, 3) points out, "the number of respondents is still three to four times larger than that of any previous study and, for the first time, large enough to examine some correspondents by country." Hess' analysis of the survey results is augmented by 146 interviews with foreign correspondents who were queried about who they are, how they do their work, and what do they report.

In contrast, Lars Willnat and David Weaver's (2003) work was based exclusively on a mail survey that yielded 152 responses, constituting roughly 5 percent of the corps of European correspondents in the U.S.; it briefly explores the correspondents' personal backgrounds, daily routines, the perceived problems in correspondents' work, job satisfaction and other factors, journalistic role perceptions, norms and values, and perceptions of reporting practices. Willnat and Weaver's (2003) findings, as are Hess', are important because they provide a glimpse of the issues that should be studied in-depth; their conclusion that "how foreign correspondents see themselves, their very capacity to do work is shaped at least in part by the larger cultural and social environment of the United States," demands further scrutiny. Their study is perhaps the most elucidating of all similar studies on the ethos and professional role perceptions, and reporting practices of the corps of correspondents covering the United States.

Murali Nair's (1991) study, based on 117 responses from foreign correspondents stationed in the Washington, D.C. area, provides demographic data and concludes that this group of journalists has lesser access to government sources than do their American counterparts, that they rely on American news outlets for information and have little contact with American journalists. A 1983 study by Shailendra Gorpade provides similar data and conclusions, as does Hamid Mowlana's (1975) survey, which found that the "typical" foreign correspondent working in the U.S. in the mid-1970s had an interest in politics, felt a "social duty" to become a reporter, and had about 12 years of experience in journalism when assigned to the United States. Donald A. Lambert's 1956 study, "Foreign Correspondents Covering the United States," also dealt with the demographics and other characteristics of the foreign journalists covering the United States.

These studies, as well as a number of American and European doctoral dissertations and MA thesis, have substantial shortcomings—their sole reliance on survey data, for example, and the absence of follow-up interviews—that do not allow for an in-depth understanding of how the correspondents do their jobs and of the reasons underlining their performance. Furthermore, without exception, the surveys were based on limited percentages of responses vis-à-vis the large pools to be studied and, perhaps more important for the contemporary student of the topic, they are from an earlier era. Still, these examinations of the topic are benchmarks for future studies.

In Europe, the scarcity of specific works dealing with European correspondents who report on the U.S. serves as a stark contrast in scholarly foci vis-à-vis what American scholars have published. General descriptions of correspondents from various European nations, such as Augusto Assia's (1966) article and Felipe Sahagun's (1986) book on Spanish foreign correspondents, and Nicole Gysin's (2000) book on German-language Swiss correspondents, provide a brief peek into the demographics and professional habits of these reporters.

Early Swedish studies deal with the image of the U.S. during the Cold War and the coverage of American foreign and domestic politics (Block, 1976). But the fundamental role of the foreign correspondents in producing and transmitting the "news" from the U.S. to Sweden is largely neglected and the research available on Swedish correspondents station in North America is at best scant. That is also true for the other European countries, with the exception of Germany where scholars are now engaged in substantial sociological research about their foreign correspondents.

Most of the available works examines the whole of the German journalistic corps serving abroad, the majority of whom are located in other Western European nations, with the second and third largest contingent covering North and South America, respectively (Junghanns, 2004; Seifert, 2002; Nafroth 2002; Gysin, 2000). In the U.S., most German correspondents are stationed on the East Coast (Marten, 1989) and "associate and fraternize with the intelligentsia" (Irmler, 1987). Aside from demographic data, German scholars have recorded the self-perception of German foreign correspondents and have found some significant differences in the definition of journalism and its practice—from the notion of objectivity to informational vs. opinion journalism and investigative vs. advocacy journalism—between correspondents covering developing and developed countries (Junghanns, 2004; Gysin, 2000; Nafroth, 2002; Kunczik, 1998).

Most German foreign correspondents see themselves as experts on the countries they cover, a perception that is seemingly averred by the increasing number of books these correspondents publish about the countries or regions they covered for a news outlet (e.g., Bertram, 1996; Lojewski, 2001 and 1991; Ruge, 2000; Scholl-Latour, 2004 a, b, c; Wickert 2004 and 2003). And, finally, in Britain, the paucity of scholarly sources on British correspondents and their work in the United States is astonishing considering the close ties, including media ones, and the shared language between the two countries.

C. Anthropological/anecdotal works. Ulf Hannerz's (2004) anthropological study of the world's foreign correspondents as producers and organizers of "flows of culture" is the latest and most wide-ranging examination of the lives and work of the unique individuals that venture into foreign lands. He combines anthropological methods with what he calls multi-local fieldwork to gain insight in the culture or "tribe" of correspondents and into the actual circumstances under which they conduct their daily work. He examines the careers of the correspondents and what he describes as the continued ordering of the activity of the reporters assigned to a foreign land, and their room to maneuver and improvise. Hannerz's contribution to the literature in the field is a fun read and one can glean some answers to a short list of important questions that go to the heart of getting a bird's eye view of this select group of individuals.

There are a number of other recent works on foreign correspondents, both scholarly and journalistic, available on both sides of the Atlantic. Wagner's (2001) work is a general study of correspondents for general circulation media and the news agencies; Matussek (1995) specifically examines the German correspondents and their coverage of the United States.

Dom Bonafede's article (Feb. 23, 1985), John C. W. Suh's (1972) work, Bob Warner's 1960 description of "The Foreign Press in the U.S.A," and Thomas B. Littlewood's (1972) article are a small sampling of works that described how the foreign press sees America. Ronald Rubin (December 1964) focused on a subgroup, the foreign correspondents who cover the work of the United Nations.

Swedish correspondents' experiences of news reporting from the Gulf War concludes that the allied countries' media got a dominant position compared with media from other countries; CNN was especially privileged and the reporting strengthened home opinion in the allied countries, while human suffering got a rather marginal position in the reports. The same study asserts that the Swedish media did not differ much from other Western media regarding how they depicted war participants.

No American study has to date replicated Rubin's (1979) seminal work on foreign correspondents covering the United States, which not only dealt with the correspondents but also with their work. Chapter IV, for example, detailed the many lenses through which European correspondents viewed the U.S. foreign policies and racial struggles, in particular, influenced by the national interests of their respective countries. Such a "nationalist" approach to covering the U.S. was specifically true of the French press, notes Rubin; the British press covered mostly American domestic news; Germany and Italy were more admiring of the U.S. and perceived it important to their protection. Rubin's study should be replicated.

The Coverage and Image of the United States in the Foreign Media

The study of the coverage of the United States and the image put forth by the European correspondents offers the richest pool of knowledge available among all the other subtopics related to European correspondents and their work. In Belgium, France, Germany, Great Britain, and Sweden, the focus on America's image in their media and of the nature of reporting on the United States takes center stage in their studies on foreign correspondence.

From the early studies of how the European press covered certain American economic crisis, to more recent studies of the same issue, the

French press's coverage of the 1987 economic downturn appears to have been more dramatic than was its coverage in 1929.[6] According to Le Texier's (2001, 141) analysis of the main national French newspapers and magazines in the 1990s, French journalists covering the economic growth in the U.S. first attempted to find the flaw that would lead to the recession and wrote about an artificial growth and a "speculative bubble." When the economic growth continued, the French media no longer denied the legitimacy of the trend but began emphasizing its negative impact on the "laisses-pour-compte" (casualties of prosperity) (Le Texier, 2001, 142).

Le Texier's (2001) study reveals what may be the paroxysm of the anti-American approach, replicating to a great extent the American Left's anti-Americanism. The 2000 U.S. presidential elections were condemned for their anti-democratic nature; America, the French press reported, was near deca-dence and George W. Bush was depicted as a "moron."

The British's media's coverage of the United States appears to be less tainted by an anti-American approach, partly because these seems to be an affinity between British and American journalism, despite some salient dif-ferences (Chalaby, 1996; Doyle and Getler, 2004), and there is a close work-ing relationship between the media in the two countries, at least according to some researchers (Goldfarb, 1999; Tunstall and Machin, 1999).

This connection between British and American media outlets may be unique and, if true to the extent claimed by some, puts a new twist to the coverage of the U.S. and to the relationship between British and American media and political elites. Goldfarb's (1999) snapshot of the channels of communication raises a question regarding the extent to which the British media's U.S.-reporting agenda is set along Transatlantic lines. That is not to say that there are no major differences between British and American jour-nalism, as is clearly demonstrated in the coverage, for example, of the Clin-ton-Lewinski scandal picked up by a British press that is more partisan and more competitive than the American press.

Understanding how British journalists report from the U.S. means under-standing their journalistic culture; and that means understanding the tabloid culture. Not all British journalists work for the tabloid press but it can be ar-gued that the more positive aspects of tabloid culture are at the heart of all British journalism. The BBC interviewer Jeremy Paxman, perhaps hinted at

---

6 See, for example, Ralf Schor (1995) and Nancy L. Green, (1988).

the tabloid swagger implicit even in his brand of serious journalism when he told a researcher:

> They [U.S. journalists] have a constitutional role and are part of the process. We don't suffer from the canker of self-importance. The media should be outside casting a quizzical and critical eye. Journalism is still a disreputable trade here. I reach for my revolver when I hear about it as a profession. We are not the same as lawyers, doctors and accountants. (Lo, 1998)

This journalistic culture that makes a priority of human interest, exclusives, sensationalism and irreverence over neutrality, balance, accuracy, completeness and fairness, might help us understand how British journalists manage to break stories in the U.S., rather than just following them, as is often the plight of foreign correspondents. They then find themselves contributing to the American news agenda as well, as the recent example of *The Observer* breaking the story about U.S. spying on the United Nations illustrates (Bright, 2003).

Researchers in Britain have a problem: an indifference to or even suspicion of and hostility to academia. In the Britain, journalists and those who study them do not have a long or fruitful shared history upon which relationships might have been built. The relationship may be easier where scholars encounter the quality/broadsheet press, but any study that ignores the tabloids will present but a fractional picture of how the U.S. is reported in Britain.

The U.S. occupies a major place in foreign news reporting in Belgium and the substantial presence of this news is also manifest in news that does not directly concern the U.S., as foreign news reports are often structured around regions or countries, such as Israel, the Palestinian territory, and Iraq, for example, where the U.S. has direct interests. A number of Belgian scholars have investigated to what extent and in what light the Belgian media present news from the U.S. or items that are closely related to it.

Deprez and Hauttekeete (2003) combine quantitative content analysis with qualitative data to examine the coverage four Flemish newspapers (*De Standaard, De Morgen, Het Laatste Nieuws,* and *Het Volk*) give to the attack on the World Trade Center Sept. 11, 2001 and conclude that the newspapers presented the U.S. in a positive light.

The American presidential elections are a popular subject for analysis in the Belgian media, as they are in other European media, and a number of researchers have examined how the representation of the American presidential elections and the candidates has developed over the years (Terryn, 2001). Modern political marketing, De Bens et al. (1990) argue, is a Belgian import from the U.S. and election campaigns have been increasingly approaching their American counterparts both in style and content, thanks in large measure to the hiring of media advisors.

The study of Belgian media coverage of the war in Afghanistan yielded the following conclusions:

- President Bush is frequently cited as a source, as are other American spokespersons, whereas Afghan political figures are cited only a handful of times (Caers, 2002).
- *De Standaard, De Morgen,* and *Het Laatste Nieuws* reported positively on the U.S. intervention in Afghanistan and the negative statements on the U.S. are too few to offset its positive image; Afghans are hardly ever cited as sources and themes such as humanitarian aid or the reconstruction of the country are seldom mentioned (Van de Spiegle, 2004).

Media coverage of the U.S. in Sweden is extensive, particularly during periods when the Americans are involved in a major international conflict, but also on such topics as major American political and economic issues, popular culture and sports. One would expect, therefore, a substantial body of research on how Swedish media represent the U.S. to their audiences. That is not the case, however.

The existing studies are mostly qualitative and quantitative content analysis of the coverage afforded certain big events. Hvtfelt and Mattsson (1992) analyzed how the Gulf War was dramatized in the Swedish media, the language the journalists used, how the major participants in the conflict were characterized, and the impact of CNN on how the war was perceived by journalists from all over the world. In a volume edited by Nordlund (1992), a variety of issues related to the Gulf War are being examined: Bobert discusses how sources were chosen; Kisch and Lundgren compare how the Gulf War and the Balkan conflict were covered; and Johannesson shows how heroes and villains were easily identifiable in the narrative of reports, turning the war into something reminiscent of a fairy tale.

Nord and Stromback (2002) studied how the major Swedish news media reported on the first five days after the attacks on the World Trade Center and on the first five days of the war in Afghanistan and found that elite U.S. sources were the dominant sources of information for the Swedish media.

Nordstrom (2002) also found American sources to be dominant in Swedish reports and that the events in New York were dramatized in the same fashion as the Gulf War was, with abstract presentations of good and evil. The dominance of American sources was also recorded in the study of the Iraq war coverage in the Swedish media, as was the dramatization and staged nature of news reports (Nordstrom, 2003; Nord et al., 2003).

Looking at the coverage of the U.S. in the Gulf War, the attack on the World Trade Center, the wars in Afghanistan and Iraq, Swedish researchers found that the image of the U.S. in the Swedish media was predominantly positive, partly because of the predominance of American sources in Swedish reporting and American news companies from which the Swedish media get their materials.

For a general and now historical description of the international coverage of nations, one should consult Buchanan and Contril (1953) and their comprehensive study of *How Nations See Each Other* and for a more recent view of the image of the U.S. in the world, Kamalipour's 1999 work is fairly comprehensive.

References

Adams, Benjamin Pettengill (1939). *You Americans: Fifteen Foreign Correspondents Report Their Impression of the United States and Its People*. NY and London: Funk and Wagnalls.

Adams, William C. (1982). *Television Coverage of International Affairs*. Norwood, NJ: Ablex Publishing Corp.

Allen, Donald Roy (1979). *French Views of America in the 1930s*. London and NY: Garland Publishing.

Alleyne, Mark D. (1995). *International Power and International Communication*. NY: St. Martin's Press.

American Institute for Contemporary German Studies (AICGS) (Jan. 9, 2004). The Media and German-American Relations: Policies, Perspectives and Presentations in Conflict. Conference proceedings. Accessed on Jan. 17, 2004 <www.aicgs.org/events/2004/01092004summary.shtml>

Ammon, Royce J. (2001). *Global Television and the Shaping of World Politics*. Jefferson, NC and London: McFarland & Company, Inc., Publishers.

Assia, Augusto (1966). "Los corresponsales en el extranjero" (Correspondents in foreign lands) in *Enciclopedia de Periodismo*, 4th Edition. Barcelona: Noguer, 369–84.

Bartholy, Heike (1992). "Barrieren in der interkulturellen Kommunikation (Barriers in intercultural communication)." In Horst Reimann, ed., *Transkulturelle Kommunikation und Wletgessellschaft: Zur Theorie und Pragmatik globaler Interaktion*. Opland, Wiesbaden: Westdeutscher Verlag, 174–191.

Barzini, Luigi (1985). *O America: When You and I Were Young*. NY: Viking Press.

Barzini, Luigi (1972). *Americans are Alone in the World*. Library Press.

Baum, Matthew A. (2003). *Soft News Goes to War: Public Opinion and American Foreign Policy in the New Media Age*. Princeton, NJ: Princeton University Press.

Bertram, Jurgen (1996). *Asien, atemlos. Als Korrespondent in einer fremden Welt*. (Asia, Breathless. Correspondent in a strange world). Hamburg, Germany: Rasch and Rohring.

Blackburn, George M. (1997). *French Newspaper Opinion on the American Civil War*. Westport, CT: Greenwood Press.

Block, E. (1976). *Amerikabilden I svensk dagspress* 1948–1968 (The Image of America in the Swedish Daily Press, 1948–1968). Lund, Sweden: CWK Gleerup.

Bobert, J. (1992). "Att redovisa kallor." In I. R. Nordlund, ed., *Svenskarna, medierna och gulkriget. Psykologiskt forsvar rapport nr. 158–1*. Stockholm: Styrelsen for psykologiskt forsvar.

Bonafede, Dom (Feb. 23, 1985). "Foreign Correspondents in Washington Tell the World About the United States," in *National Journal*: 421–25.

Boyd-Barrett, Oliver and Terhi Rantanen, eds. (1998). *The Globalization of News*. Thousand Oaks, CA: Sage Publication

Boyd-Barrett, Oliver (1980). *The International News Agencies*. London: Sage Publications.

Bright, M. (March 9, 2003). "Nation Shall Speak Peace Unto Nation." *The Observer*. Accessed April 20, 2003. <www.observer.guardian.co.uk/iraz/story/0%2C12239%2C9 10725%2C00.html>

Brogan, Patrick (Jan. 1, 1989). *Foreign Correspondents in Washington*. Occasional Paper. Washington, D.C.: Media Studies Project, Woodrow Wilson International Center For Scholars.

Brooks, John Graham (1909). *As Others See Us*. NY: The MacMillan Company.

Buchanan, William and Hadley Contril (1953). *How Nations See Each Other: A Study in Public Opinion*. Urbana: University of Illinois Press.

Burchett, Wilfred (1969). *Passport: An Autobiography*. Melbourne, Australia: Thomas Nelson.

Caers, F. (2002). *De Amerikaanse strijd tegen het internationale terrorisme: een inhoudsanalyse van het Amerikaans-Afghaans conflict in Vlaamse kranten*. Unpublished MA thesis: Gent: Communication Sciences Department, Gent University.

Merrill, John C. (1979). *The Imperative of Freedom: A Philosophy of Journalistic Autonomy*. New York: Hastings House.

Chalaby, J. (1996). "Journalism as an Anglo-American Invention." *European Journal of Communication*, 11(3):303–26.

Cohen, Bernard C. (1963). *The Press and Foreign Policy*. Princeton, NJ: Princeton University Press.

Cohen, Y. (September 1995). "Foreign Press Corps as an Indicator of International News Iinterest." *Gazette*, 56(2): 89–100.

Cooper, Kent (1942). *Barriers Down*. NY: Farrar and Rinehart.

Council on Foreign Relations (2001). The Report of an Independent Task Force on Public Diplomacy. Washington, D.C.

Demers, David (2002). *Global Media. Menace or Messiah*. Cresskill, NJ: Hampton Press.

Deprez, A. and L. Jauttekeete (2003). "Courage under Fire: How did the Flemish Newspapers Cover the September 11 Attack?," Unpublished paper. Gent: Communication Sciences Department, Gent University.

Des Champs, Jean (1990) *The Life and "Memoirs secrets" of Jean Des Champs (1707–1767): Journalist, minister, and man of feeling.* Amsterdam/London: Holland University Press

Dizard Jr., Wilson P. (2004). *Inventing Public Diplomacy. The Story of the U.S. Information Agency.* Boulder and London: Lynne Rienner Publishers, Inc.

Donsbach, Wolfgang (1995). "Lapdogs, Watchdogs and Junkyard Dogs." *Media Studies Journal* 9(4): 17–30.

Donsbach, Wolfgang and Bettina Klett (1993). "How Journalists in Four Countries Define a Key Term of Their Profession," in *Gazette* 51:53–83.

Dorsch, Petra E. (1974/75). "Isolationismus oder Weltoffenheit? Zur Auslands-berichterstattung von "Boston Globe" und "Suddeutscher Zeitung," (Isolationism or Opening to the World? The foreign correspondence of the Boston Globe and the Suddeutscher Zeitung). *Publizistik, 00000* 19/20, 901–924.

Doyle, L. and M. Getler (May/June 2004). "Brits vs. Yanks. Who Does Journalism Right?" in *Columbia Journalism Review,* 3:44–49.

Duvergier de Hauranne, Ernest (1990). *Les Etats-Unis pendant la guerre de Secession. Recit d'un journaliste francais* (The United States during the war of secession. The story of a French journalist). Paris: Calmann-Levy.

Duvergier de Hauranne, Ernest (1974). *A Frenchman in Lincoln's America—Huit mois en Amerique: Lettres et notes de voyage, 1884–1865* (Eight months in America: Travel letters and notes, 1884–1865). Chicago: Lakeside Press.

Eco, Umberto (1986). *Travels in Hyperreality.* New York: Harvest Books.

Ehrenreich, Susanne (2005). *Images of the USA in Selected German Newspapers After 9/11 and During the Wars in Afghanistan and Iraq.* University of Regensburg. Thesis (unpublished).

Eigenmann, Simone Eva (2003). *Die Informationsführung der amerikanischen Regierung im Irakkrieg 2003 und die Auswirkungen auf die Schweizer Korrespondenten.* Journalism Institute of Fribourg University, Switzerland. Thesis (unpublished).

Eisendrath, Charles R. (November/December 1976). "Foreign Correspondence: A Declining Art." *Columbia Journalism Review,* 14–18.

Elasmar, Michael G., ed. (2003). *The Impact of International Television. A Paradigm Shift.* Mahwah, NJ and London: Lawrence Erlbaum Associates, Publishers.

Elliot, Kim A. (Autumn 1981). "World News Coverage of U.S. and International Broadcasters." *Journalism Quarterly* 58: 444–49. Reprinted in L. John Martin and Ray Eldon Hiebert, eds., *Current Issues in International Communication* (1990). NY: Longman.

Entman, Robert M. (2004). *Projection of Power. Framing News, Public Opinion, and U.S. Foreign Policy.* Chicago and London: The University of Chicago Press.

Ehrenreich, Susanne (2005). *Images of the USA in Selected German Newspapers after 9/11 and During the Wars in Afghanistan and Iraq.* University of Regensburg, Germany. Thesis (unpublished).

Evans, S (2001). "The Biggest Story of my Life." *British Journalism Review,* 12(4): 7–11.

Faure, Christine and Tom Bishop (1992). *L'Amerique des Français* (The America of the French). Paris, France: Editions Francois Bourin.

Fischer, Heinz Dietrich (1992). *Outstanding International Press Reporting: Pulitzer Prize Winning Articles in Foreign Correspondence, Vol. 1*: 1928–45; Vol. 2: 1946–62; Vol. 3: 1963–1977; Vol. 4: 1978–1989. Berlin, Germany: Walter De Gruyter, Inc.

Fraser, Matthew (2003). *Weapons of Mass Distraction. Soft Power and American Empire.* NY: Thomas Dunne Books (St. Martin's Press).

Gagnon, Paul A. (1962). "French Views of the Second American Revolution." *French Historical Studies* 2 (4): 430–449.

Ghorpade, Shailendra (1984). "Foreign Correspondents Cover Washington for World." *Journalism Quarterly* 61:667–71.

Ghorpade, Shailendra (1984). "Foreign Correspondents and the New World Information Order." *Gazette* 33:203–08.

Ghorpade, Shailendra (Autumn 1984). "Sources and Access: How Foreign Correspondents Rate Washington, D.C." *Journal of Communication* 34(4):32–40.

Giffard, C. Anthony (2000). "International Agencies in Global Issues: The Decline of the Cold War News Frames." In Abbas Malek and Anandam P. Kavoori, eds., *The Global Dynamics of News: Studies in International News Coverage and News Agendas.* Samford, Conn: Ablex Publishing Corp.

Gilboa, Eytan (2003). "Television News and U.S. Foreign Policy: Constraints of Real-Time Coverage." *The Harvard International Journal of Press/Politics* 8(4): 97–113.

Gilboa, Eytan (2003). *Media and Conflict: Framing Issues, Making Policy, Shaping Opinions.* Transnational Publishers, Inc.

Ginneken, Jaap van (2003) *Understanding Global News. A Critical Introduction.* London, Thousand Oaks, New Delhi: Sage Publications.

Golan, Guy and Wayne Wanta (2003). "International Elections on US Network News: An Examination of Factors Affecting Newsworthiness." *Gazette* 65 (1): 25–39.

Goldfarb, M. (1999). "Our President/Their Scandal: The Role of the British Press in Keeping the Clinton Scandals Alive." The Joan Shorenstein Center on the Press, Politics and Public Policy. Working paper series, Harvard University, 2000–5.

Gramling, Oliver (1940). *AP, The Story of News.* NY: Farrar and Rinehart.

Green, Nancy L. (1988) "Leçons d'octobre 1929, 1987. La presse française et americaine face aux deux crises boursières" (Lessons of October 1929, 1987. The French and American press confront the two stock exchange crisis). *Esprit*, 143: 91–110.

Gysin, Nicole (2000). *Der direkte Draht zur Welt? Eine Untersuchung uber Auslandskorrespondentinnen und-korrespondenten Deutschschweizer Printmedien* (The instant line to the world? An examination of foreign correspondents for the German-Swiss print media). Berner Texte zur Medienwissenschaft, 5. Bern, Switzerland: Institut fur Medienwissenschaft, Universitat Bern.

Hafez, Kai (2002). *Die politische Dimension der Auslandsberichterstattung* (The political dimension of foreign correspondence). Bd.1: Theoretische Grundlagen. Baden-Baden: Nomos Verlagsgesellschaft.

Hafez, Kai (2002). "Journalism Ethics Revisited: A Comparison of Ethics Codes in Europe, North Africa, the Middle East, and Muslim Asia." *Political Communication,* 19, 225–250.

Hamilton, John Maxwell (2009), *Journalism's Roving Eye. A History of American Foreign Reporting*. Baton Rouge: Louisiana State University Press.
Hamilton, John Maxwell and Eric Fenner (September/October 2003). "The New Foreign Correspondence." *Foreign Affairs 82* (5):131–38.
Hamilton, John Maxwell and Eric Fenner (2004). "Redefining Foreign Correspondence." *Journalism, 5*(3): 301–21.
Hannerz, Ulf (2004). *Foreign News. Exploring the World of Foreign Correspondents*. Chicago and London: The University of Chicago Press.
Hannerz, Ulf (April 24, 2001). "Among the Foreign Correspondents: Reflections on Anthropological Styles and Audiences." Presented at the Vega Symposium on The Death and Rebirth of Anthropology, in honor of Sherry B. Ortner. Swedish Society for Anthropology and Geography, Stockholm.
Hannerz, Ulf (2002). "Among the Foreign Correspondents: Reflections on Anthropological Styles and Audiences." *Ethnos 67* (1): 57–74.
Hartwell, Dickson (1952). *Off the Record: The Best Stories of Foreign Correspondents*. NY: Doubleday.
Heil, Jr., Alan L. (2003). *Voice of America. A History*. NY: Columbia University Press.
Herrscher, R. (2002). "A Universal Code of Journalism Ethics: Problems, Limitations and Proposals." *Journal of Mass Media Ethics*, 17:277–289.
Hess, Stephen (1996). *International News & Foreign Correspondence*. Washington, D.C.: The Brookings Institution.
Hess, Stephen (2005). Through Their Eyes. Foreign Correspondents in the United States. Washington, D.C.: Brookings Institution.
Hess, Stephen and Robert L. Stevenson (1997). "International News and Foreign Correspondents." *The American Journal of Sociology*, 102(4): 1187–89.
Hohenberg, John (1995). *Foreign Correspondence: The Great Reporters and Their Times*. Syracuse, NY: Syracuse University Press (first published in 1964).
Hull, Dana (Oct. 1, 2004). "Foreign Relations: Journalists from Afar Are Dismayed by the End of a Convention Mainstay." *American Journalism Review, 26*(5): 20–22.
Hvitfelt, H. and K. Mattsson (1992). Gulfkriget—Ett mediedrama I tva akter (The Gulf War—A Media Drama in Two Acts). *Psykologiskt forsvar* 158–2. Stockholm, Sweden: Styrelsen for psykologiskt forswar.
Irmler, Gerhard (1987). "A Look at the Image of the United States in the West German Media." In Lore Amlinger, ed., *Deutschland und die Vereinigten Staaten—Gefahr und Hoffnung im Wander der gegenseitigen Wahrnehmung*. Chapter 5. Stuttgart: Akademischer Verlag.
Jarausch, Konrad (1986). "Das amerikanische Deutschlandbild in drei Jahrhunderten" (The Image of Germany in America in three centuries). In Klaus Weigelt, ed., *Das Deutschland and Amerikabild: Beitrage zum gegenseitigen Verstandnis beider Volker*. Forschungsbericht 50. Konrad-Adenauer-Stiftung. Melle: Knoth Verlag.
Jervis, Robert (1970). *The Logic of Images in International Relations*. NY: Columbia University Press.

Johannesson, K. (1992). "Kriget som en saga." I R. Nordlund, ed., *Svenskarna, medierna och gulkriget*. Psykologiskt forsvar rapport nr. 158–1. Stockholm: Styrelsen for psykologiskt forsvar.

Johnston, Karin L. (2004). *Clashing World and Images: Media and Politics in the United States and Germany*. AICGS Issue Brief <www.aicgs.org/Publications/ PDF/issuebrief1.pdf>

Joseph, Franz M., ed. (1959) *As Other See Us: The United States Through Foreign Eyes*. Princeton, NJ: Princeton University Press.

Junghanns, Kathrin (2004). *Merkmale und Selbstverstandnis von deutschen Auslandskorrespondenten*. Technische Universitat Ilmenau. Thesis (unpublished).

Kamalipour, Yahya R. (1999). *Images of the U.S. Around the World*. Albany: State University of New York Press.

Kamps, Klaus (1998). "Nachrichtengeographie. Themen, Strukturen und Prasentation internationaler Ereignisse: ein Vergleich" (The geography of news. Themes, Structures and Presentation of international events: a comparison). In Klaus Kamps and Miriam Meckel, eds., *Fernsehnachrichten* (Television News) Oplanden, Germany: Westdeutscher Verlag, 275–94.

Kellerman, Barbara (Spring 1990). "Henry Brandon, Special Relationships: A Foreign Correspondent's Memoirs from Roosevelt to Reagan." *Presidential Studies Quarterly*, 20(2): 390–91.

Kettle, Martin (August 23, 2002). "Monica to George, It's a Foreign Land." *The Guardian Weekly*, www.guardian.co.uk/Gweekly/Story/0,540855,00.html Accessed Dec. 17, 2004.

Kevin, Deidre (2003*). Europe in the Media. A Comparison of Reporting, Representation, and Rhetoric in National Media Systems in Europe*. London and Mahwah, NJ: Routledge.

Kirat, M. and D. Weaver, (1985) "Foreign News Coverage in Three Wire Services: A Study of AP, UPI, and the Nonaligned News Agencies Pool." *Gazette*, 35(1): 31–47.

Kisch, C. and C. Lundgren (1992). "Gulfen och Balkan." I. R. Nordlund, ed., *Svenskarna, medierna och gulkriget*. Psykologiskt forsvar rapport nr. 158–1. Stockholm: Styrelsen for psykologiskt forsvar.

Knight, A. (1998). "Covering the Global Village: Foreign Reporting on the Internet." *Media Asia*, 25(2), 71–77.

Knight, T. (Jan. 21, 1978). "Now Newsmen Become Pawns of Superpowers." *U.S. News & World Report,* 226: 35–36.

Knightly, Phillip (2000). *The First Casualty. The War Correspondent as Hero and Myth-Maker from the Crimea to Kosovo*. Baltimore, MD: The Johns Hopkins University Press (first published in 1975).

Kruckeberg, Dean, and Katerina Tsetsura (2004). "International journalism ethics." In A.S. de Beer and J.C. Merrill, eds., *Global Journalism*, 4th edition. Pearson A & B, pp. 84–92.

Kruglak, Theodore E. (1974) *The Foreign Correspondents: A Study of the Men and Women Reporting for the American Information Media in Western Europe*. Westport: Greenwood Press.

Kunczik, Michael (1998). "'Seiltanzer' in Krisengebieten—Auslandsberichterstattung im Fernsehen," (Tightrope walker in crisis regions—foreign correspondence in television) *Sudfunkhefte*, 25:317–43.

Lambert, Donald A. (Summer 1956). "Foreign Correspondents Covering the United States." *Journalism Quarterly*, 33: 349-356.

Large, David (1990). "America in the consciousness of the Germans." In Frank Krampikowski, ed., *Amerikanischens Deutschlandbild und deutsches Amerikabild in Medien und Erziehung*. Baltmannsweiler: Padag.Verl. Burgbucherei Schneider, 199–210.

Lennon, Alexander T.J. (2003). *The Battle for Hearts and Minds. Using Soft Power to Undermine Terrorist Networks*. Cambridge, MA and London: The MIT Press.

Le Texier, Emmanuelle (2001). "L'Amerique au miroir de la presse francaise (1998–2000)," (America in the mirror of the French press, 1998–2000). *The Tocqueville Review/La Revue Tocqueville*, 22(1): 139–61.

Levo-Henriksson, Ritva (1987). Foreign News Coverage and Factors Influencing It; Focusing on the New York Times and Some Leading Nordic Newspapers. In *Ten Years of American Studies: The Helsinki Experience*. Helsinki, SHS: 313–332.

Littlewood, Thomas B. (April 15, 1972). "Exploring the Mysterious West, or How the Foreign Press Corps Sees America." *Saturday Review*, 23–27.

Lo, J. (1998). "In Britain, Rottweilers Attack." *Nieman Reports*, 52(3). Accessed April 20, 2005 <www.nieman.harvard.edu/reports/98-3Nrfall98/Lo_Britain.html>

Lojewski von, Wolf (2001). *Live dabei*. Bergisch-Gladbach, Germany: Lubbe Verlag.

Lojewski von, Wolf (1991). *Amerika: Der Traum vom neuen Leben* (America: The dream of a new life). Hamburg, Germany: Hoffmann and Campe.

Lonnendonker, Julia, Pia Nitz and Sonja Stamm (2006), Transatlanting Reporting. Work Routines and Self Perceptions of US and German Foreign Correspondents. *Working Papers in International Journalism*. Editor Gerd G. Kopper. Bochum/Freiberg, Germany: projectverlag.

Lubman, Sarah (Spring 1992). "Foreign Correspondents." *Nieman Reports XLVI*(1):55–58.

Mackay, C. (1887). *Thought the Long Day*. London, UK: n.p.

Maisonrouge, J.G. (1981). "Regulation of International Information Flows." *The Information Society*, 1(1): 17–30.

Malek, Abbas, ed. (1997). *News Media and Foreign Relations. A Multifaceted Perspective*. Norwood, NJ: Ablex Publishing.

Malek, Abbas and Anandam P. Kavoori, eds. (2000). *The Global Dynamics of News: Studies in International News Coverage and News Agendas*. Stamford, Conn.: Ablex Publishing Corp.

Manheim, Jarol B. (1994). *Strategic Public Diplomacy and American Foreign Policy. The Evolution of Influence*. NY and Oxford: Oxford University Press.

Marchetti, D. (2004) "La fin d'un Monde? Les transformations du traitement de la 'politique etrangere' dans les chaines de television francaises grand public. In L. Arnaud and C. Guionnet, eds., *Les frontieres du politique*. Rennes, France: Presses Universitaire de Rennes, pp. 49–77.

Marten, Eckhard (1989). *Das Deutschlandbild in der amerikanischen Auslandsberichterstattung: Ein kommunikationswissenschaftlicher Beitrag zur Nationenbildforschung* (The German image in American foreign correspondence). Wiesbaden: Dt.-Univ.-Verlag, 1.

Matussek, Matthias (1995). "Die wahrheit uber Amerika. Der Job des Auslandskorrespondenten (The Truth about America. The job of the foreign correspondents)." *Der Spiegel* (Special Edition), 94.

Meckel, Miriam (1998). "Internationales als Restgrosse? Zur Auslandsberichterstattung in Fernsehnachrichten." In Klaus Kamps and Miriam Meckel, eds., *Fernsehnarchrichten-Strukturen, Funktionen, Prozesse.* Opland, Germany: Westdeustcher Verlag, 257–274.

Medientenor (2004). "Supermacht mit Imageproblemen: Das negative Amerikabild erschwert eine sachliche Auseinandersetzung." In *Medientenor Forschungsbericht* Nr. 143. Bonn, Germany: Medientenor.

Meier, Werner A. (1984). *Ungleicher Nachrichtenaustausch und fragmentarische Weltbilder. Eine empirische Studie uber Strukturmerkmale in der Auslandsberichterstattung.* Frankfurt and NY: Lang.

Mikich, Sonia (2003). "Geistige Provinzialisierung: Eine Zustandsbeschreibung." In Claudia Cippitelli and Axel Schwanebeck, eds., *Nur Krisen, Kriege, Katastrophen? Auslandsberichterstattung im deutschen Fernsehen* (Dokumentation der 21. Tutzinger Medientage). Munich, Germany: Verlag Reinhard Fischer, 117–127.

Milligan, Susan (Sept. 1, 1995). "A post Cold War Chill (East European Journalists' Difficulty in Obtaining Visas to Western Countries." *American Journalism Review,* 17(7): 15–16.

(August 1992). "Mirror on the U.S. Will Voters Stick with Bush? Foreign Correspondents Offer their Predictions." *World Press Review,* 39(8): 38.

Moisy, Claude (1996). *The Foreign News Flow in the Information Age.* Discussion Paper D-23. Cambridge, MA: The Joan Shorenstein Center on the Press, Politics and Public Policy, Harvard University.

Morrow, Edward R. (1967). *In Search of Light.* NY: Knopf.

Mowlana, Hamid (Summer 1975). "Who Covers America?" *Journal of Communication,* 25 (3): 87–91.

Mowlana, Hamid (1985). *International Flow of Information. A Global Report and Analysis.* Paris, France: UNESCO (Reports and Papers on Mass Communication, Nr. 99).

Nacos, Brigitte L, Robert Y. Shapiro and Pierangelo Isernia, eds. (2000). *Decision Making in a Glass House: Mass Media, Public Opinion, and American and European Foreign Policy in the 21ˢᵗ Century.* Lanham, MD: Rowman & Littlefield Publishers.

Naemeka, Tony and Jim Richstad (1980/81). "Internal Control and Foreign News Coverage—Pacific Press Systems." *Communication Research* 7–8:

Nafroth, Katja (2002). Zur Konstruktion von Nationenbildern in der Auslandsberichterstattung: Das Japanbild der deutschen Medien im Wandel. *Aktuelle Medien—und Kommunikationsforschung,* Vol. 15. Munster, Germany: LIT.

Nair, Murali (1991). "The Foreign Media Correspondent: Dateline Washington, D.C." *Gazette* 48: 59–64.

Napoli, Jim (2001). "American Journalism and the French Press." *Harvard International Review on Press/Politics,* 6(2): 104–112

Nohrstedt, S.A. (1992). "Utanfor Poolerna. Svenska korrespondenters erfarenheter av nyhetsrapporteringen fran kriget vid Persiska viken." I. R. Nordlund, ed., *Svenskarna, medierna och gulkriget*. Psykologiskt forsvar rapport nr. 158–1. Stockholm: Styrelsen for psykologiskt forsvar.

Nord, L., A. Shehata and J. Stromback (2003). *Fran osaker kalla*. Stockholm, Sweden: Styrelsen for psykologiskt forsvar.

Nord, L. and J. Stromback (2002). *Tio dagar som skakade varlden—En studie av mediernas beskrivningar av terrorattackerna I USA och kriget I Afghanistan hosten 2001* (Ten Days that Shook the World—A Study of the Media's Descriptions of the Terror Attacks in the US and the War in Afghanistan, Autumn 2001). Stockholm, Sweden: Styrelsen for psykologiskt forswar.

Nordlund, Roland, ed. (1992). *Svenskarna, medierna och gulfkriget* (The Swedes, the Media and the Gulf War). Psykologiskt forswar 158–1. Stockholm, Sweden: Styrelsen for psykologiskt forswar.

Nordstrom, Gert Z. (1992). "Krigsutbrottet och de svenska massmediebilderna." In R. Nordlund, ed., *Svenskarna, medierna och gulkriget*. Psykologiskt forsvar rapport nr. 158–1. Stockholm: Styrelsen for psykologiskt forsvar.

Nordsrom, Gert Z. (2002). *Terrorkriget I kvallspressen* (Terror War in the Evening Press). Stockholm, Sweden: Styrelsen for psykologiskt forswar.

Nordsrom, Gert Z. (2003). *Irakkrigets andra dag. En jamforelse mellan SVT och tidningspressen den 21 mars 2003*. Stockholm: Styrelsen for psykologiskt forsvar.

Nye, Jr., Joseph S. (2004). *Soft Power. The Means to Success in World Politics*. NY: Public Affairs.

O'Heffernan, Patrick (1991). *Mass Media and American Foreign Policy: Insider Prespective on Global Journalism and the Foreign Policy Process*. Norwood, NJ: Ablex Pub.

Pan, Zhongdang and Gerald M. Kosicki (1993). "Framing Analysis: An Approach to News Discourse." *Political Communication*, 10: 55–75.

Pedelty, Mark (1995). *War Stories: The Culture of Foreign Correspondents*. New York: Routledge.

Pedelty, Mark (1996). "War Stories: The Culture of Foreign Correspondents." *Media, Culture & Society* 18(3): 509– 511

Perlmutter, David D. (1998). *Photojournalism and Foreign Policy: Icons of Outrage in International Crisis*. Westport, CT: Praeger Publishers.

Perry, David K. (1987). "The Mass Media and Audience Generalization About Groups of Foreign Countries." *World Communication*, 16(2): 101–120.

Perry, David K. (1987). "The Image Gap: How International News Affects Perceptions of nations." *Journalism Quarterly*, 64:416–33.

Perry, David K. (1990). "News Reading, Knowledge About, and Attitudes Toward Foreign Countries." *Journalism Quarterly*, 67:353–58.

Portes, Jaques (1990). *Une fascination reticente. Les Etats-Unis dans l'opinion francaise 1870–1914* (A hesitant fascination. The United States in French Public Opinion 1870–1914). Nancy, France: Presses Universitaires de Nancy.

Reese, S. (2001). "Understanding the Global Journalist: A Hierarchy-of-Influence Approach." *Journalism Studies*, 2(2): 173–187.

Reigosa, Carlos Gonzales (1997). "El periodista en su circunstancia." *Alianza Editorial*, 117–145.

Remond, Rene (1962). *Les Etats-Unis devant l'opinion française 1815–1852* (The United States in front of French public opinion 1815–1852). Paris, France: Armand-Colin.

Reston, James (1967). *The Artillery of the Press: Its Influence on American Foreign Policy.* NY: Harper & Row.

Riffe, Daniel (1984). "International News Borrowing: A Trend Analysis." *Journalism Quarterly,* 61:142–48.

Riley, T. (May 1981). "Access to Government Information: An International Perspective." *Journal of Media Law and Practices,* 2(1):92–100.

Robinson, Piers (2002). *The CNN Effect. The Myth of News, Foreign Policy and Intervention.* London and NY: Routledge.

Roger, Philippe (1996). *Rêves & cauchemars americains. Les Etats-Unis au miroir de l'opinion publique française* (1945–1953). Paris: Septentrion presses universitaires.

Rubin, Barry (1977). *International News and the American Media.* Beverly Hills and London: Sage.

Rubin, Barry (1979). *How Others Report Us: America and the Foreign Press.* Beverly Hills: Sage.

Rubin, Ronald (December 1964). "The U.N. Correspondent." *Western Political Quarterly* 17, 531–615.

Ruge, Gerd (2000). *Sibirisches Tagebuch* (Siberian Diary). Munich, Germany: Droemer Knaur.

Rupnik, Jacques (1988). "Anti-Americanism and the Modern: The Image of the United States in French Public Opinion." In John Gaffney, ed., *France and Modernization.* London: Avebury, 189–205.

Rupnik, Jacques and Muriel Humbertjean (1986). "Image(s) des Etats-Unis dans l'opinion publique" (The Image(s) of the United States in Public Opinion). In Jacques Rupnik and Muriel Humbertjean, *L'Amérique dans les têtes. Un siècle defascination.* Paris: Hachette, 101–23.

Russell, William Howard (1863). *My Diary North and South.* Boston and New York: T.O.H.P. Burnham.

Ryle, John (July 27, 2001), "Tales of Mythical Africa. Tropical baroque, African reality and the work of Ryszard Kapuscinski." *Times Literary Supplement.*

Sahagun, Felipe (1986). *El Mundo fue Noticia. Corresponsales espanoles en el extranjero. La informacion internacional en Espana* (The World in News. Spanish foreign correspondents. International information in Spain) Madrid: Fundacion Banco Exterior.

Sala, G.A. (1865). *My Diary in America in the Midst of War.* London, UK: Tinsley Brothers.

Schenk, Birgit (1987). "Die Struktur des internationalen Nachrichtenflusses. Analyse empirischer Studien" (The Structure of International News Flows. The Analysis of Empirical Studies). *Runkfunk und Fernsehen,* 35: 36–54.

Schmidt, Dagmar and Jurgen Wilke (1998). Die Darstellung des Auslands in den deutschen Medien. Ergebnisse einer Inhaltsanalyse 1995" (The presentation of the world in the German media. The results of a content analysis 1995). In Sigfried Quandt and Wolfgang Gast, eds., *Deutschland im Dialog der Kulturen. Medien—Images—Verstandigung.* Schriften der DguK Nr. 25, Konstanz 1998: 167–181.

Schneider, Beate (1984). "Von Friedensfursten und Brandstiftern: Massenmedien und Internationale Politik." *Publizistik,* 29: 303–323.

Scholl-Latour, Peter (2004a). *Der Fluch des neuen Jahrtausends.* Munich, Germany: Goldmann.

Scholl-Latour, Peter (2004b). *Weltmacht im Treibsand* (Superpower in Quicksand). Berlin, Germany: Propylaen.

Scholl-Latour, Peter (2004c). *Kampf dem Terror—Kampf dem Islam?* Berlin, Germany: Ull-stein-TB.

Schor, Ralf (1995). "Les Etats-Unis vus de la droite. La crise americaine de 1929 à travers la presse française de droite." *Revue d'histoire moderne et contemporaine*, 42(4): 568–76.

Seib, Philip (1997). *Headline Diplomacy. How News Coverage Affects Foreign Policy.* London and Westport, CT: Praeger.

Seib, Philip (2002). *The Global Journalist. News and Conscience in a World of Conflict.* Lanham, MD and Oxford: Rowman & Littlefield Publishers.

Seifert, Katrin (2002). *Die Konstruction Ruslands in der deutschen Auslandsberichterstattung 1985–1995: Studien zum Wandel der deutschen Wahrnehmung Ruslands* (The presentation of Russia in German foreign correspondence 1985–1995: Studies of the change in German perceptions of Russia). Berlin, Germany: Wissenschaftlicher Verlag.

Seldes, George (November 1934). "The Poisoned Springs of World News." *Harpers,* 169(1014): 719.

Serfaty, Simon, ed. (1990). *The Media and Foreign Policy.* NY: St. Martin's Press.

Smith, Phillip (Sept. 18, 1995). "War Stories: The Culture of Foreign Correspondents." *In These Times 19*(21–22): 46.

Snyder, L. and R. Morris, eds. (1949). *A Treasury of Great Reporting.* NY: Simon & Schuster.

Sreberny-Mohammadi, Annabelle, Kaarle Nordenstreng, Robert Stevenson and Frank Ugboajah, eds. (1985). *Foreign News in the Media: International Reporting in 29 Countries.* Final Report for UNESCO by the International Association for Mass Communication Research. Paris, France.

Sreberny-Mohammadi, Annabelle, Dwayne Winseck, Jim McKenna & Oliver Boyd-Barrett (1997). *Media in Global Context. A Reader.* London, NY, Sydney and Auckland: Arnold.

Strobel, Warren P. (1997) *Late-Breaking Foreign Policy: The News Media's Influence on Peace Operations.* Washington, DC: United States Institute of Peace.

Strack-Zimmermann, Marie-Agnes (1987). "Bilder aus Amerika: Eine zeitungswissenschaftliche Studie uber die USA-Berichterstattung im Zweiten Deutschen Fernsehen (ZDF)" (Pictures from America: A journalism study of the coverage of the USA in the ZDF television channel). *Kommunikationswissenschaft und Publizistik* (Communication Sciences and Journalism), Vol. 9. European University Studies, Series XL. Frankfurt am Main, Bern, NY, Paris: Peter Lang.

(Sept. 29, 1934). "Study of International News Urged." *Editor & Publisher,* 67(2):9.

Suh, Chung Woo (1971). *The Socio-Professional Aspects of Foreign Correspondents in the United States: A Study of International Communications.* Ph.D. Dissertation, University of Minnesota.

Suh, John C.W. (April 15, 1972). "126 Foreign Correspondents Talk about Work in America." *Editor & Publisher,* 27–30.

Sullivan, Stacy (Spring 1999). "New Wars, New Correspondents." *Media Studies Journal,* 13 (2): 84–90.

Sussman, Gerald and John A. Lent, eds. (1991). *Transnational Communications. Wiring the Third World.* London, Newberry and New Delhi: Sage Publications.

Sussman, Leonard R. (Oct. 2, 1978) "Who Rules the World's News?" *Newsweek,* 15.

Szu, J., David Weaver, V. Lo, C. Chen, and W. Wu (1997). "Individual, Organizational and Societal Influences on Media Roles Perceptions: A Comparative Study of Journalists in China, Taiwan and the United States." *Journalism & Mass Communication Quarterly* 74(1): 84–96.

Taylor, Philip M. (1997). *Global Communications, International Affairs and the Media since 1945.* NY and London: Routledge.

Terryn, A. (2001). *Van Kennedy vs Nixon tot Bush vs Gore: de rol van de media bij presidentsverkiezingen.* Unpublished MA thesis. Gent: Communication Sciences Department, Gent University.

Thorein, Stig (1972). *The News Cycle: Variations in the Flow of Foreign News to News Agencies and Newspapers in Sweden. Beredskapsnaimnden foir Pskologiskt Foirsvar.*

Tuch, Hans N. (1990). *Communicating With The World. U.S. Public Diplomacy Overseas.* NY: St. Martin's Press.

Tulloch, Christopher David (2004). *Corresponsales e el extranjero: mito y realidad.* Pamplona: Eunsa.

Tunstall, J. and D. Machin (1999). *The Anglo-American Media Connection.* NY: Oxford University Press.

UNESCO (1985) Foreign *News in the Media: International Reporting in 29 Countries.* Reports and Papers on Mass Communication, Nr. 93. Accessed June 10, 2006 at unesdoc.unesco.org/images/0006/000652/065257eo.pdf

Van den Spiegle, A. (2004). *Analyse van de berichtgeving over internationale conflicten in de Vlaamse dagbladpers. Casestudy de US vs Afghanistan.* Unpublished MA thesis. Gent: Communication Sciences Department, Gent University.

Wagner, Martin (2001). *Auslandskorrespondent/in für Press, Radio, Fernsehen und Nachrichtenagenturen* (Foreign correspondent for the Press, Radio, Television and News Agencies). Munich, Germany: List Verlag.

Warner, Bob (May 28, 1960). "The Foreign Press in the U.S.A." *Editor & Publisher,* 66.

Weigelt, Klaus, ed. (1986) *Das Deutschland und Amerikabild: Beitrage zum gegenseitigen Verstandnis beider Volker* (The Image of Germany and America: Contributions to the Mutual Understanding of Both Peoples). Forschungsbericht 50. Konrad-Adenauer Stiftung. Melle: Knoth Verlag.

Weisenien, John (Oct. 23, 1982). "Intimidation—Overseas Reporters Facing Intimidation." *TV Guide,* 1543:4–10.

Wickert, Ulrich (2003). *Zeit zu Handeln?* (Time for Act?). Munich, Germany: Heyne.

Wickert, Ulrich (2004). *Alles Uber Paris* (Everything about Paris). Hamburg, Germany: Europa Verlag.

Wilhelm, John (Spring 1963). The Re-appearing Foreign Correspondent: A World Survey." *Journalism Quarterly* 40: 147–68.

Wilke, Axel (1994). *Die Volker und gemeinschaftsrechtliche Schutz der Tatigkeit des Auslandskorrespondenten* (The protection of foreign correspondents in international law). Berlin: Springer Verlag.

Wilke, Jurgen (1986). "Auslandsberichterstattung und internationaler Nachrichtenflus in Wandel" (Changing Foreign Coverage and International News Flow). *Publizistik,* 31(1–2): 53–90.

Wilke, Jurgen (1987). "Foreign News Coverage and International News Flow over Three Centuries." *Gazette,* 39:147–180.

Wilke, Jurgen and Bernhard Rosenberger (1994). "Importing Foreign News: A Case Study of the German News Service of the Associated Press." *Journalism Quarterly,* 71(2): 421–432.

Willnat, Lars and David Weaver (2003). "Through Their Eyes. The Work of Foreign Correspondents in the United States." *Journalism,* 4(4):403–22.

Wolfsfeld, Gadi (2004). *Media and the Path to Peace.* Cambridge, UK: Cambridge University Press.

Yoder, A. (1981). "The News Media and One World." *Political Communication and Persuasion,* 1 (3):217–230.

Yu, Frederick T.C. (Fall/Winter 1981/82). "International News Flow Problem—What Can Be Done about It?" in *Journal of International Affairs,* 35: 189–97.

Yu, Frederick T.C. and John Luter (Spring 1964). "The Foreign Correspondent and his Work." *Columbia Journalism Review:* 5–12.

Zschunke, Peter (2000). *Agenturjournalismus: nachrichtenschreiben im Sekundentakt* (Agency journalism: newswriting in a split second). Konstanz: UVK Medien.

CHAPTER 2

Theoretical Perspectives and Research Methods in Studies of Foreign Correspondence

Charles C. Self

U.S. Studies

Most of what we think we know about foreign correspondents is gleaned from biographies, autobiographies, personal accounts, and fictional representations of the life and work of those covering other countries for citizens back home. A mythology of foreign correspondence permeates popular thinking and finds its way into professional accounts.

While a number of systematic, scientific attempts to describe the work of the foreign correspondent have been attempted, in the United States, these have been mostly descriptive studies derived from surveys of those doing work as foreign correspondents or have been content analysis studies attempting to examine what is being reported by the foreign correspondents. Some have been studies of related social processes such as foreign policy formation or news agency. The most cohesive theoretical work has been in international news flow. That work has tended to focus at the macro-organizational or cultural level and has not focused on foreign correspondence itself. A very few studies have been theoretically grounded attempts to find underlying concepts and principles governing foreign correspondence.

Most of the direct scientific approaches to foreign correspondence have used survey methodologies, personal interviews, and content analysis. Much of it has focused on correspondents posted abroad from major industrialized countries. Some has focused on foreign correspondents posted in the United States. Systematic studies aimed at developing theoretical propositions testing specific hypotheses or searching for generalizable principles have been more rare.

The Foreign Correspondence Surveys

A series of surveys have attempted to describe foreign correspondents and their work over the years. In the United States these surveys may be divided into two types: those focused on correspondents working in the United States for news organizations abroad and those focused on correspondents from the United States posted overseas.

Foreign Correspondents Stationed in the United States

Six major studies have produced a picture of correspondents stationed in the United States reporting for news organizations abroad.

The earliest of these studies was conducted by Lambert in 1956. Lambert patterned his study on an earlier study of U.S. Washington correspondents conducted by Leo Rosten in 1937. That study was published as *The Washington Correspondents* in 1937. Rosten interviewed 154 of the correspondents from around the Unitd States working in Washington, D.C., in order to develop his questionnaires. He then selected 203 correspondents from the 497 listed in the 1936 *Congressional Directory*. He sent two biographical questionnaires and received 127 replies to the first and 107 to the second. He was able to learn a great deal about the demographic characteristics, work habits, and attitudes of the domestic Washington correspondents. This study of American reporters in Washington became the model for most of the studies that followed of foreign correspondents in the U.S. and of U.S. correspondents abroad.

Following Rosten's example, Lambert sent a mail questionnaire in 1956 to 250 foreign correspondents from abroad posted in the United States and received 111 responses. He believed this to be a census of all correspondents in the U.S. at that time. He found that most correspondents were male (105 and only 6 female) with a median age of 44, about half had a college education (53.6%) and 21% had graduate work, and 80.9% were married. Most worked in New York or Washington, D.C., and three quarters were full-time. They were experienced journalists (18 years, 9 as foreign correspondents) and wrote mostly about foreign affairs. Three quarters said their writing was "interpretative" while 20% said it was "straight factual." The correspondents depended most heavily upon American news media as sources and most were relatively happy in their work. They found access to sources to be adequate (63.1%) or excellent (34%).

This survey set a pattern for studies of foreign correspondents that has varied little over the intervening years.

The second major study was conducted in 1970 and published in 1972 by John Chung Woo Suh as research for a doctoral dissertation (1971) at the University of Minnesota. It used a mail survey to collect demographic data from 126 foreign correspondents selected from 870 individuals stationed in the United States and probed for information about their professional attitudes and work habits. It also found that most of the correspondents were male, experienced and well educated.

The third study was by Hamid Mowlana in 1975. He used a mail survey sent to 300 foreign correspondents (one-third of those listed by the USIA's Foreign Press Center) and received 103 responses. He found that most of these correspondents had entered journalism for "serious" reasons, were experienced, produced five to seven stories a week and stayed mostly in Washington or New York. He found that the correspondents were well educated, socially unorthodox, liberal, and had strong professional connections.

The fourth study was conducted in 1983 by Shailendra Ghorpade, who published her results in a report and three separate articles that appeared in 1983 and 1984. The mail survey study was of 480 Washington-based foreign correspondents (317 replied). One report focused on the demographics, organization characteristics, media use, and views of the foreign correspondents about U.S. media reporting of foreign news. It confirmed much of what had been found in earlier studies. A second report focused on how accessible various sources in the United States were to these correspondents. It compared the responses of first world and third world correspondents about the sources they use in their reports and their perceptions of how available government officials were to them. It found that foreign correspondents, especially those from developing countries, had trouble gaining access to U.S. government sources.

The fifth study was by Nair in 1991. His mail survey was sent to a skip sample of Washington-based foreign correspondents and netted a 46 percent return rate for 117 usable responses. He examined demographic and social characteristics of the correspondents and their perceptions of New World Information Order issues. As with earlier studies, he found that the correspondents were mostly male, older, well educated, experienced and mostly focused on economic and political news. He found that the correspondents filed 2,000 to 4,000 words per week, had little access to officials and depended heavily on "borrowed news" from U.S. media. Respondents perceived a bias in U.S. media against the third world as alleged in NWIO debates.

The sixth and most recent study, "Through Their Eyes: the Work of Foreign Correspondents in the United States," was done by Willnat and Weaver in 2003. They reported the results of a study of 1,550 U.S. based foreign Correspondents (152 completed responses for a 17 percent response rate). They sent a mail questionnaire that asked about 1) professional background, 2) work routines, 3) perceived problems in the correspondents' work, 4) job satisfaction and job factors, 5) journalistic role perceptions, and 6) perceptions of reporting practices. The authors compared the results with those of an earlier Weaver and Willnat study of U.S. journalists (1996). Much of what they found confirmed findings from earlier studies. However, they reported "a growing dissatisfaction with access to official news sources in the United States," more women among the foreign correspondents in their study, and a greater dependency upon new technologies reshaping some of the work of these correspondents. They found significant differences in demographics, job satisfaction, practices, problems, and role perceptions of foreign correspondents when compared to local U.S. journalists. The foreign correspondents were older, better educated, and more experienced than the U.S. journalists. They also reported more job satisfaction and were news junkies. They reported problems with access to government officials, placed more emphasis on "analysis and interpretation" in their reporting, and said they were helping develop the "intellectual and cultural interests" of their readers through their reporting.

These findings are surprisingly consistent across time. They do reveal a growing dissatisfaction with access to U.S. government officials and they do reveal larger numbers of women in more recent studies.

U.S. Foreign Correspondents Posted Abroad

Similarly, a series of eight descriptive studies in the United States have been made of foreign correspondents from U.S. media who are stationed abroad.

The first of these was a pair of studies by John William Maxwell conducted in 1954 and published in *Journalism Quarterly* in 1956. The main study was a survey sent to full-time American and foreign national correspondents for American newspapers, news agencies, news magazines, radio and television throughout the world. It elicited 209 responses, thought to be 55 to 60 percent of all correspondents. It found that nearly one-third of the

American correspondents had at least one foreign-born parent and that two-thirds came from business or professional families. A third were from the Northeast United States and nearly one-third grew up in cities. More than 60 percent held college degrees and 90 percent had attended college. A third spoke at least one language besides English and 80 percent received their first post abroad before they were 35 years old.

The second was Kruglak's 1955 study of the European correspondents for American news media. At the time, three-quarters of all U.S. media correspondents worldwide were posted to Europe. Kruglak compiled his population from the accredited correspondent lists of press offices and international organizations based in Europe. It included full-time employees who were U.S. citizens, foreign nationals working for U.S. media, and part-time stringers working for U.S. media. He sent a questionnaire to the entire list of 396 correspondents and received 277 usable responses. He followed this with extensive personal interviews with 96 of the correspondents. He found that most of the correspondents were in their 20s and 30s, three-quarters of them had higher education degrees, and almost all (98.1 percent) were men. The book provides a detailed account of the work, environment, characteristics, and attitudes of the correspondents.

The third study was Wilhelm's 1963 article, which attempted to compile a comprehensive list of all foreign correspondents working for U.S. media in the early 1960s. His report, titled "The Reappearing Foreign Correspondent: A World Survey," was assembled with the help of nearly 100 people in 84 countries. He found 515 American correspondents writing for U.S. media and an additional 718 local nationals working for U.S. Media. The number of Americans was 75% higher than the 293 correspondents reported in 1950 by Russell Anderson in an essay in the *Michigan Alumni Quarterly* lamenting the decline of foreign correspondence after World War II. Wilhelm found that the correspondents were not distributed evenly across the globe. They were concentrated in London (with 73 American correspondents), Rome (49), Paris (48), and Tokyo (47). However, he reported finding 14 new news bureaus in Latin America and 20 new correspondents in Africa. He still found many areas of the world with no correspondents or bureaus.

The fourth study was Leo Bogart's survey of 503 active members of the Overseas Press Club conducted in 1967 (206 completed responses). The sample included correspondents from around the world and was balanced for Europe and non-Europe-based journalists. The survey focused on demographics and lifestyle, but also include questions about the attitudes of the journalists toward their jobs and their profession. The study found that the respondents were experienced, well-educated, older reporters. Most correspondents (80 percent) reported that they worked in an established bureau with several other correspondents. About 20 percent said they maintained close relationships with nationals (more in Europe than in other areas). Most correspondents said that they communicated well in the language of the country in which they are stationed. Two of three said they personally read the local press. Most correspondents believed that they had less freedom of access where they worked than did foreign correspondents working in Washington. Most of the correspondents expressed satisfaction with their jobs as foreign correspondents.

The fifth survey was Kliesch's 1991 study, "The U.S. Press Corps Abroad Rebounds: A 7th World Survey of Foreign Correspondents." This was a census of more than 1,700 journalists representing U.S. news media abroad. Kliesch found that the number of U.S. correspondents abroad had jumped from 676 to 1,734 and that they were more widely distributed around the world. He also found more women correspondents—25 percent up from 10 percent he found in an earlier study in 1975.

The sixth study was the major 1996 survey and content analysis made by Steven Hess and his team for the Brookings Institute. The book-length report is an excellent compilation of facts about foreign correspondents, what gets covered, the backgrounds of the foreign correspondents, the technologies they use and the problems they face. It was based on two types of data: 1) surveys of the content of articles over three years (1978, 1988, and 1992) in three newspapers and two news magazines, and of the transcripts of the evening broadcasts of CBS, ABC, and NBC from the Vanderbilt Television News Archive, and 2) 404 responses to a 10-page mail questionnaire sent to journalists (U.S. media and Reuters) outside the United States in 1992 and 370 additional responses to that questionnaire from former foreign correspondents. The study also included a good deal of data for context drawn from secondary sources.

The seventh major report was Weaver's 1998 book *The Global Jouranlist: News People Around the World*. This is a compilation of 23 separate reports of mostly surveys of journalists in different countries around the world. It is roughly a replication of the Weaver and Wilhoit study *American Journalist* in 19 countries. While it is not focused specifically on the work of foreign correspondents, it does provide a useful context for understanding the work of foreign correspondents across the globe.

The eighth and most recent study was Wu and Maxwell's 2004 survey of 354 foreign correspondents drawn from 4,825 names of U.S. foreign correspondents collected over 20 years by Dr. Ralph Kliesch of Ohio University. The survey looked at 1) demographics, 2) working requirements, 3) impacts of the Internet, and 4) differences in news topics between U.S. and foreign nationals representing U.S. media abroad. The researchers found that more foreign nationals are being used by U.S. media; more experience among the foreign correspondents than among typical domestic U.S. reporters; a well-educated corps; more non-white correspondents (though still low); that foreign nationals are paid less than U.S. correspondents; a still Euro-centered corps; more Internet-oriented correspondents; less travel; fewer hours per week of work; lower morale (and a perception that editors want too light a fare); and a perception that new topics are needed in coverage.

These findings give a wonderfully evocative description of foreign correspondents in the U. S. and of U. S. correspondents abroad. They offer insights into their lives, their background, their work conditions, and their attitudes. However, the studies are mainly descriptive and lack a strong theoretical focus that might develop the constructs and principles needed to understand how foreign correspondence works and what drives the work of the foreign correspondent.

Studies Supporting Knowledge about the Work of Foreign Correspondents

These survey methods for directly describing foreign correspondents and their work have been supplemented by studies that indirectly add to our understanding of foreign correspondents and how they work.

These studies fall into three categories: content analysis studies, studies of news agencies, and studies of international news flow.

Content Studies

Many of the important content studies have some overlap with the surveys; they are grounded in empirical methods that are primarily descriptive. Most are based on content analysis of print or broadcast media. A few examples illustrate this type of research.

One example of this kind of study is John Adams' "What the Foreign Correspondent Does for a Newspaper's Readers," published in *Journalism*

Quarterly in 1966. The study examined the impact on coverage of a newspaper's having its own correspondent. It was a study of three pairs of newspapers—one newspaper in each pair had its own foreign correspondent, the other did not. The study examined newspaper content to see if this made a difference in coverage. It found that having a foreign correspondent resulted in more foreign news stories, of greater length, with more specific sources, dealing with more significant topics and more background and analysis.

A second example of these content studies is study published in 1981 by Kim Andres Elliott. It was a content tracking study focused on counting the number of news items on two major U.S. broadcasts and five international broadcasts originating outside the U.S., but aimed at U.S. audiences. The study found that over a five-day period, 55 world news items not covered by the U.S. media would have been heard on these foreign broadcasts.

Daniel Riffe published a third example of content studies in *Journalism Quarterly* in 1984. The research was a content analysis of the *Chicago Tribune* and the *New York Times* taken from an 11-year period. It found a shrinking international news hole and slightly growing use of news "borrowing" (from locally produced news reports in local media overseas or in government media reports). However, the percent of such borrowing was small (less than 20 percent) and correspondents were thought to exercise judgment in selecting the items to borrow.

In 1988, Catherine Cassara looked at U.S. newspaper coverage of human rights in Latin America from 1975 to 1982 by analyzing the content of four prestige newspapers in the United States. She found that Carter administration policies emphasizing human rights did seem to significantly increase coverage of human rights issues, supporting an agenda-building theory of foreign news coverage.

The Stephen Hess book (1996) described earlier included significant chapters examining the content of the work of the foreign correspondents. This research was focused examination of articles in three separate years in three newspapers and two news magazines and of transcripts of the evening news broadcasts of CBS, ABC, and NBC taken from the Vanderbilt Television News Archive.

A final example is Melissa A. Johnson's 1997 content analysis of 515 index citations from 34 U.S. newspapers in order to study the role of geographic proximity, cultural proximity, and organization on the quantity of stories about Mexico. She found that "cultural proximity" influenced the number of stories published, but that geographic proximity did not. She also found that the size of the newspaper and its organizational characteristics had influenced the lengths of stories published.

These examples show the usual approach of content analysis studies to foreign correspondence. The studies attempt to find patterns in stories selected from the stream of reports generated from abroad for domestic media. They then attempt to deduce the impact of this correspondence on readers and viewers of domestic media to find relationships between the work of the foreign correspondents and the responses of those consuming the work of those correspondents.

However, they contribute only indirectly to our understanding of the work of the foreign correspondent and leave little data upon which to construct a systematic understanding of what drives foreign correspondence or the work of the foreign correspondent.

News Agency Studies

A second indirect approach to studying foreign correspondence is to examine the organizational structures within which the correspondents work. The most common approach to this type of study is to examine the structure of the major news agencies, especially the major international news agencies.

These studies are best illustrated by the impressive review, *International News Agencies*, by Oliver Boyd-Barrett. It it is a sweeping review of the structure, functions and role of the four "world agencies." The review examines their domestic and international role, their competition with each other and with other agencies, their structures and processes, their threats and conflicts in a changing environment. The focus of the book is on the agencies, not on individual reporters.

International Flow of Information

A third approach peripherally related to our grasp of the work of the foreign correspondent is the area of the international flow of news and information. In 1985, Mowlana created a model of international news flow based on the interaction of technology and information sources. He found that production and distribution of information generally flows from richer northern countries to poorer southern countries creating a gap made worse by technology hardware and software lags.

De Bens and Kelly (1992) have found that this imbalance has been exacerbated by recent technological and marketing developments in Internet media. They report that cable and satellite communication has accelerated the impact of countries with high production values on their neighbors.

While these approaches have value in understanding the impact of foreign correspondence on other cultures, they leave opportunities for more research focused specifically on the processes and principles of foreign correspondence itself.

Histories, Biographies, and Essays

The history of foreign correspondence is dominated by two seminal works: John Hohenberg's *Foreign Correspondence: The Great Reporters and Their Times* and Phillip Knightley's *The First Casualty: The War Correspondent as Hero and Myth-Maker from the Crimea to Kosovo*. Hohenberg has written a powerful history of foreign correspondence by focusing on major personalities from the 1700s through the 1960s. His account is driven by accounts of the personalities who established foreign correspondence and those who practiced it.

Knightley's work is centered on unifying theme: that truth inevitably falls victim to propaganda, government manipulation and patriotic fervor during times of conflict. He tracks war correspondence during conflicts from the Crimean War to the conflict in Kosovo and shows how coverage has been riddled with falsehoods and half-truths often misleading the public into supporting policies they would otherwise have repudiated.

These seminal works have been supplemented by a number of biographies and essays by correspondents themselves. These works describe first hand the experiences of the correspondence including the problems the faced and their techniques for overcoming these problems. However, such personal accounts provide little help in developing the systematic analysis required for theory building.

Theoretical Studies

These approaches to understanding foreign correspondence are largely descriptive. They adopt a limited effects set of assumptions and have drawn from only a narrow range of theoretical possibilities for developing a more systematic understanding of the work of the foreign correspondent. The surveys and content studies are quantitative in approach with limited aspirations of contributing to theory building about foreign correspondence. The histories, biographies, and essays generally are not focused on generating theory.

The news agency and international news flow studies have resulted in theoretical models, but are structured to address questions at a macroorganizational level and say little about the practice of foreign correspondence itself.

A limited number of both qualitative and quantitative studies have been mounted to contribute to theory building in the field. However, they have been sporadic and have not yet produced a coherent theoretical foundation for the field. Quantitative studies of foreign correspondence specifically aimed at testing theoretical propositions are relatively rare.

We do have a few examples. Millissa A. Johnson's 1997 article "Predicting News Flow from Mexico" was a content analysis of 515 index citations from 34 U.S. newspapers. It sought to test the relationship of geographic proximity, cultural proximity, and organization characteristics to the quantity of stories about Mexico. It found that cultural proximity influenced the number of stories covered while geographic proximity did not. It also found that the size of the newspaper and its organizational characteristics tended to influence the lengths of stories reported.

Similarly, Catherine Cassara's "U.S. Newspaper Coverage of Human Rights in Latin America, 1975–1992: Exploring President Carter's Agenda-Building Influence" used content analysis of coverage in four prestige newspapers in the United States to see if efforts by the Carter administration did seem to significantly increase coverage of human rights issues, supporting an agenda-building theory of presidential influence on foreign news coverage.

The Willnat and Weaver study cited earlier, while primarily a descriptive study, did have some questions aimed at exploring whether the characteristics of foreign correspondents might influence them to place more emphasis on "analysis and interpretation" as a part of their decisions to cover events.

A later chapter in this book will examine a series of theoretical studies related to foreign correspondence. They do not bear directly on our understanding of the work of the foreign correspondent, but they suggest how established theoretical paradigms might be brought to bear on research about foreign correspondence. Among the most important of these are "gatekeeping" studies, "agenda setting theory" and "framing analysis."

However, the broader fields of research in journalism, mass communication, and communication studies has generated a broad range of theoretical perspectives in the last half of the 20th century. These approaches offer a full spectrum of research methodologies and theoretical paradigms that might be brought to bear on foreign correspondence. The possibilities are grounded in sets of assumptions about units of analysis, ontological perspectives, research values, and epistemological parameters.

Broadly speaking, these sets of assumptions may be described as quantitative perspectives or qualitative perspectives. Both approaches are discussed in succeeding chapters of this book.

Briefly, the quantitative perspectives first define independent and dependent variables, then operationalize the presence of each variable in order to count specified units for observation, apply arithmetic/statistical analytic techniques to the observed frequencies, and examine the resulting manifestations of patterns for causal relationships. Quantitative approaches depend upon experimenter-defined units of analysis and search for the relationships among them that cause human behavior.

The qualitative perspectives generally identify constructs rather than variables, examine "texts" or "speech acts" rather than countable units, apply contextual analytic techniques rather than statistical or arithmetic analysis, and seek narrative themes, processes, or deep structures as representations or essences of human experience rather than causal relationships to human behavior. Qualitative approaches depend upon not-previously-defined constructs of analysis in order to comprehend, synthesize, and recontextualize human experience.

The result is a wide range of theoretic/methodological options for the study of mass and human communication. These options include theories of human behavior that search for causes in the structure of the human mind (Gestalt), the conditioning of human experience (Behaviorism), the structure of mediation (Information Theory), and the structure of social experience (cognitive theory). They include objective structural approaches (systems theory) and subjective structural approaches (symbolic interactionism and framing theory). They include cultural theories, social constructionism and postmodernism.

Few studies based on these more recent paradigms have been mounted to examine the work of foreign correspondents.

Ken Stark and Estela Villanueva did publish a study called "Cultural Framing: Foreign Correspondents and Their Work" in 1992 that examined 75 books by and about foreign correspondents and supplemented it with interviews with six foreign correspondents. Their analysis was done from a cultural framing theoretical perspective examining the role of culture in the work of the foreign correspondents. They found that fewer than half of the printed sources (44%) referred explicitly to culture. In the interviews, the authors found an unconscious awareness of four types of cultural influences that were articulated once they were introduced by the interviewer.

Jin Yang published "Framing the NATO Air Strikes on Kosovo Across Countries: Comparison of Chinese and U.S. Newspaper Coverage" in 2003. The "framing" study sought to test the hypotheses that Chinese and U.S. coverage reflected the national interests of each country based on framing key terms and themes reflected in the text of newspaper coverage. It found that the national interest of each country was reflected in the coverage.

Wayne Wanto and Yu-Wei Hu published "The Agenda-Setting Effects of International News Coverage: An Examination of Differing News Frames" in 1993. They compared the coverage of 15 categories of international news in four news media "with the level of public concern with international problems as recorded by all 41 Gallup organization's most important problem polls conducted from 1975 to 1990." They found that the way that news reports are framed "may determine the magnitude of salience cues."

Elfriede Fursich and Anandam P. Kavoori published "Mapping a Critical Framework for the Study of Travel Journalism" in 2001. It was an essay that laid out a framework for studying travel journalism and three theoretical perspectives for studying its impact including periodization including the interplay of modernity and post-modernism, power and identity of cultural imperialism, and how tourism cultivates the phenomenology of experience.

In 1995, Mark Pedelty published *War Stories: The Culture of Foreign Correspondents*. This participant observation study by a cultural anthropologist examined foreign correspondents covering the war in El Salvador. The author adopts a social constructionist approach. He explains the work of the correspondents from within what he calls (from Michel Foucalt and Louis Althusser) the "disciplinary apparatuses that pattern many of their actions." He argues that professional practices shape their work and produce the discourse or text of their reports.

In 2002, Giokvanna Dell'Orto published *Giving Meaning to the World: The First U.S. Foreign Correspondents, 1838–1859*. This book reports a "discourse analysis" of newspaper congressional and foreign correspondence "text" driven by theories of the social construction of reality. The author especially cites the work of James Carey as guiding his research. It searches for the cultural antecedents of meaning in the work of the foreign correspondents derived from the foreign cultures in which they work.

These works use recent theoretical perspectives to understand the work of foreign correspondents. However, the studies are isolated and often are grounded in broader cultural, social and organizational issues. They demand to be followed up with additional studies in order to achieve the kind of coherent theoretical explanation of foreign correspondence made possible at the beginning of the 20th century. In fact, as Wu and Hamilton (2004) have pointed out, recent trends in this area including the growth of the Internet, the increasing dependence upon foreign nationals by international news organizations, and the reduction in investment in support for foreign news bureaus and traditional foreign news correspondents. These trends make it ever more difficult for descriptive studies to adequately explain the processes and principles at work in foreign correspondence. These developments call for new thinking about how to study these issues.

The following chapters will outline the studies that have been conducted to this point. They will offer suggestions about new ways to develop theories of foreign correspondence. They will suggest that this area demands coherent theory building using the full range of theoretical perspectives available to build our understanding of the specific processes and principles of foreign correspondence apart from the work being done in related areas of news flow, news agency, and social impact of foreign news. This specific work on foreign correspondence can have a lasting impact on our understanding of all these related areas and is important in its own right.

References

Adams, John B. (Summer 1966). "What the Foreign Correspondent Does for a Newspaper's Readers." *Journalism Quarterly,* 43:2. 300–304.

Anderson, Russell F. (Dec. 9, 1950). "The Disappearing Foreign Correspondent." *The Michigan Alumnus Quarterly Review,* LVCII:10 1–12.

Bogart, Leo (Summer 1968). "The Overseas Newsman: A 1967 Profile Study." *Journalism Quarterly,* 45:2. 293–306.

Bonafede, Dom (Feb. 23, 1985). "Foreign Correspondents in Washington Tell the World about the United States." *National Journal,* 421–425.

Boyd-Barrett, Oliver (1980). *The International News Agencies.* Beverly Hills, CA: Sage.

Boyd-Barrett, Oliver and Rantanen, Terhi (eds.) (1998). *The Globalization of News.* London: Sage.

Brogan, Patrick (1989). *Foreign Correspondents in Washington.* (Occasional Paper/Media Studies Project). Washington, D.C.: Woodrow Wilson International Center for Scholars.

Cassara, Catherine. (Autumn 1998). "U.S. Newspaper Coverage of Human Rights in Latin America, 1975–1982: Exploring President Carter's Agenda-Building Influence." *Journalism and Mass Communication Quarterly,* 75:3. 478–486.

Dell'Orto, Giovanna (2002). *Giving Meanings to the World: The First U.S. Foreign Correspondents, 1838–1859.* Westport, CT: Greenwood Press.

Elliot, Kim Andrew. (Autumn 1981). "World News Coverage of U.S. and International Broadcasters." *Journalism Quarterly,* 58:3. 444–449.

Etheredge, Lloyd S. (ed.) (1998). *Selected Writings of Ithiel de Sola Pool.* New Brunswick, N.J.: Transaction Publishers.

Fursich, Elfriede and Kavoori, Anandam P. (2001). "Mapping a Critical Framework for the Study of Travel Journalism." *International Journal of Cultural Studies,* 4:2. 149–171.

Ghorpade, Shailendra ((1983). *Survey of Washington-based Foreign Correspondents, 1983.* Chapel Hill: University of North Carolina Center for Research in journalism and Mass Communication.

Ghorpade, Shailendra (Autumn 1984). "Foreign Correspondents Cover Washington for the World." *Journalism Quarterly.* 61:3. 667–71.

Ghorpade, Shailendra (Autumn 1984). "Sources and Access: How Foreign Correspondents Rate Washington, D.C." *Journal of Communication.* 34:4. 32–40.

Hachten, William (1992). *The World News Prism: Changing Media* of International Communication (3rd ed.). Ames, IA: Iowa State University Press.

Hamilton, John Maxwell and Jenner, Eric (2004). "Redefining Foreign Correspondence." *Journalism,* 5:3 301–321.

Hess, Stephen (1996). *International News & Foreign Correspondents.* Washington, DC: The Brookings Institute.

Hess, Stephen (2005). *Through Their Eyes: Foreign Correspondents in the United States.* Washington, DC: Brookings Institution Press.

Hess, Stephen, and Stevenson, Robert L. (1997). "International News and Foreign Correspondents." *American Journal of Sociology,* 102:4. 1189–1189.

Hohenberg, John (1964). *Foreign Correspondence: The Great Reporters and Their Times.* New York: Columbia University Press.

Johnson, Melissa (Summer 1997). "Predicting News Flow from Mexico." *Journalism and Mass Communication Quarterly,* 74:2. 315–330.

Kennedy, Liam and Lucas, Scott (2005). "Enduring Freedom: Public Diplomacy and U.S. Foreign Policy." *American Quarterly,* 57:2, 309–333.

Kliesch, Ralph E. (Winter 1991). "The U.S. Press Corps Abroad Rebounds: A 7th World Survey of Foreign Correspondents." *Newspaper Research Journal,* 12:1. 24–33.

Knight, Alan (1998). "Covering the Global Village: Foreign Reporters and the Internet." *Media Asia,* 25:2. 71–77.

Knightley, Phillip (2000). *The First Casualty: The War Correspondent as Hero and Myth-Maker from the Crimea to Kosovo.* Baltimore: The Johns Hopkins University Press.

Kruglak, Theodore E. (1955). *The Foreign Correspondents: A Study of the Men and Women Reporting for the American Information Media in Western Europe.* Geneva: E. Droz.

Lambert, Donald A. (Summer 1956). "Foreign Correspdents Covering the United States." *Journalism Quarterly,* 33:2. 349–356.

Maxwell, John William (Summer 1956). "Foreign Correspondents Abroad: A Study of Backgrounds." *Journalism Quarterly,* 33:2. 346–348.

Mowlana, Hamid (Summer 1975). "Who Covers America?" *Journal of Communication,* 25:3. 86–91.

Mowlana, Hamid (1985). *International Flow of Information: A Global Report and Analysis.* Paris: UNESCO.

Nair, Murali (July 1991). "The Foreign Correspondent: Dateline Washington, D. C." *Gazette,* 48:1. 59–64.

Pedelty, Mark (1995). *War Stories: The Culture of Foreign Correspondents.* New York: Routledge.

Riffe, Daniel (1984). "International News Borrowing: A Trend Analysis." *Journalism Quarterly,.* 61:1. 142–148.

Rosten, Leo (1997). *The Washington Correspondents.* New York: Harcourt, Brace.

Silva, Tony (ed.) (2001). *Global News: Perspectives on the Information Age.* Ames, IA: Iowa State University Press.

Sreberny-Mohammadi, Annabelle; Winseck, Dwayne; McKenna, Jim; and Boyd-Barrett, Oliver (1997). *Media in Global Context.* London: Arnold.

Stark, Kenneth and Villanueva, Estela (August 1992). "Cultural Framing: Foreign Correspondents and Their Work." Paper presented at the annual meeting of the Association for Education in Journalism and Mass Communication, Montreal, Canada.

Suh, Chung Woo (1971). "The Socio-Professional Aspects of Foreign Corresponents in the United States: A Study of International Communications." Ph.D. Dissertation, University of Minnesota.

Suh, John C. W. (April 29, 1972). "126 Foreign Correspondents Talk About Work in America." *Editor & Publisher,* pp. 27–28, 30.

Wanta, Wayne, and Hu, Yu-Wei (1993). "The Agenda-Setting Effects of International News Coverage: An Examination of Differing News Frames." *International Journal of Public Opinion Research,* 5:3. 250–264.

Weaver, David (ed.) (1998). *The Global Journalist: News People Around the World.* Cresskill, N.J.: Hampton Press.

Wilhelm, John (Spring 1963). "The Re-appearing Foreign Correspondent: A World Survey." *Journalism Quarterly,* 40:1 147–168.

Wilnat, Laras and Weaver, David (2003). "Through Their Eyes. The Work of Foreign Correspondents in the United States." *Journalism,* 4:4. 403–422.

Wu, H. Denis, and Hamilton, John Maxwell (2004). "U.S. Foreign Correspondents: Changes and Continuity at the Turn of the Century." *Gazette: The International Journals for Communication Studies,* 66:6. 517–532.

Yang, Jin (2003). "Framing the NATO Air Strikes on Kosovo Across Countries: Compairson of Chinese and U.S. Newspaper Coverage." *Gazette: The International Journal for Communication Studies. 65*:3. 231–249.

CHAPTER 3

Political Economy of Foreign Correspondents

Gerd G. Kopper & Benjamin J. Bates

Few professions within the media industry have so directly followed historical political, economic and technological developments as has the position of foreign correspondents. From the outset, their jobs and duties have been instigated by the economic needs of news and news media, and whose practice was shaped by advances in communication and information technology. Foreign correspondents thus find their work directly affected by shifts in the political and cultural framework of their markets and society; their work can be viewed as an application of specific framing and ideology in terms of background contexts of economy, technology, political systems and cultures. Thus, it would seem useful to consider the *political economy of foreign correspondents*—that is, how theory can inform essential aspects of the development and utilization of foreign correspondents as a specialty in journalism. Such an examination can also allow us to consider the implications of continuing technological, market, and political developments, and what this might mean for the profession and the industry.

Before proceeding, we have to note an interesting concurrence: It so happens that the rise of professional journalism, and the use of foreign correspondents in particular, coincided with the very beginning of "political economy" as a new term for the start of the science of economy under the auspices of international free trade, a market economy, and the intense beginning of industrialization. The rise of technology and industrial processes was rapidly applied to journalism with the development of steam presses and the major urban daily. This expansion of the size and scope of newspapers industrialized and professionalized journalism and refocused "news" not only as a communication tool, but an economic product in search of value. Economic value came from reports of events near and far, creating demand for both news and correspondents.

Interestingly, Karl Marx earned some of the little money that he ever earned as a freelance foreign correspondent, sending articles to Horace

Greeley's *New York Tribune*, founded in 1841. This was not coincidental; the use of foreign correspondence also provided an opportunity to frame reporting to reflect the needs and interests of publishers and readers as well as the correspondents themselves. As the rise of news agencies standardized and commoditized non-local news reporting (Boyd-Barrett, 1980), the foreign correspondent provided alternative perspectives and insights, adding value through their insights and writing skills. There exist voluminous archives of the work of foreign correspondents who worked in Europe, having sent news and reports across the Atlantic that were intimately intertwined with the advance of the new science called political economy and its ramifications and sincere conflicts (cf. List, 1996).

With these shared roots, the application of theoretical insights from political economy should not bypass the intellectual history of this tradition and its links with foreign correspondence. The historical development of political economy suggests that one must include, among the essential factors of social dynamics, elements of infrastructure development, labor markets as well as the press. Knies (1883) was one of the forerunners of doing research in this area. And it is within the political economy background that his student Weber—within the context of the new discipline of sociology that he helped to develop—started the first large-scale project of empirical research concerning content production of the press. Political economy, thus, is an inherent part of the development of the establishment of a particular work role of foreign correspondents.

In exploring the political economics of foreign correspondents, this chapter will try to integrate theoretical insights with an overview of the development of the profession. We will, however, not enter into one special segment of the political economic discourse tied in with foreign correspondence, i.e., the grand-scale questions of macro-politics and macroeconomics of the international communication order. There has been a long-standing and tight-fisted international debate about pivotal phenomena of this problem area starting within the UNESCO context during the second half of the 1970s. UNESCO, the organization for culture and education of the United Nations, based in Paris (France), ultimately inaugurated an International Commission for the Study of Communication Problems under the chairmanship of Irish Nobel Laureate Sean McBride in 1978. Its final report (McBride, 1980) drew marked attention as well as severe counter-polemics. The facts presented, however, clearly indicated that there existed a type of underdevelopment in communication, information and global news flows—next to social, cultural and economic dimensions of imbalance among highly industrialized countries and the Third World (Stevenson & Shaw, 1984). A political agenda emerged, calling for a "New World Information Order" (NWIO) that eventually triggered the exodus of the United States of America from UNESCO at the beginning of 1985 (further insight in Preston et al., 1989). This debate largely ended in 1988/89 with the end of the cold war.

The general situation, in many respects, has changed during the last 40 years; however, the overall structures of imbalance in the availability of global news still exists. The "digital divide" brought about by new means of global information exchange like Internet services constitutes only one element of the continuing historic dilemma of information inequality that is bound by the issue of global diversity and disparity in general (Norris, 2001).

The three instrumental questions guiding our analysis will be:

• What do the empirical changes in the work profile and professional perspective of foreign correspondents tell us about basic changes in the structure of political and economic ground rules and frameworks in the international context applicable to foreign correspondence (and vice versa)?

• To what extent, and with what kind of implications, has technology changed processes underlying the professional processes of foreign correspondents?

• What role does the economy in general and micro economic developments within the media industry play within the changing nature of foreign correspondents?

At the very end we shall also ask what one might learn by theoretical introspection of this type about possible future developments within this sector of journalistic work. This, however, because of the surprising lack of research in this area, will just be a rather tentative and speculative extrapolation, based on our observations and analyses. Nevertheless, it gives some direction as to where one might find fruitful avenues of future research in this area.

In order to address these questions, we will start by considering the various theoretical approaches within political economy, in order to extract those concepts and implications that are most useful in developing and examining the political economy of foreign correspondents. We will then apply that approach to the evolution of the profession of foreign correspondence over time, showing how a range of economic, social, and political forces has shaped it, including the rise of communication and media technologies. We will do this in four steps:

- briefly depict the economic motivation for foreign correspondence as a distinctive news form, in order to establish a foundation for further analysis of specific factors;
- examine the role of industrial and technological developments over time on the journalistic practices and norms for foreign correspondence, in part a result of changing economics and markets;
- outline the general structural developments within the media system as well as the socio-cultural surroundings that had an impact on the professional work of foreign correspondence; and
- focus on some particularly valuable theoretical elements of political economic thinking within this sector that could steer further research into very fruitful areas.

Political Economy Approaches and Journalism

Our approach to political economic analysis tries to focus on those types of theoretical thought that have developed, since the rise of industrialization within the Western world. The analytical considerations that we will be using rely on a broad and inclusive understanding of political economy; one that is not bound by one singular school of thought. We see our assignment to be more of a kind of meta-layer observation and reflection within the sphere of theory, exploring relationships and structures rather than testing the relative appropriateness of a particular perspective, or identifying a specific impact. We want to be open to the entire spectrum of schools of thought, and utilize what is helpful in understanding the evolution of foreign correspondence.

Thus, we will draw on foundational literature to identify and develop key concepts and approaches shared by the various approaches, and are appropriate for examining the particular issues and perspectives associated with the profession of foreign correspondence, rather than emphasizing current applications of those approaches. We can start with the basic concern of political economics—social change and historical transformation. Within the various theories and approaches, certain useful themes about the impact of industrialization emerge:

- The treatment of the role of individual work was refocused from job characteristics (such as rules of inherited positive and negative disposition, systems of privileges and grants, and boundaries set by artisans' conclaves) to considering economic and political forces of markets and the development of labor markets. This shifting emphasis has been applied to writers being employed by news organizations (Altschull, 1984; Boyd-Barrett, 1980; Fenby, 1986; Hannerz, 2004; Hess, 2005; Huteau, 1992; McLee, 1937; Schudson, 1978; Schwarzlose, 1989).
- The emphasis on free trade redefined the fundamental understanding of the political economy of states. There emerged a new type of self-identified collectivity, no longer determined by feudal elites but by international trade markets (including for quite a long time that for slave labor) and the prosperity that they implied. Power and identity were increasingly defined in economic and market terms (for an overview of Marxist approaches, see Bottomore, 1983).
- Science and technological development shifted into a new role at the turn of the 18th and 19th century within the Western hemisphere, gaining increasing weight as a prime force of industrialization and social prosperity, including the development of military technology as one of the major ingredients of winning an edge over competing or conflicting states during an era of new empires (for examples, see Berghahn, 1994 (Germany); Czitrom, 1982 (USA); Flichy, 1995).

Another fundamental concept of political economics is that of *praxis*, the role of human actions, such as professional behaviors, in society. This suggests the value of examining foreign correspondence as practice. The centrality of this focus is furthered by the political economic emphasis on ideology; particularly Gramsci's (1971) notion of hegemony and the Frankfurt school's emphasis on the role of the cultural industry in political economy (Adorno & Horkheimer, 1979). These suggest that power and control may be manifest through internalization of ideology into practice, in defining the norms of professions and behaviors. These suggest the value of examining not only the evolution of practice, but also the degree to which practices can incorporate ideology. There is strong potential for such an approach, as one of the main values of foreign correspondents is their ability to differentiate their reporting from the more normalized product of international news agencies.

The foundations of political economic theory and thought were laid on the background of these principal developments. In fact, much of political economic theory of today is still very deeply, and often directly, rooted in concepts grounded in the 19th century (Lower, 1987). Thus, it is not surprising that whatever theoretical work might have a bearing on this sector does not *directly* refer to foreign correspondence as a specific area within professional journalism. Existing political economic thinking, thus, has only rather indirect relationship to the practical work of foreign correspondents (cf. theoretical work to overcome traditional types of political economic thinking within this sphere: Dröge & Kopper, 1991). Our effort in this analysis, thus, is a pioneering effort to collect elements of theoretical thinking of political economy relevant to this field of study and to try to juxtapose the 19th-century roots of political economy with more modern applications to journalism as a profession and industry (cf.: Fenton, 2005; Johnston, 1998; Reese, 2001; Schudson, 1978).

In order to follow these questions there has to be a common ground on which to position the establishment of general patterns of specific change in foreign correspondence within the international media industry. This overview can only be rather cursory and extremely abbreviated because we have to press more than two hundred years of succinct historical development concerning this sphere into just a few paragraphs—and we have to leave out even the most abbreviated type of coverage of some of the essentials of this development (an intense study to relate the contextual dimensions cf. Leidinger, 2003).

We are basing our sense of political economy—as our conceptual framework for theoretical inspiration—on one particular historical element, i.e., the advent of modern rational thinking and its application and expression in the world of modern economy, again construed on progress in technology, energy supplies, the idea of free trade, internal and external markets, and a constant dynamics towards industrialization as experienced for more than 150 years (for an instructive overview into one practical side of this process, cf.: Hills, 1988). This emphasis on the beginning of a *new* type of economy is not accidental. It is also attached to the rise of new types of political organization in many societies in the Western hemisphere—increasing representative organization built on electoral proceedings; party organizations; the increase of general suffrage; first general regulation of economic processes outside of customs and taxes etc. (for data, see Mitchell, 1980). A demand for a new type of general public information is an element of the very process of modernization that starts with industrialization. Looking into the history of modern press development, including how news agencies quickly transformed into worldwide operating organizations (Fenby, 1985; Read, 1992; Schwarzlose, 1989), one can follow certain trends that directly relate to époques of general political and economic development.

Economic Foundations of Foreign Correspondence

To start, we need to consider the basic economics of news. This could, of course, lead back to eons of development history of humankind, which we are not prepared to do in such a short introspection. It has to be made clear, though, that there is an economy of information, obviously attached to the use of applying written symbols to acts and decisions worth to be fixed for ulterior memory (Assmann, 2006). Information and knowledge have value (Arrow, 1984; Lamberton, 1971), and journalism and media have value deriving from their ability to bring such knowledge and information to consumers (cf. Doyle, 2002; Lacy & Simon, 1993). More relevantly for journalism, that value is often linked to concepts of newsworthiness, such as novelty (timeliness) and/or its usefulness (relevance) (Bates, 1988, 1990). And more importantly from our perspective, these are also areas where foreign correspondence can provide competitive advantage to newspapers within home markets.

The differentiated product that foreign correspondents provide is information and knowledge from distant locations. In the earliest manifestation of journalism, having a foreign correspondent gave papers two distinct advantages. First, the paper could receive timely news reports from their agents without having to wait for normal news flows. Second, having their own correspondent meant that the reporter could select those stories of particular relevance to the paper's readers, and frame them so as to maximize their value and utility to their home news audience.

By framing, we refer to the expansion of the fundamental objective news story in ways that add meaning and value. This may be accomplished through the use of distinctive literary styles and approaches of a writer, the placing of the story within a context particularly appropriate to the media or its audience, the incorporation of analysis and interpretation, and even the incorporation of specific cultural perspectives and/or ideology. This last type of differentiation also embraces the concept of framing in news, the use of language and style that derives from and supports particular perspectives, cultural values and norms, and/or ideology. Framing has a long history as a theory of media effects (Scheufele, 1999; Watson, 2007; Wicks, 2005), and is of particular focus to political economic approaches, fitting in with their notions of the role of media in promoting ideology and hegemony (Carragee & Roefs, 2004; Holstein, 2003).

While this suggests value for foreign correspondents, one also has to consider that there are costs involved, and that there are competitive sources for news and information. From an economic perspective, use of foreign correspondents over time depends on whether their added value outstrips costs and the value of alternative information sources. These factors can change with shifts in technology, public attitudes and preferences, and social and political needs. This is where the shift into political economics is crucial; it places emphasis on examining those changing factors and their impact on the profession.

As a quick example, the rise of the telegraph and news agency significantly reduced the "timeliness" value of foreign correspondents. The news agency could spread its costs across multiple papers, and provide timely basic reports more cheaply. Thus, the focus of foreign correspondents shifted to the value they provided through gatekeeping and framing. That is, in finding stories that would be of particular interest to readers that were outside the normal news judgments of the international agencies or by incorporating a distinctive frame for the story that added value to the objective agency news report. This frame could encompass distinctive styles and approaches, greater analysis, or placing the story in ideological context.

The Rise of Practice in Foreign Correspondence

As noted above, there was an early use of foreign correspondents in the 19th century. This earliest uses focused initially on the value of timeliness, in getting the news earliest. With the rise of the telegraph and press agencies, the individual correspondent lost that competitive advantage (Boyd-Barrett 1980), at least when it came to straight news reports. Some larger papers, in more competitive markets, could still achieve value from the second source: the distinctive focus and style of a particular correspondent. The emphasis and value came from the correspondent as much as from the underlying basic information (Dell'Orto, 2002). There remained a bit of a market for foreign correspondence, but arguably more from a columnist rather than a reporter. The telegraph and the rise of news agencies thus shifted the role of the foreign correspondent. However, as competitive pressures encouraged further standardization of news products, the value and demand for foreign correspondents waned.

News in the modern journalistic sense, as a rather differentiated product (within different sections of different press media) arrived at its most rationalized and culturally pre-formatted pattern within various countries in the early 1920s. Journalism rose as a distinct profession, with a variety of beats and with standard practices developed to rationalize production. The standards and norms of press agencies provided a model, while the rise of advertising as a funding source provided the motivation for objectification in the search for the mass audience. The growing international competition among news agencies in this era fed the emerging emphasis on distant news and information from an increasingly accessible world. While many processes were normalized, there was still a role, albeit more limited, for differential framing, particularly in support of some publishers' social or political agendas. In contrast to regular reporters, foreign correspondents were often expected to provide a distinct style and perspective, making them a prime source for integrating cultural frames and ideologies into news flows. This would suggest that foreign correspondents would play a particularly important role in the political economy of news, and in the emerging concepts of public diplomacy and soft power (Nye, 2008).

The peak development of industrialization within the sector of the news agencies, including the application of "new" technology (e.g., photo transfer), enabled a new role for the 'gentleman' foreign correspondent—as the elite outpost for the media able to pay for such services (out of a multitude of examples, cf. Schäfer, 1994). During this period, which ends with the entrance of the U.S.A. into World War II, but finds some continuity, at least, in some highly regarded stations (e.g., Moscow, London, Paris, Tokyo), some elite correspondents gained measurable political influence (Hamilton, 2009; Heald, 1988). There exists a vast collection of histories (cf. Dell'Orto, 2002; Hamilton, 2009) and autobiographies of these types of correspondents worldwide in most countries of the Western hemisphere, particularly linked to background insights into the higher grounds of politics. The Library of Congress, for example, collects unpublished biographical material of this echelon of U.S. American correspondents. We will come back to the procedural point of development that is to be recognized concerning its theoretical value: Here one can clearly recognize a differentiation among working layers in foreign correspondence.

It is at this stage, during the 1920s, that there emerges a minimal international standard of news production, in the sense of reliability, precision and optimal use of space and time. It is from then on that one can observe a further differentiation within the context and function of types of foreign correspondence: There is a certified role for the correspondent specialized in hard news and actuality, mostly working for the wire agencies and there is more of an elite role for correspondents for the larger quality press (which could afford outposts in areas of particular interest). Also, there evolved a new type of traveling reporter, inheriting the tradition of the traveling correspondent cum adventurer. While initially focused on exploiting particular writing styles (e.g., Mark Twain's jaunt through Europe), this role was increasingly attached to visual elements (photography, then video) as technological improvements reduced the costs of newsgathering equipment (and of transmitting their output to home news media). This modernized version of the "special correspondent"—somebody with special access, special talents and/or special reputation to increase readership and audience at "special" occasions—helped news organizations create value through product differentiation (for further development, cf. Hamilton & Jenner, 2003).

However, it is not the basic description of the process of functional differentiation that, though being interesting, drives our consideration of the political economics of foreign correspondence. Rather, it is the insight it provides into the theoretical concept of layer-bound development as principal characteristic of the political economy of news and information. Following such a theoretical concept leads us to a fruitful conceptual design that allows us to integrate the dynamic factors of market development, technical progress, and institutional adaptations by the media organizations (to state just some of the essential re-constructive analytical dimensions). Again, this is but one example of theoretical perspective and an illustration of its immediate reward. There might be and there are, numerous more, to be looked after.

News, which can be seen as a product of economic modernization and as a commodity and service of mass demand, therefore has to be viewed as a differentiated and mass-marketed form of daily public information that, in fact, sees further dynamic development on an increasing spectrum of layers of demand. One can analyze these by further narrowing the specifications of the layers (e.g., economic news wire; general affairs news; sports news, entertainment news, etc.) or along a variety of other dimensions; for example, according to format patterns, market trends, production and distribution modes, competition structures, etc.

One leading observation, so far, is that if an ulterior stage of rationalization of the format pattern has been reached—which is the case of general wire news format within the era of the 1920s—the dynamic development is one based on central economic criteria. That is, one has to arrive at leadership in particular markets in order to stabilize markets and to build a quality brand and thus serve entrepreneurial continuity. This dynamic pattern, again, implies that—following Schumpeter's uncontested rule of the modern entrepreneurial economy—that the competitive development within the general news sector, including that of foreign correspondence, in the long run is one of *market layer development.*

In other words, given the maturation of a news format and the daily routines of material production and delivery, there is little economic chance that an additional reader, listener, or viewer will be attracted to the medium or channel because of what comes in as a daily product. Attracting audience in a competitive environment requires increasing the attractiveness and value of the product. This can be accomplished most easily on newly established layers of presentation within a medium or channel—including new layers for news generated content presentation.

But here again, what was once been considered new and most attractive will, after some time, stagnate and become routine and mundane. Further theoretical reflection will, hence, suggest that a further type of differentiation has to be developed. Minor tinkering and improvements of existing routine is not a long-term solution to competitive markets. That requires a different type of differentiation; one directly geared to market development. One can best seek out and maintain new value by creating and/or developing new market niches. It is at this point those theoretical perspectives, such as risk management (Spaeth, 2004), can serve as a starting element for further rewarding insight.

It is in this way that one sees a particular dynamic concerning the general management of the information flow. There is a constant structurally determined push towards the further rationalization of the news production process (many empirical studies from the inside of news organizations have made this evident; cf. Neumann, 1997). After an ever-evolving stagnation of particular format patterns incurred through rationalization efforts, a re-shaping and differentiation in the form of market layer development starts. This turns out to be a consistent ingredient of what, in the end, and after more discoveries might be termed a general "law of actual news production."

Are there implications, already at this stage of insight, for the under-standing of the general role and function of the foreign correspondent? In many cases there are, however, mostly rather tragic ones. Empirical research has shown that there are many examples of an organization not being com-petitively oriented within this segment of information service. And there are cases of correspondents not really interested in a thorough reflection of their function, set by daily routines. This leads to seemingly endless stretches of time when there is just routine filing of news in the most rationalized format (detailed presentations through various studies collected in Kopper, 2006a).

Self-reflection within the news industry will rarely dive deeply into the core area of the production economy and its political context, lest it get trapped within the particular stagflation of market layer development. And it is because of this that the there exists residual theoretical insights that rely on the inclusion of stagnant format patterns. Typically, these arguments follow this pattern: 'Information can have value to people, and news organizations have value to the extent that they bring valuable information to its audiences. And value lies in a combination of relevance, utility, and novelty. And it is here where the foreign correspondent can create value: by searching out news and information in foreign locales, but from the perspective of the in-terests and frames of the home news organization.'

Recent developments in the field directly illustrate how this type of in-ner-organizational thinking might concomitantly justify even standardized routine types of news production. The tremendous shift that occurred within this information segment through the rise of Internet-based services provides an example. The Internet provides access to a more than ample range of news (of relevance, utility and novelty), in large part free of charge to every-body worldwide. More importantly, it allows direct access to foreign news sources, bypassing the gatekeeping of the local media source. The rise of the Internet, in fact, can provide an economic rationale to cancel many routine correspondents' posts globally (Hamilton & Jenner, 2004; Kopper, 2006b).

With the ability of Internet based material to be re-produced and re-posted (experiments have proven that this is routinely possible, cf. Kopper, 2006a: 47f.), the added value of the foreign correspondent to the paper is in jeopardy. While the Internet may increase the social value generated by the correspondent's material by enhancing its distribution and use, it simultane-ously hampers the ability of the firm employing the correspondent to exclu-sively capture that value. Simple economic calculation will show that the value of traditional foreign correspondence to the news organization is much too low, relative to the costs of alternative information sources and the declining ability to capture added value. The embrace of the Internet as a delivery mechanism by international news agencies for international news on the Internet is not only impressive; it is transformative (Paterson, 2005).

While basic economics might suggest that the traditional market for foreign correspondence has declined, the profession still exists. One reason might be that the decision to use foreign correspondents is not a purely financial one (Kopper, 2006b). The use of foreign correspondents and their work may serve other purposes; it may well create real value for the news organization in other ways. Value may accrue from the use of foreign correspondents as a mechanism to provide prestige, or even as an avenue for training staff. Value might also be derived from the use of their differentiated products for social or political influence, or the building of ideology. One might also want to consider whether new markets for their work have developed.

What these excursions demonstrate is an insight into the fact that political economy and its theory within this field of study is not simple-minded economy with a little touch of political perspective. There is more to the matter. And one central element of what begets the "more" of it is the immense impact of changes over time, especially those, implied by technological developments. Though an economic interest already existed when early news exchange systems started to operate in the 16th and 17th century in Europe as postal messenger services, one has to clearly see that the news concepts underlying modern actuality-based information systems is one that implies rigorous rationalization of the gathering, formatting, transfer and distribution processes, plus just as rigorous content standardization practice in terms of a clear understanding of what has to be considered important, as well as of priority and immediacy on both sides of the market. Both rationalization and standardization are elements of the market driven production processes that start in the area of consumer articles parallel to the development of news agencies in the modern sense during the first half of the 19th century. This parallel is not brought about by accident. These processes of adaptation are ingredients of modern economic thinking that started during that time, influencing the entire socio-cultural environment, including journalism. One of the classics to demonstrate the necessity of a re-integration of political thought into economics, and one with relevance to our subject area, is Hirshman (1970; for the appreciation and context, also Pies & Leschke, 2006).

Rationalization of the operative environment of news production and standardization of formats and content production are central elements of determining the basic political economic framework of the development of the international news organization systems that configure the daily work of foreign correspondents, up to the present (cf. Hess, 1996). Political economy comes into play as well. News organizations help to shape consciousness, through their ability to select what does and does not get transmitted to audiences, as well as their framing of news and information (Stark & Villanueva, 1992, Wicks, 2005). In this sense, political economy is also concerned with the ability to control information and information flows, which will also change over time and with technology (for critical aspects, cf. Fenton, 2005; Hamilton & Jenner, 2003; Hannerz, 2004).

These enter into a description and analysis of the development of news organizations in terms of an understanding of the theoretical implications derived from the constant dynamics of change over a period of well over 200 years. A thorough examination is not possible within this analytic essay. We have, therefore, attached a historical outline of the major technological developments with a direct effect on the role and function of foreign correspondence (Appendix I). A similar outline addresses the major points of change in the area of media organization and media structure (Appendix II). Theoretical hypotheses can be introduced at each of those points listed in the appendices. To our knowledge this, to this date, is very much unexplored territory in the study of foreign correspondence.

Looking back at the various foci of empirical insight into the political economy of foreign correspondents, it becomes clear that there exist three unique ways to develop and apply theoretical thinking to the phenomenon and work of foreign correspondents:

- The first is to make use of the evident parallels in the development of economic, industrial and political environments constituting the basis of this segment of professional work in journalism. We can follow the technical shifts that have fostered the modernization process, using a focus of insight and application that integrates essential elements of the context created within the environment of foreign correspondence invoked by the economy, by politics, and by technological developments. This then would lead to an applied evaluation of links and impacts at certain key points of economic history and, furthermore, extend the sharp analytical reflection that already exists at the intersections of economic and technological dynamics. There exists a rich literature within this scholarly segment of an integration of economic, historical and political analysis outside the English-speaking world, e.g., in France, in Italy, and in Germany in the Northern countries. Much of this work has not been translated into English. The theoretical approaches following this methodological line one would have to describe as contextual in-depth developmental theoretical focus.

- The second approach will leave out much of the re-constructive historical emphasis and concentrate on the broad spectrum of dynamic developments within the media industry itself. And it will do so, foremost, on an international and comparative scale. The theoretical challenge within this line of thinking, again, resides in the intriguing span of knowledge necessary to cover all media sectors and the entire set of technical progress that is on the way at a particular timeline within the entire media industry. For example, empirical research has delivered proof that a new journalistic format, the 'photo illustrated reportage' was created within a most dynamic and booming reconstruction period of Berlin in the years 1928/1929 (Walker, 1991). This format was further developed into especially new ways of bringing foreign countries, peoples, and cultures into a new 'realistic' perspective of the mass public that, so far, did not have 'immediate visible' access into foreign and international spheres. This new format became, afterwards, a basic concept for the success of mass publications in the United Kingdom (*Saturday Evening Post*), and in the USA (*Life*). Further development outside Germany became immensely enforced through the emigration from Germany of large groups of creative journalists, only a couple of years later, having been key developers in this area. The emigration was due to the rule of National Socialism (NSDAP) as of January 1933. In this way, a new type of foreign correspondent was born in the early 1920s. Somebody who was a step removed from the normal, routinized, production and delivery of actual news out of foreign quarters. Instead, the new type of foreign correspondent was an adventurous combination of photographer, socializing jack-of-all-trades, writer and reporter; in some instances, even developed into a recognizable brand for the magazines he was working for. From our perspective, the import of this new development lies in the fact that a new type of division of labor had arisen in the area of foreign correspondence: an increasing sharp line was be drawn between the precision style of daily actuality reporting from a country or world area, and a more illustrated and personalized, even entertaining, type of story-telling. This was a new product and market niche, not merely a tweaking of the market layer, which created a new demand that expanded from that time on. This example presents all the ingredients needed for a different type of theoretical approach emphasizing the horizontal staging area of dynamic developments within the media industry itself. A theoretical focus following this line of thought has to incorporate consideration of complex ramifications over a vast spectrum of media sectors and underlying management decisions within the entire industry. The political economic aspects involved, and the example above, make this very clear. Analysis must consider a second layer of causal ingredients that, at different points in time, might span even an entire range of countries, like in this case the clearly completely different socio-political situations in Germany, in the United Kingdom, and in the United States of America. One might call this type of theoretical approach a transversal developmental model focused on industry analysis. So far, we have not seen much effort to evolve questioning into this direction, except from minor, though very rewarding pilot studies. Some implications of such new approach for a trans-national type of media economy in Europe are outlined and collected in Heinrich and Kopper (2006).

• The third theoretical approach seems, from the outset, to be the most banal one: It follows the clear lines of economic theory on the one hand, and political science theory on the other hand. It will include several aspects that have sprung up within these large disciplinary branches, like institutional economics (to mention just one impressive example). So far, not much work is available within a clear economic or political science focus. That there is a large missing link to be called political economy, within this special sector of analysis, we have already mentioned at several occasions. The analytical reward of focusing on the phenomenon and work of foreign correspondents, using clear-cut economic and/or political science questions, will likely be quite substantial. And there is evidence that many studies already existing in these disciplines render theoretical implications that can be used in the field of foreign correspondence with great reward. Instead of offering a long list we, at this stage, just introduce one example: risk management (cf. Spaeth, 2004). The few cases where such applications have been started show the kind of high reward in terms of substantial insight to be gained (e.g., Kopper, 2006b). Precision analysis following theoretical questions stemming from economics and/or political science will help to bring light into a number of areas within the field that, concerning the research results available, tend to offer rather ambiguous interpretations. Again, to illustrate this through an example: when studies of U.S. correspondents working out of Europe (Hannerz, 2004) and foreign correspondents in the U.S. (Hess, 2005) shows that their number has been reduced, and that their reporting areas have been enlarged much beyond past limits, there are interpretations by the interviewed correspondents referring to economic factors within the media industry as well as a shift of interest of home editors and audiences (Lönnendonker, Nitz, & Stamm, 2006). These two explanations leave the researchers somewhat unable to reach broader conclusions, because they are based more on superficial considerations than any thorough theoretical grounding. The first explanation looks only at overall performance (i.e., if profits decline, then cut costs), for example, not what foreign correspondents contribute to overall value or what editorial strategy may be most effective in an increasingly competitive environment. The failure of this research area to consider theory and issues of value more deeply limits their ability to provide an integrated analysis of the situation. An increase in contextual introspection would relate more of the general political economy in such a case (one example of many: Röttger, 1997) and hence open a wider spectrum of possible answers.

The central question, awaiting more thorough theoretical analysis, would have to be what grounds are there for any kind of economic argument? A straightforward and clear-cut type of theoretical approach is still largely missing. As has already been stressed, what is missing here in the field is an analysis based on economic and political science theory.

Looking back over the development and evolution of foreign correspondence (as a particular type of information gathering, news production, and interpretation of the world outside), all the while trying to understand the major theoretical ramifications of technological change, the evolving structures of media systems, institutional frameworks and political contexts involved, one is inclined to fall back on one reticent and a bit snobbish remark of British economists reflecting on the term "political economy." For them, political economy reflects "an early title" for the subject area of economics; political economy "now has an old-fashioned ring to it but usually emphasizes the importance of choice between alternatives in economics which remains, despite continuing scientific progress, as much of an act of art as a science" (Bannock, Baxter & Davis, 1987: 129). For them, of course, macro and micro economic aspects were the major concern. The application of this somewhat ironic insight, however, to the micro level of foreign correspondence can lead to the challenging assumption that the entire process of professional development might be subsumed as a general sum of manifold economic decisions determining the specific working environment. Reconstructing the basic patterns that formed the underlying decision-making process forming this specific development, thus, will render rewarding theoretical insight. The theoretical implications have been tried out in Dröge and Kopper (1991).

From our perspective, the most rewarding theoretical approach within economics for such an examination is the subfield of institutional economics. Within this framework, a number of the old questions asked under the heading of "political economy" re-emerge within a fresh and suitable perspective, because institutional economics "focuses on power, institutions, technology, process and similar concepts" (Samuels, 1991: 116). As has been made clear in our observations, various advances in technology have had major impacts on the fundamental nature and practice of the work of foreign correspondents over time. It is within the concepts of institutional economics that one finds a long-standing and rich theoretical approach for examining these, and, hence, an adequate conceptual framework for examining technology and its implications for change (e.g., for one of the early perspectives, Lower, 1987).

There is one important element in foreign correspondence and its political economy foundations that has remained unchanged over time, which is the impact that this type of news has had within the financial and economic sector itself. Starting from the early lettered dispatches in the feudal times, news and information went from one sensitive market to another via post, impacting economic actions in those markets. We see similar effects under the most modern circumstances, with highly automatic and computer supported news services plus correspondents' analyses (cf. Joyce & Read, 1999) widely available and regularly triggering significant market swings.

A simplified model, thus, of understanding the political economy of foreign correspondence could follow the theoretical implications of the news processes within the sphere of finances and economic information. It is at this front that the initial applications of new technologies, over the centuries, had the first impact and forced systematic and structural changes within the entire news environment. And we find in economic history rich material to show that, consistently, the use of foreign correspondence followed the economic expansion of countries (for Japan, see Kuwahara, 1990). Shifts in world perspective have also led to a changes in the logistics of foreign correspondence, as has been the case for the USA recently (Lönnendonker, Nitz, & Stamm, 2006).

So far, an integral and encompassing trans-disciplinary perspective concerning news processes and news results within the financial and economic area has not emerged. Therefore we tend to find rather pure, i.e., disciplinary economic analysis, also in cases where the total news process and its understanding would be of particular value (e.g., Veronesi, 1999).

One outcome of our observation will have become quite clear: when explaining the thrust, but also the dilemma, of major theoretical approaches possible under the general umbrella of political economy in the rather unexplored area of foreign correspondence, it is obvious that the type of theory preceding new research will have to become much better retrieved, clarified and put to use. A truly international cooperation of researchers will tremendously enhance this task. The variety of trans-cultural differences in understanding and using even the latest instruments of technology in foreign correspondence indicate the degree of insight to be gained by, first of all, an inclusion of all relevant perspectives available. Issues like "rationalization" within the professional environment of foreign correspondents, follow a very diverse spectrum of leading foci that tends to extend from view points of business administration to those of cultural heritage. This research field, hence, offers an enormous potential for rewarding inroads in theoretically engaged and innovative forms of trans-disciplinary international work (e.g., Kopper, 2008).

And this might, in most cases, be a task without much immediate or direct support through an ongoing debate on the very premises of the problem area. At the end of our observations we shall point this out, again, by showing the direct implications of changes in practical reality and the impact on theory building.

It will only be possible to advance into new directions within this area when the necessary research follows a proper and thorough theoretical preparation. We shall illustrate this by a practical example. In an age of global implications of national and supra-national policies and, generally, of political and economic changes because of their intermingled cross-implications beyond national horizons, there is increasing empirical evidence that the type and spread of information concerning such issues has new impact (Kuzyk & McCluskey, 2006; Swinnen & Francken, 2006). By the same token, however, the use of the media for political protests and by new actor groups creating events of such new dimension to be covered for the purpose of worldwide distribution raises fundamentally new questions with regard to foreign correspondence its role and implications. To assess these through new types of empirical research one has, first of all, develop a theoretical approach concerning the very nature of these changes within their new political and economic implications.

As some of the examples might have already shown, it will not be sufficient to simply re-interpret existing descriptive statistics, the results of empirical studies based on interviews, or surveys, etc. Starting from a new theoretically founded platform within the political science frame of analysis would require substantially new approaches in terms of methodologies, research instruments, and measures. However, to outline those is not our immediate purpose.

This overall analysis of the political economy of the work of foreign correspondents has shown that central elements of theory applicable to this important segment of the modern news world has never been rigorously applied and turned into pertinent questions for research—and also practical understanding. It remains for that work to begin.

References

Adorno, T., & Horkheimer, M. (1979). The culture industry: Enlightenment as mass deception. In J. Curran, M. Gurevitch, & J. Woollacott (Eds.), *Mass Communication and Society*. Beverly Hills, CA: Sage

Altschull, H. J. (1984). *Agents of Power. The Role of the News Media in Human Affairs*. London: Longmans.

Arrow, K. J. (1984). *The Economics of Information* (Collected Papers of Kenneth J. Arrow, Vol. 4). Cambridge, MA: Belknap Press.

Assmann, J. (2006). *Religion and cultural memory*. Stanford, CA: Stanford University Press.

Bannock, G., Baxter, R. E., & Davis, E. (1987). *The Penguin Dictionary of Economics, 4th ed.* London, Penguin.

Bates, B. J. (1988). Information as an economic good: Sources of individual and social value. In V. Mosco and J. Wasko (Eds.), *The Political Economy of Information* (pp. 76–94). Madison, WI: University of Wisconsin Press.

Bates, B. J. (1990). Information as an economic good: A re-evaluation of theoretical approaches. In B. D. Ruben & L. A. Lievrouw (Eds.), *Mediation, Information, and Communication. Information and Behavior. Volume 3* (pp. 379–394). New Brunswick, NJ: Transaction.

Berghahn, V. R. (1994). *Imperial Germany, 1871–1914. Economy, Society, Culture and Politics.* Providence: Berghahn Books.

Bottomore, T. (1983). *A history of Marxist Thought.* Cambridge, MA: Harvard University Press.

Boyd-Barrett, O. (1980). *The International News Agencies.* London: Constable.

Carragee, K. M., & Roefs, W. (2004): The neglect of power in recent framing research. *Journal of Communication, 54*(2), 214–233.

Czitrom, D. J. (1982). *Media and the American Mind from Morse to McLuhan.* Chapel Hill, NC: University of North Carolina Press.

Dell'Orto, G. (2002). *Giving Meanings to the World: The First U.S. Foreign Correspondents, 1838–1859.* Westport, CT: Greenwood Press.

Doyle, G. (2002). *Understanding Media Economics.* London: Sage.

Dröge, F. & Kopper, G. G. (1991). Der Medien-Prozess. Zur Struktur innerer Errungenschaften der bürgerlichen Gesellschaft [The media process. On the structure of symbolic assets of bourgeois society]. Opladen: Westdeutscher Verlag.

Fenby, J. (1986*). The International News Services.* New York, NY: Schocken.

Fenton, T. (2005). *Bad News: The Decline of Reporting, the Business of News, and the Danger to Us All.* New York, NY: Harper Collins.

Flichy, P. (1995). *Dynamics of Modern Communication: The Shaping and Impact of New Communication Technologies.* London: Sage Publications.

Gramsci, A. (1971). *Selections from the prison notebooks* (translated by Q. Hoare & G. N. Smith). London: Lawrence & Wishart.

Hamilton, J. M. (2009). *Journalism's Roving Eye: A History of American Foreign Reporting.* Baton Rouge, LA: Louisiana State University Press.

Hamilton, J. M., & Jenner, E. (2003). The new foreign correspondence. *Foreign Affairs, 82*(5), 131–139.

Hamilton, J. M., & Jenner, E. (2004). Redefining foreign correspondence. *Journalism, 5*(3), 301–321.

Hannerz, U. (2004). *Foreign News: Exploring the World of Foreign Correspondents.* Chicago: University of Chicago Press.

Heald, M. (1988). *Transatlantic Vistas: American Journalists in Europe.* Kent, OH: Kent State University Press.

Heinrich, J., & Kopper, G. G. (eds.) (2006). *Media Economics in Europe.* Berlin: Vistas.

Hess, S. (1996). *International News & Foreign Correspondents.* Washington, DC: The Brookings Institution.

Hess, S. (2005). *Through Their Eyes: Foreign Correspondents in the United States.* Washington, DC: The Brookings Institution.

Hills, R. L. (1988). *Papermaking in Britain 1488–1988.* London: Athlon Press.

Hirschman, A. O. (1970). *Exit, Voice and Loyalty: Responses to Decline in Firms, Organizations and States.* Cambridge, MA: Harvard University Press.

Holstein, L. (2003). *In Defense of Framing Theory: Bringing Hegemony Back.* Paper presented at the ICA conference, San Diego, 2003.

Huteau, J., & Ullmann, B. (1992). *AFP. Une histoire de l'Agence France Presse, 1944–1980.* Paris: Laffont.

66   UNDERSTANDING FOREIGN CORRESPONDENCE

Johnston, C. B. (1998). *Global News Access. The Impact of New Communication Technologies.* Westport, CT: Praeger.

Joyce, M., & Read, V. (1999). The impact of inflation news on financial markets. Bank of England. Quarterly Report, vol. 39, 1/2, 48–59.

Knies, K. (1883). *Die politische Ökonomie vom geschichtlichen Standpunkt. Nachdruck* [Political economy under perspective of history. A Reprint.]. Saarbrücken: VDM Müller.

Kopper, G. G. (ed.). (2006a). *"How are you, Mr. President?"—Nachrichtenarbeit, Berufswirklichkeit und Produktionsmanagement an den Korrespondentenplätzen deutscher Medien in den USA. Arbeitsbuch für Medienpraxis und Forschung.* ["How are you, Mr. President?" News work, professional reality and production management at correspondents' sites in the U.S.A. A work book for practice in the media and for research.] Berlin: Vistas.

Kopper, G. G. (2006b). Work of German foreign correspondents in the USA and Internet based rationalisation options. A case study at Washington, D.C., USA. In: G. G. Kopper (ed.), *"How are you, Mr. President?"—Nachrichtenarbeit, Berufswirklichkeit und Produktionsmanagement an den Korrespondentenplätzen deutscher Medien in den USA. Arbeitsbuch für Medienpraxis und Forschung.* ["How are you, Mr. President?" News work, professional reality and production management at correspondents' sites in the U.S.A. A work book for practice in the media and within research.] Berlin: Vistas, pp.119–140.

Kopper, G. G. (2008). Aktueller Fernsehjournalismus, Industriepolitik und Journalistenausbildung [TV News Journalism, Industrial Policy, and Journalism Training]. In: L. Hausmann, S. Kretschmar, S. Opitz, & H. Röper (eds.) *"Wir müssen mehr experimentieren." Journalistenausbildung zwischen Wissenschaft und Praxis.* ["More experiments needed"—Journalism Training Between Communication Science and Practice] Dortmund: OVM 2008. S. 239–264.

Kuwahara, T. (1990). *Kigyo kokusai no shiteki bunseki* [Japanese business abroad in historical perspective]. Tokyo: Moriyama.

Kuzyk, P., & McCluskey, J. J. (2006). The Political Economy of the Media: Coverage of the Lumber Tariff Dispute. *The World Economy*, 29 (5), 655–667.

Lacy, S., and Simon, T. F. (1993). *The Economics and Regulation of United States Newspapers.* Norwood, NJ: Ablex.

Lamberton, D. M. (1971). *The Economics of Information and Knowledge: Selected Readings.* New York: Penguin.

Leidinger, C. (2003). *Medien—Herrschaft—Globalisierung. Folgenabschätzung zu Medieninhalten im Zuge transnationaler Konzentrationsprozesse.* Münster: Westfälisches Dampfboot [Media—Power—Globalization—Assessing the impact on media content as a result of transnational processes of concentration. < also Doctoral Thesis Univ. of Münster>]

List, F. (1996). *Outlines of American Political Economy: In Twelve Letters to Charles J. Ingersoll.* Ed. of commented reprint: Michael Liebig. Wiesbaden: Böttiger.

Lönnendonker, J., Nitz, P., & Stamm, S. (2006). Transatlantic reporting. Work routines and self perception of US and German correspondents. Working Papers in International Journalism (Ed: G. G. Kopper). Bochum: Projekt Verlag.

Lower, M. (1987). The concept of technology within the institutional perspective. *Journal of Economic Issues, 21*, 1147–1176.

McBride, S. (Ed.) (1980). *Many voices, one world*. Paris: UNESCO.

McLee, A. (1937).*The daily newspaper in America*. New York, N.Y.: Macmillan.

Mitchell, B. R. (1980). *European Historical Statistics, 1750–1975*, 2ⁿᵈ ed. London.

Mosco, V. (1996). *The Political Economy of Communication*. London: Sage.

Neumann, S. (1997). *Redaktionsmanagement in den USA. Fallbeispiel "Seattle Times."* Dortmunder Beiträge zur Zeitungsforschung 55. München: Saur. [Editorial management in the USA. Case study of the "Seattle Times." No 55, Dortmund Contributions to Newspaper Research. Also Doctoral Dissertation, University of Dortmund].

Norris, P. (2001). *Digital Divide: Civic Engagement, Information Poverty, and the Internet Worldwide*. Cambridge, UK: Cambridge University Press.

Nye, J. S., Jr. (2008). Public diplomacy and soft power. *The Annals of the American Academy of Political and Social Science, 616*, 94–109.

Paterson, C. (2005). News agency dominance in international news on the Internet. In D. Skinner, J. R. Compton, & M. Gasher (eds.), *Converging Media, Diverging Politics: a Political Economy of News Media in the United States and Canada*. Lanham, MD: Lexington.

Pies, I., & Leschke, M. (eds.) (2006). *Albert Hirschmans grenzüberschreitende Ökonomik. Tübingen: Mohr Siebeck* [Albert Hirschman's economy passing beyond borders. Proceedings of a congress at Wittenberg 2005]

Preston, W., Jr., Herman, E. S., & Schiller, H. I. (1989). *Hope and Folly. The United States and UNESCO, 1945–1985*. Minneapolis: University of Minnesota Press.

Read, D. (1992). *The Power of News. The History of Reuters*. Oxford: Oxford University Press.

Reese, S. D. (2001). Understanding the global journalist: a hierarchy-of-influence approach. *Journalism Studies, 2*(2), 173–187.

Röttger, B. (1997). *Neoliberale Globalisierung und eurokapitalistische Regulation* [Neoliberal globalizing and euro-capitalist regulation]. Münster: Westfälisches Dampfboot

Samuels, W. J. (1991). Institutional Economics. In D. Grennaway, M. Bleaney, & I. Stewart (eds.), *Companion to contemporary economic thought* (pp. 105–118). London, New York: Routledge.

Schäfer, U. P. (1994). *Ludwig Kircher als Korrespondent der Frankfurter Zeitung 1920–1923* [Ludwig Kircher as correspondent of the „Frankfurter Zeitung" 1920–1923]. Frankfurt/Main, Lang.

Scheufele, D. A. (1999). Framing as a theory of media effects. *Journal of Communication, 49*(1), 103–122.

Stevenson, R.L., & Shaw, D. L. (1984): *Foreign News and the New World Information Order*. Ames: Iowa State University Press.

Schudson, M. (1978). *Discovering the News: A Social History of American Newspapers*. New York, NY: Basic Books.

Schwarzlose, R. A. (1989). *The Nation's Newsbrokers: Vol. 1 The Formative Years, from the Pre-Telegraph to 1865; Vol. 2 The Push to Institution, from 1865 to 1920*. Evanston, IL: Northwestern University Press.

Spaeth, M. (2004). Womit handelt die Medienindustrie und ihr Managemment? Ein Beitrag zur Risikoverarbeitung in der Medienindustrie aus sozialwissenschaftlicher Perspektive. Dissertation (unveröffentlicht) Univ. München. [What does the media industry and its management trade? A contribution to risk management in the media industry through a social science perspective. Unpubl. Doctoral Dissertation, University of Munich.]

Stark, K., & Villanueva, E. (1992). *Cultural Framing: Foreign Correspondents and Their Work*. Paper presented at AEJMC conference, Montreal, 1992.

Swinnen, J. F. M., & Francken, N. (2006). Summits, riots and media attention: The political economy of information on trade and globalisation. *The World Economy 29* (5), 637–654.

Veronesi, P. (1999). Stock market overreaction to bad news in good times. A rational expectation equilibrium model. *Review of Financial Studies*, 12 (5), 975–1008.

Walker, A. (1991). Die Fotoreportage in den Illustrierten der Weimarer Zeit. Zur Entwicklung einer journalistischen Gattung. Eine exemplarische Untersuchung anhand der Jahrgänge 1928 und 1929 der „Berliner Illustrirten Zeitung" und der „Münchener Illustrierten Presse". Diplomarbeit Journalistik (unveröffentlicht), Universität Dortmund. [The photo reportage in the illustrated weeklies of the German Weimar Republic. On the development of a journalism format. An exemplary empirical study of the publication years 1928 and 1929 of "Berliner Illustrirte Zeitung" and "Münchener Illustrierte Presse". Diploma Journalism thesis (unpublished), Univ. of Dortmund.]

Watson, J. (2007). Representing realities: An overview of news framing. *Keio Communication Review, 29,* 107–131.

Wicks, R. H. (2005). Message framing and constructing meaning: An emerging paradigm in mass communication research. In P. J. Kalbfleisch (Ed.), *Communication Yearbook 29*. Mahwah, NJ: Lawrence Erlbaum.

CHAPTER 4

Foreign Correspondents and Ethnography: Research Practices, Methods, and Texts

Ralph Beliveau and Julia Lönnendonker

I. Introduction

> No text can do everything at once. The perfect ethnography cannot be written.
> —*Norman K. Denzin:* Interpretive Ethnography:
> Ethnographic Practices for the 21ˢᵗ Century, *p. 287.*

> It is all too easy to assume that a credible proposition is a reality....There can never be a definitive fact of any kind. But between the definitive fact and the presumed but undemonstrated reality lies a wide range of possibilities, and it is into this murky middle ground—into the world of what has probably really happened in the world—that the historical social sciences are called to work. Deductive models serve us ill. Common knowledge is at best a source of possible correct perceptions and is itself an object of study. This is why fieldwork (in the loosest, broadest sense of the term) is our eternal responsibility.
> —*Immanuel Wallerstein:* The Uncertainties of Knowledge *(2004), pp. 182-183.*

Understanding the work of foreign correspondents entails understanding and accounting for how they see and communicate about their world. How we choose to pursue such an understanding is a choice of great significance. In this chapter, we would like to argue the case for understanding foreign correspondents through ethnographic fieldwork.

Consider for a moment three different approaches to the question of developing a scholarly understanding of the work of foreign correspondents. One group of studies might take statistical approaches to the questions at hand. Hypotheses produce survey questions, surveys collect data, and data is collated and analyzed. The analysis would give us a general knowledge of how foreign correspondents work as a group. The impetus toward social scientific thinking defers in many ways to the kind of generalizable information

that comes from such studies. From these generalizations comes the conclusion of forming general laws of ideology or behavior for the group.

Such an approach has been called nomothetic, from the Greek *nomos* or
laws. This notion argues that if any single person is to be studied as part of a
group, the goal is to ascertain their individual combination of "universal
laws" which are understood in relation to the group. In the case of the specific group we are concerned with—foreign correspondents—the acts of an
individual foreign correspondent are understood in so far as they represent
their representation of a larger group.

The second and third approaches to understanding we might consider, on
the other hand, seek knowledge that is idiographic rather than nomothetic,
focusing in the *idios* or the private or personal. This notion argues that we get
to know the acts of individuals in and of themselves. What we come to understand we put into a complex picture of the individual and her or his situation. Rather than seeing the "law" in operation among a group, we see how
all of the "laws" or beliefs of that individual example are integrated into their
cultural situation. The kind of study here seeks depth, and sees the present
against a context of complex experiences that played their role at some point
in the past, contributing to a single individual or a single subcultural point of
view.

To get to that level of analysis requires a methodological choice that
must thread a difficult path. On the one hand, it must be close to the subject
under study so it can gain a sufficient level of detail about the subject to put
together individual choices and actions into larger patterns. On the other
hand, it must maintain a kind of observational detachment that produces
knowledge that is meaningful beyond the specific observer or scholar. In
other words, what the researcher sees in the observation should not be just a
reflection on the specific researcher.

A second approach might conduct this close observation through careful
historical accounts of the social conditions that affect the lives of foreign correspondents. When we settle on the foreign correspondent as the subject of
the close observation and analysis we can observe that several different kinds
of pressures have played into their mix of professional and personal choices.
One could document their education and training, personal experience with
news throughout their lives, desire for travel, the genesis of their interest in
another culture, etc. To be complete, the account would need to include professional pressures, whether commercial or aesthetic, which locate these correspondents in or among larger media organizations. This study is

fundamentally historical in design seeking understanding through an account of significant details, both known and unknown to the foreign correspondent as a subject.

This kind of study was proposed by the Annales School, which was founded in 1928 by Marc Bloch and Lucien Febvre. The most famous work of this School was done by Ferdinand Braudel in the 1940s (Braudel, 1973). This movement seeks a kind of comprehensive history, attending to structural details of the smallest dimension to build a thorough picture. Ultimately, as Alan Megill argues, the coherence that is brought to the subject in the production of history is brought by the practice of historical investigation itself (Megill, 2004, p. 212). While this particular school of history, focusing on comprehensive detail as a way of accounting for the subject, is less influential in and of itself, it had a profound effect on the way cultural history is practiced through the last 50—75 years of historical writing. The Annales School is worth noting because it attempted to shore up the relationship between history and other social sciences. In that sense, it attempts to bridge between the *nomos*/laws and the *idios*/personal. For the study of foreign correspondents, the result would be somewhere between a historical and a sociological account. It gains in terms of the possibility of an explanation outside of the understanding of the foreign correspondents themselves, since they may not be fully conscious of all of the influences that produce their journalistic work. But gaining the more objective perspective is limited because of what is specifically left out; the consciousness of the foreign correspondents themselves.

The third approach is ethnography. This approach is more purely idiographic, and thus more ideally situated to understand the reflexive side of foreign correspondents, without necessarily producing an idiosyncratic individual account. We want to argue that a well-grounded, rigorous and methodologically sophisticated way to gather such a picture becomes available through ethnography. In this chapter, we will define ethnography with a particular eye toward its application studying foreign correspondents; we will discuss the research process, materials and methods that are deployed in conducting ethnographic research practice; we will discuss what ethnography and journalism have to do with each other, in terms of the way each constructs a picture of the world, assumes that there are certain advantageous ways of communicating the details of that world, and reflects on their mutual practices to do their work better; and finally give examples of ethnographic field work applied to the research of foreign correspondents.

II. Ethnography: Process

The discussion of ethnography must bring together some minor differences in use between some North American and some European understandings. The U.S. notion of an 'ethnographer' can encompass a complete scholarly identity, where in some places the European notion is more strictly considered a question of technique rather than identity:

> In the US, being an ethnographer means utilizing certain methods of research, engaging certain analytical strategies and perspectives, and seeking certain audiences for one's work. In contrast, it seems that, among Europeans, ethnography equals participant observation, thus describing a technique of qualitative inquiry (…) rather than a scholarly identity. (Kusenbach, 2005, p. 3)

A Dutch researcher says, "another label for this style of research work is 'participant observation'" (Have, 2004, p. 7).

But the other significant difference has to do with limits on methodology. U.S. ethnographers are not strictly contained within qualitative methods, where European scholars see a more dedicated link between ethnography and qualitative research.

In either case, however, a common definition can be offered. Krotz describes:

> In general one can say that ethnography is a super ordinate concept for a whole range of different empirical access routes to the social and cultural reality of human beings, thus a whole collection of research strategies. All these methods have in common, that they are aimed at the exhibition of cultural structures and processes. (Krotz, 2005, p. 251).[1]

Krotz adds:

> The data collection aims at the reconstruction of the sense and impact of social action. In the process, participant observation and non-participant observation as well as interviews and conversation are the most important methods of investigation, in addition to the experiences and reflections of the ethnographer. (Krotz, 2005, p. 281)

Ethnography offers procedures and methods, but does not oblige the researcher to any single set or procedure. As Lindlof states (1995, p. 19), "Ba-

---

1 All translations by the authors.

sically ethnographers will turn to any method that will help them to achieve the goals of good ethnography." The ethnographer benefits from the flexible application of different methodological approaches, even taking advantage of the opportunity to innovate in the way interviews are structured, and the way informants and subjects are positioned within the ethnography. Rigor is accomplished through the way the ethnographer incorporates explanations of the research procedure into the work. Transparency replaces procedural conformity, which is most easily understood against the background of the area's history.

An understanding of ethnography requires an understanding of the developments of knowledge in the fields of sociology and anthropology. Both of these larger fields research problems of definition, and specifically investigate the idea of self and other. Historically it was not always the case to develop a balanced representation of the self and other.

Such a balance was lacking because the identity of the anthropological or sociological researcher was determined by professional training (Clifford, 1988, pp. 24-25). By the mid-1930s, an international consensus had developed on how this kind of research was done. The researcher would enter the "field" where the object of study was located. Researchers were trained to engage in a period of intense observation and writing, developing cultural descriptions of the "other." Such observations required long and intense periods of relocation into the context of the culture. This observation and note-taking period is referred to as fieldwork:

> "Fieldwork is one answer—some say the best—to the question of how the understanding of others, close or distant, is achieved. Fieldwork usually means living with and living like those who are studied. In its broadest, most conventional sense, fieldwork demands the full-time involvement of a researcher over a lengthy period of time (typically unspecified) and consists mostly of ongoing interaction with the human targets of study on their home ground." (Van Maanen, 1988, p. 2)

In the field the researcher translates his or her observations into a series of fieldnotes, reflections on fieldnotes, and subsequent analysis of fieldnotes to find cultural patterns of the specified other. Although the length of time in the field is not specified, some scholars argue that a researcher should not skimp on traditional ethnographic practices, and remain committed to long-term, in depth, site-specific work that allow for the maturation of the material that is collected and the analyses of the patterns found (La Pastina, 2005, p.

147). The accumulation of these analyses of patterns, typically structured into some kind of a larger account, make up an ethnography.

The practices of ethnographic observation—as could be gathered from the "-graph" part of the name—are ultimately practices of writing, practices of translating the observed world into words and sentences. Some of this writing is intended to absorb and manifest the observations, and are written primarily for the use of the ethnographic observer. The audience is not yet included in this writing in any direct sense, although that ultimate aim toward that audience is always influential in the process of looking for social and cultural patterns and developing descriptions of them out of the observations, memories, and fieldnotes. These are methodologies that are grounded in reading and writing. As such, these methodologies share many of the same communication problems as foreign correspondents do in their work. This is not to say that the professional practices and constraints are the same, but it does bring attention to such practices and conventions. Researchers are usually bound by some kind of written output, and are aware of the constraints that allow their research work to reach a targeted academic audience.

The practices of ethnographic observation have a participatory dimension as well. There is, in fact, a history of using participant observation methodology to understand the operation of media organizations (Hansen et al., 1998, pp. 38-43). Participant observation may not fundamentally change the operation of the media organization, but the presence of the ethnographer becomes an undeniable component of the field. Subjects are usually informed and consent to the presence of the researcher, both as a practical matter and as an ethical grounding for the actions of the ethnographer. In addition, as Lene Tanggaard writes, "All types of talk are coproduced. Even an interviewer who tries to ask relatively few questions is part of a coproduction of meaning when setting up an interview or undertaking an informal conversation as part of fieldwork studies" (2009, p. 1510). The ethnographer has a complex sense of agency, pulled in one direction be the desire to secure a deep understanding of the ethnographic subject, and pulled in another direction to make her or his own thinking on the ethnographic process a material component of the account, since it was indeed a material component of the conversation. Contemporary ethnography is increasingly invested in the intellectual account of the ethnographer.

These notions support the basic idea that ethnography is a term that means two things at once. It is, first a systematic process of observation. Second the term refers to the (usually) written product of that observation.

Ethnography is both a process and a product (Tedlock, 2003, p. 165). Ethnographers and others in anthropology and sociology, as well as education and nursing, have also come to problematize the authority of any single account. Over the past 20 years, critical and feminist ethnography have argued for "the diversity of possible ethnographies" (Williams, 2008, p. 245).

The researcher working with foreign correspondents occupies a unique position in relation to this process/product binary. The correspondent is involved in a similar pursuit, where their life as a "correspondent"—their experience as a process—finds its fulfillment in their production of journalistic "correspondence," which is a specific and targeted transformation of their process in the written result of their activities. Traditional ethnographic work observes a different kind of product, since what is observed is the product "culture" unified with the process of producing it (i.e., the lives the method observes).

At the same time, ethnography with foreign correspondents has limits as far as participant observation goes. Since its origins with Malinowski in the 1920s ethnographic fieldwork has been concerned with developing an understanding of the point of view of the "native" under observation. The ethnographer arrived at this understanding through observation, but not from a distance. Instead the ideal ethnographic method uses "participant observation," where the ethnographer occupies the role of the person in that cultural position. Participant observation is thus limited since the ethnographer is not likely to produce journalism in the same way the foreign correspondent produces stories. However, the experience of the milieu of the foreign correspondents, as individuals and as a group, would still allow for some development of participant observer data.

The gains of the combination of observation and participation, however, are numerous (Hansen et al., 1998, pp. 44-46). The ethnographic observer is well positioned to see the usually invisible side of the world of foreign correspondents, those parts of the process that fall outside of their conscious decision-making. Observation of the correspondent's routine also allows access to the material that is ventured but never completed, stories that are abandoned, spiked, or overtaken by other priorities. Observation and participation offers the opportunity to test claims that arise in the ethnographer's thinking, hypotheses about the work, the routine, or the product that can be tested against events. Ethnography also affords the opportunity to investigate circumstances that, in practice, are more chaotic than might be implied by a shaped narrative that seeks clarity:

...[T]he processes of cultural production and consumption are likely to be less clean, less tidy, more happenstance, more leaky than theorists sometimes acknowledge. Attending to both the routine and the contingent nature of media production, in all its complexity, dents the idea that cultural production is a smooth running operation, and points to the 'mediatedness' of cultural processes. (Hansen et al., 1998, p. 46)

Understanding the work of foreign correspondents through ethnographic work requires an account of both the successes and the failures, an idea of how things go when they go well, and how they go when they go poorly. Both of these aspects of the work, as well as the analysis of the produced work itself, and the reflections the correspondents offer on the published work, are an important area to include in the ethnographic product.

III. Ethnography: Product

Ethnographers produce ethnographies. Ethnographies are representations, specific uses of language within particular sets of expectations that are intended to communicate a sense—arguably verifiable—that a trained ethnographic observer has to offer about an observed subject.

The problems connected to ethnographies are directly connected to how the communication takes place, and the desired result. Fortunately for researchers, types of ethnographic work have broadened considerably over the last 30 years, finding a place in a variety of disciplines including education, social work, and communication in its varied formations of mass communication, speech communication, media studies, etc. We might consider three different kinds of communication that arise out of an ethnography (Clifford, 1988, p. 62). First, an ethnography might strive for a documentary moment, offering a set of 'social facts' as evidence for an interpretation that argues for a pattern arising out of the set of facts. The task of the ethnography is to present documentation of observed pieces of culture, and attempt to keep tight reigns over the move to interpretation. This shares a kind of basic set of possibilities with journalism if both are understood to deploy language as transparently as possible. Both kinds of writing share a desire to present a notion of disinterestedness or objectivity in their means of communication. Often these characteristics are addressed in the way writers are trained to connect their observations with their means of representation. Ethnographies in this more traditional paradigm should be produced through a scientific approach that structures research questions, uses them to guide the method of selection of data, and arrive at "scientifically supportable interpretations of their data" (Le Compte & Schensul, 1999, p. 150).

Consider as a comparison, the way the *Associated Press Broadcast News Handbook* presents a notion of objectivity:

> "The reporter's job is to observe events and to tell people about them....By defini-tion, the act of informing the members of such a society is the act of separating fact from opinion....There is no doubt that reporting and writing by definition involve making choices about which facts to use. Supremely important are the criteria used to make the selections....If a reporter includes those facts that support a given view-point and leaves out those facts which support a competing viewpoint, that's bias. If, however, the story reports each relevant viewpoint (there may be more than two), giving each the weight it had in the event being covered, that's what newspeople call objective." (Kalbfeld, 2001, pp. 27-28)

Note how this definition suggests that the representation of "facts" through language is not problematized to a great degree. Language use can fall into categories of fact or opinion, and a reporter sensitive to the differ-ence is similar to an ethnographer operating in a documentary mode. Thoughtful people in either activity are certainly sensitive to the complicated way language can reflect subjective interpretations. The point is that each approach, in a documentary frame of mind, tries to limit the markers of an individual perspective in the representation. Clearly the researcher studying foreign correspondents would need to consider her or his own assumptions and definitions about their jobs, their understanding of the articulation be-tween knowledge and communication, and the relationship between observ-ing and informing. Ethnographic research is appropriately sensitive to its attempts to reach across cultures. In many instances the standards and defini-tions of the role of journalism are critical to seeing how they cover a similar goal of moving information between cultural groups.

A second kind of ethnography might offer a picture that is more experi-ential than documentary. The ethnography would detail the way a person experiences the world being studied. This participant observation approach can be found in the ethnographic work of Mark Fishman (1980, 1997). For some of his work Fishman became a reporter on an alternative weekly news-paper for seven months, followed by three months observing the daily work routines of three journalists (1997, pp. 213-214). Out of these experiences Fishman represents the patterns that he finds in the activities of journalists, the way they see events, identify 'newsness' and importance, and decide to act on events. His conclusions point to the way different bureaucracies interact with each other (pp. 217-227).

A third kind of ethnography is hermeneutic in orientation. Such an approach begins to discuss some of the complex issues of language and epistemology that ground the reader's understanding of the ethnographic text. The metaphor of ethnography as text is perhaps most clearly expressed by Clifford Geertz in his production and discussion of the Balinese cockfight (1973, p. 448). Geertz shifts the analysis of cultural form from an organism metaphor to a text metaphor. He suggests that the ethnography produces a "thick description" (Geertz, 199, p. 10), a complex symbolic structure that 'says something.' The focus shifts, he argues, from a formulation of social mechanics to a formulation of social semantics. Culture is examined as an assemblage of texts. This perspective on ethnography becomes significant as a text practice, even possibly extending to arguments about the relationship between text forms from fieldnotes, to journal article, to short story (Wolf, 1992). In this context, ethnographic research is more a matter of interpretation and not only of observation and description (Krotz, 2005, p. 255).

Such a textual understanding might become more useful, however, if the text is seen as representing a more important moment of dialogue (Clifford & Fischer, 1999, p. 30). Dialogue suggests an active process of exchange between the ethnographer and the subject, reconstructed into a dialogic experience between the ethnography and the reader. Communication is not dependent on empathy or sympathy, but instead extends to a notion of communicative exchange.

As we consider the possibilities of the production of ethnographies of foreign correspondents we can see the potential impact of such a shift. The activity is less centered on the production of particular media artifacts and more concentrated on the way foreign correspondence is lives as a process of negotiation between cultures.

IV. What do ethnography and journalism have in common?

"Foreign correspondents are a sort of anthropologist, or an anthropologist is a sort of foreign correspondent, to the extent that they engage in reporting from one part of the world to another." (Hannerz, 2004, p. 4)

Hannerz presents the question of similarities and differences between ethnographers and journalist. The most obvious similarity between the two groups is that they both live in a culture which is not their own. Krotz observes that "the ethnographer always has to live 'between' two cultures" (Krotz, 2005, p. 269). The same is true for foreign correspondents. Beyond that also Krotz's (2005, p. 269) fear that "where ethnographers develop too much sympathy for their counterpart and get used to everyday live too much, they jeopardize to loose the distance to what they research" holds true for foreign correspondents. This sacrifice of distance is described as "going native" among communication scientists.

Anthropology might even have been influenced by journalistic methods in the investigation of real-life settings. For example, one of the founders of the famous Chicago School, Robert E. Park, had had a career as a journalist working for newspapers. This encounter with journalism influenced his later work in sociology. He believed that a sociologist was "a kind of super-reporter, like the men who write for *Fortune*...reporting on the long-term trends which record what is actually going on rather than what, on the surface, merely seems to be going on" (Park, 1950, pp. vii-ix).

Another similarity between ethnographers and journalists is that both groups translate their experiences into writing. More recently, journalists tend to write books about the countries or regions they once covered appearing as experts (e.g., see Bertram, 1996; Buhrow & Stamer, 2006; Grill, 2005 & 2007; Lojewski, 2001 and 1991; Ruge, 2000; Scholl-Latour, 2004 a, b, c, 2005, 2007 a, b; Wickert, 2003 & 2004). These narratives also often resemble documentary ethnographies in style and content. Often, too, the style of writing of a journalistic reportage and an ethnography resembles each other (Dreßler, 2008, p. 31).

The development of a comparative understanding of ethnography and journalism as parallel practices dedicated to writing means that one can be used to reflect on the other. The development of scholarly research, the practices of ethnography, and the construction of news can be compared, contrasted, and analyzed to the extent that they can shed light on each others' strengths and weaknesses.

Some researchers even rationalize that journalists should acquire the methods of ethnography. Cramer and McDevitt demand that "journalists should use this powerful tool (Ethnography; addendum by the author) for observing and documenting social life" (Cramer & McDevitt, 2004, p. 127).

V. Examples of ethnographic studies of journalists / foreign correspondents

In recent years, ethnography has moved into the focus of communication sciences (Krotz, 2005, p. 259). Media ethnography, however, has mostly developed at the receiving end of the information flow. So far, only seldom the production of transnational media structures has been studied (Hannerz, 1998). This would, however, be a valuable starting point for research since the production of media can be understood as a social and cultural act. Dracklé writes that journalists—as well as other media producer's—have a certain culturally affected perception; they interpret and express cultural knowledge, when they produce media products for their readers and viewers (Dracklé, 2005, p. 200). Hahn, Lönnendonker, and Schröder (2008, p. 44) call foreign correspondents "context transmitters between cultures" and compare their task to that of intercultural translators.

One of the first ethnographies researching a media production site is Powdermaker's (1950) account of the movie production in Hollywood. Powdermaker undertook this study "to understand and interpret Hollywood, its relationship to the dreams it manufactures, and to our society" (Powdermaker, 2002, p. 162). She spent a year living in Hollywood as a participant observer and interviewed approximately 300 people as representatives of the various functional groups such as producers, writers, directors, and actors.

Ethnography has more recently also been used in the study of newsroom organizations. Fishman (1980, p. 3), who was mentioned already before, researched "the social facts that journalists produce every day and the methods they employ to generate them." His central concern is the creation of news and therewith the work routines of journalists and the methods by which they transform their experiences into news stories. For that purpose he became a reporter on an alternative weekly newspaper for seven months, followed by three months observing the daily work routines of three journalists (Fishman, 1997, pp. 213-214). Out of these experiences Fishman represents the patterns that he finds in the activities of journalists, the way they see events, identify 'newsness' and importance, and decide to act on events. His conclusions point to the way different bureaucracies interact with each other (pp. 217-227). Fishman's work arises as much out of his experiences as out of his observations. He notes:

This, my first experience as a journalist, allowed me to observe beat reporters working for other media in the community. More important, my experiences as an apprentice journalist provided data that no veteran newsworker could have told me and that is only clear to the novice: the invisible background knowledge one has to know in the first place to determine "what's going on" in a setting in order to 'see' news in it. (Fishman, 1997, p. 213)

This description notes one of the strong advantages of ethnographic work undertaken experientially. The researcher has the opportunity to experience the consciousness of the type under study. Thus, one might want to structure the study of a foreign correspondent through a combination of observation and participation as a foreign correspondent.

Most recently, Angela Dreßler (2008) has studied the work of German foreign correspondents in Singapore, Israel and the United States. Her work comprises participant observation phases of a few weeks in broadcast newsrooms in these three countries as well as interviews with 28 German foreign correspondents. Dreßler portrays the work of journalistic news production with a focus on the work of the foreign correspondents at the three news centers'.

Baisnée and Marchetti (2004) researched the production of European news in the pan-European news channel *Euronews*. They spent several days observing in the editorial office of the channel in Ecully, took part in editorial conference, and interviewed about 20 employees of the news channel. Additionally, they interviewed former employees of the channel, and subjected the material to both document and literary analysis. The authors argue for an ethnographic approach because their main focus lays on the research of journalistic restraints and their effects on the transmitted information.

Overall, however, ethnographic studies of foreign correspondents are very rare. Pedelty (1995) researched the environment of war correspondents in the war in El Salvador. He spent a year observing and interviewing journalists in the press office for the accredited journalists and followed them to the war scenes they covered. He describes that as an anthropologist "it feels odd observing those in the act of observing others, writing about their writings about others" and that also the journalists would demonstrate ambivalence of being studied (Pedelty, 1995. p. 5).

With his book, Pedelty attempts to explain why journalists behave as they do, explaining their work within the 'disciplinary apparatus' that pattern many of their actions (Pedelty, 1995, p. 5). He tries to investigate the news production process and the cultural and social circumstances under which news are produced. Pedelty comes to the conclusion that foreign correspondents are socialized by their peers and "seek the healing salve of ritual" (Pedelty, 1995, p. 233). He argues that by "keeping alive the myths of war correspondence, journalists retain and renew their desire to break rank with discipline, to tell their stories and make news that matters." According to Pedelty, at present paper is wasted "on redundant versions of an institutionalized story that neither illuminates nor ameliorates—news as official quote and cliché" (Pedelty, 1995, p. 234).

Hannerz (2004, 2001 a, 2001 b) uses a rather unusual approach in his studies of foreign correspondence. He shows that what one knows about the outer world, is mainly determined by the personalities of a small number of foreign correspondents. His main goal is to reproduce how the correspondents generate the news they deliver to their home media. The description of the relations between the work of the journalists, the journalist's behaviour among each other and with colleagues from their own news organizations, effectively produces a 'picture of the world'. Hannerz describes his methodology as "anthropologist multisite or multilocal fieldwork" (Hannerz, 2004, p. 11) being more focused on interviews than observation. For his book Hannerz conducted in-depth interviews with about 70 foreign correspondents at different news spots around the world. When asking the correspondents about their work routines, work situation, and their journalistic products, he was "on site" so that he "could at least catch some glimpses" of their reporting landscape himself (p. 7).

IV. Conclusion

Ethnography as a valuable method to study the news production processes, work processes and underlying structures of foreign correspondence. We have demonstrated in this chapter how the worlds of the journalist and the ethnographer are quite similar.

There is some overlap of audience between the two groups. Perhaps the result is not to the complete satisfaction of the individuals on either end. Journalists often feel that space constraints deny them the ability to tell the story in the detail and depth that are the luxurious territory of the ethnographer. Ethnographers, on the other hand, do not benefit from the same audience numbers and social significance that is often the starting point for a foreign correspondent. Their work functions within a discipline, and reaches outside of it only to the extent that the world of researcher/practitioners find such a process helpful.

But the possibilities for understanding the work of foreign correspondents might offer an outlet of a greater reach than the ethnographic researcher is accustomed. The recent developments in reflexive ethnography concern themselves with these continuing discussions. As George Marcus offers,

> The crucial turn, it seems to me, has been the new positions taken toward self-critical reflexivity in ethnographic writing. The sometimes heated debate over the desirability of reflexivity marks the opening up of the ethnographic tradition to new possibilities, to a departure from the ideology of objectivity, distance, and the transparency of reality to concepts, toward a recognition of the need to explore the ethical, political, and epistemological dimensions of ethno graphic research as an integral part of producing knowledge about others. (1994, p. 392)

We can take the notion Marcus introduces and apply it to the intersection of journalism and ethnography. This means that researchers would have the opportunity not just to understand the routines and practices of foreign correspondents, but also to examine the epistemological notions that inform their work. The greatest strengths of ethnography arise out of the way if offers the opportunity to look at a subject's understanding of the world from an alternate perspective. The ability to use that difference between the foreign correspondent and the ethnographer to understand how communication works in both cases suggests a level of inquiry with great potential for illuminating the intersection.

References

Bertram, J. (1996). *Asien, atemlos. Als Korrespondent in einer fremden Welt.* Hamburg: Rasch & Röhring.

Baisnée, O. & Marchetti, D. (2004). La production de l'information «européene» Le cas de la chaîne paneuropéenne d'information Euronews. In D. Marchetti, *En Quête D'Europe: Médias européens et médiatisation de L'Europe.* Rennes: Presse Universitaires Rennes.

Braudel, F. (1973). *The Mediterranean and the Mediterranean World in the Age of Philip II.* (S. Reynolds, Trans.) 2 vols. New York: Harper and Row.

Buhrow, T. & Stamer, S. (2006). *Mein Amerika—dein Amerika.* Reinbeck bei Hamburg: Rasch & Röhring.

Clifford, J. (1988). *The Predicament of Culture: Twentieth Century Ethnography, Literature, and Art.* Cambridge, Massachusetts: Harvard University Press.

Clifford, J. & Marcus, G. E. (1988). *Writing Culture: The Poetics and Politics of Ethnography.* Berkeley: University of California Press.

Cramer, J. M. & McDevitt, M. (2004). Ethnographic Journalism. In S.H. Iorio (Ed.), *Qualitative Research in Journalism: Taking It to the Streets.* Mahwah, NJ: Lawrence Erlbaum Associates.

Dracklé, D. (2005). Vergleichende Medienethnografie. In A. Hepp, F. Krotz, & C. Winter (Eds), *Globalisierung der Medienkommunikation: Eine Einführung.* Wiesbaden: Verlag für Sozialwissenschaften.

Dreßler, A. (2008). *Nachrichtenwelten. Hinter den Kulissen der Auslandsberichterstatung. Eine Ethnographie.* Bielefeld: Transcript Verlag.

Fishman, M. (1997). News and Nonevents: Making the Visible Invisible. In D. Berkowitz (ed.), *The Social Meanings of News: A Text Reader.* Thousand Oaks, California: Sage Publications.

Fishman, M. (1980). *Manufacturing News.* Austin, Texas: University of Texas Press.

Geertz, C. (1973). *The Interpretation of Cultures.* New York: Basic Books.

Geertz, C. (1991). *Dichte Beschreibung* (2nd ed). Frankfurt am Main: Suhrkamp.

Grill, B. (2005). *Ach, Afrika. Berichte aus dem Inneren eines Kontinents.* München: Goldmann.

Grill, B. & Hippler, S. (2007). *Gott, Aids, Afrika.* Köln: Kiepenheuer & Witsch.

Hahn, O., Lönnendonker, J., & Schröder, R. (2008). Auslandskorrespondenten als Kontextvermittler zwischen den Kulturen—Interdisziplinäres Theoriemodell journalistischen Transfers und translatorischer Äquivalenz. In O. Hahn, J. Lönnendonker & R. Schröder, *Deutsche Auslandskorrespondenten. Ein Handbuch.* Konstanz: UVK-Verlag.

Hannerz, U. (2004). *Foreign News: Exploring the World of Foreign Correspondents.* Chicago: The University of Chicago Press.

Hannerz, U. (2001 a). *Among the Foreign Correspondents: Reflections on Anthropological Styles and Audiences.* Paper presented at the Vega Symposium on "The Death and Rebirth of Anthropology," in honour of Sherry B. Ortner. Swedish Society for Anthropology and Geography, Stockholm, April 24, 2001.

Hannerz, U. (2001 b). Dateline Tokyo: Telling the World about Japan. In *Asian Media Productions.* London: Curzon Press.

Hannerz, U. (1998). Transnational Research. In H. R. Bernhard (ed.), *Handbook of Methods in Cultural Anthropology.* Walnut Creek, California: AltaMira Press/Sage.

Hansen, A., Cottle, S., Negrine, R., & Newbold, C. (1998). *Mass Communication Research Methods.* New York: New York University Press.

Have, P. (2004). *Understanding Qualitative Research and Ethnomethodology.* London/Thousand Oaks/New Delhi: Sage Publications.

Kalbfeld, B. (2001). *Associated Press Broadcast News Handbook.* New York: McGraw-Hill.

Krotz, F. (2005). *Neue Theorien entwickeln: Eine Einführung in die Grounded Theory, die Heuristische Sozialforschung und die Ethnographie anhand von Beispielen aus der Kommunikationsforschung.* Köln: Herbert von Halem Verlag.

Kusenbach, M. (2005, September). Across the Atlantic: Current Issues and Debates in US Ethnography. *Forum Qualitative Sozialforschung / Forum: Qualitative Social Research*

[Online Journal], 6(3), Art. 47. Available at: http://www.qualitativeresearch.net/fqs-texte/3-05/05-3-47-e.htm [12/13/2005].

La Pastina, A. (2005). Audience Ethnographies: A Media Engagement Approach. In E. W. Rothenbuler & M. Coman (Eds.), *Media Anthropology*. Thousand Oaks, California: Sage.

Le Compte, M. D. & Schensul, J. J. (1999). *Designing & Conducting Ethnographic Research*. Walnut Creek, California: AltaMira Press.

Lindlof, T. R. (1995). *Qualitative Communication Research Methods*. Thousand Oaks, California: Sage.

Lojewski von, W. (1991). *Amerika: Der Traum vom neuen Leben*. Hamburg: Ho.mann & Campe.

Lojewski von, W. (2001). *Live dabei*. Bergisch-Glad-bach: Lübbe Verlag.

Machin, D. (2002). *Ethnographic Research for Media Studies*. London: Arnold Publishers.

Marcus, G. E. (1994). On Ideologies of Reflexivity in Contemporary Efforts to Remake the Human Sciences. *Poetics Today*, Vol. 15 No. 3 (Autumn 1994), pp. 383—404. Stable

Marcus, G. E. & Fischer, M. M. J. (1999). *Anthropology as Cultural Critique: An Experimental Moment in the Human Sciences, 2ⁿᵈ Ed.* Chicago: University of Chicago Press.

Megill, A. (2004). Coherence and Incoherence in Historical Studies: From the Annales School to the New Cultural History. *New Literary History, 35,* 207—231.

Park, R. E. (1950). *Race and culture*. Glencoe, Illinois: Free Press.

Pedelty, M. (1995). *War Stories: The Culture of Foreign Correspondents*. New York: & London: Routledge.

Powdermaker, H. (1950). *Hollywood the Dream Factory: An Anthropologist looks at the Movie-Makers*. Boston: Little, Brown and Company.

Powdermaker, H. (2002). Hollywood and the USA. In K. Askew & R. R. Wilk, *The Anthropology of Media*. Malden, Massachusetts: Blackwell Publishing.

Ruge, G. (2000). *Sibirisches Tagebuch*. München: Droemer Knaur.

Scholl-Latour, P. (2004 a). *Der Fluch des neuen Jahr-tausends*. München: Goldmann.

Scholl-Latour, P. (2004 b). *Weltmacht im Treibsand*. Berlin: Propyläen.

Scholl-Latour, P. (2004 c). *Kampf dem Terror—Kampf dem Islam?* Berlin: Ullstein-TB.

Scholl-Latour, P. (2005). *Weltmacht im Treibsand. Bush gegen die Ayatollahs*. Berlin: Ullstein-TB.

Scholl-Latour, P. (2007 a). *Rußland im Zangengriff*. Berlin: Ullstein-TB.

Scholl-Latour, P. (2007 b). *Zwischen den Fronten. Erlebte Weltgeschichte*. Berlin: Propyläen.

Tanggaard, L. (2009). The Research Interview as a Dialogical Context for the Production of Social Life and Personal Narratives. *Qualitative Inquiry*, 15, 1498—1515.

Tedlock, B. (2003). Ethnography and Ethnographic Representation. In N. K. Denzin and Y. S. Lincoln (Eds.). *Strategies of Qualitative Inquiry (2ⁿᵈ Ed.)*. Thousand Oaks, California: Sage Publications.

Van Maanen, J. (1988). *Tales from the Field: On Writing Ethnography*. Chicago: University of Chicago Press.

Wickert, U. (2003). *Zeit zu Handeln?* München: Heyne.

Wickert, U. (2004). *Alles über Paris*. Hamburg: Europa Verlag.

Williams, A. (2008). Ethnography. In R. Watson (Ed.), *Nursing Research: Designs and Methods*. Edinburgh: Churchill Livingstone.

Wolf, M. (1992). *A Thrice-Told Tale: Feminism, Postmodernism, and Ethnographic Responsibility*. Stanford, California: Stanford University Press.

CHAPTER 5

Theoretical Frameworks Guiding the Study of International News: Gatekeeping, Agenda Setting and Framing

Peter J. Gade and Dave Ferman

Renowned American journalist Walter Lippmann (1922), writing shortly after the end of World War I, recognized that media were largely responsible for the "pictures in our heads" about the world outside. The media's influence in creating these pictures increases when the public is unable to witness events for themselves (McCombs, 1981; Wanta et al., 2004), which is the case with international news. This leaves nearly all the world's citizens reliant on media for their knowledge of the world and perceptions of cultures other than their own.

Until a short decade ago, international news was created almost exclusively by foreign correspondents working for a select few European and U.S. news agencies and news organizations. Today, the vast reach of the Internet as a tool for international journalism, from news agencies to the blogosphere, continues to reshape how and where foreign correspondents do their jobs, the resources available to them, and even who they are (Wu & Hamilton, 2004). The growth of national and regional media in non-Western nations, combined with the Internet's ability to disseminate news without regard for national boundaries, has created more international news sources and the potential for a more diverse and egalitarian flow of information and news across the globe (Friedman, 2007). Citizen-created content, especially during disasters such as the 2005 London bus and subway bombings, has contributed to dramatic and timely coverage of international events (Gordon, 2007). The control that news agencies have over international news flow has been reduced (Boyd-Barrett & Rantanen, 2004). But not so fast. Even as the Internet's global impact on news continues to grow and creates an uncertain future, recent studies of international news suggest the major Western agencies that have long dominated international news flow continue to have significant influence (Paterson, 2006; Wu, 2007; Chang et al., 2009).

The decision-making processes used by journalists and news organizations to determine what news to share with their audiences can be broadly described as "gatekeeping" (White, 1949; Shoemaker & Reese, 1996), and the effects of news coverage on the audience's sense of reality have been considered through several paradigms and theories, the most common and accepted being agenda setting and framing (McCombs & Shaw, 1972; Entman, 1993). Wanta et al. (2004) explain the relationship between gatekeeping and agenda setting in the context of international news:

> "News selection is at the heart of the agenda-setting process since the issues that fail to pass through the gatekeepers of the news also fail to give salience cues regarding the relative importance of the issues. This is especially true of international news events that happen beyond the direct experience of most news consumers." (p. 365)

This chapter explores the theoretical approaches that have guided the study of international news. Although international news has drawn the attention of scholars for nearly a half century, somewhat surprising is that much of this research is disconnected from the study of foreign correspondents. As Charles Self noted in an earlier chapter, most studies of foreign correspondents have been primarily descriptive, focused on correspondents' demographics, personal values, and the individual nature of their work. The study of international news has been more conceptual from the outset, exploring social, economic and political factors that are related to the creation, framing, dissemination and effects of international news. It should also be noted up front that the approaches used to study international news have been diverse, which at times has led to a lack of conceptual clarity and agreed-upon measures, producing inconsistent findings. The studies reviewed in this chapter are not an exhaustive list, but they reflect the primary theoretical approaches and create a type of historical narrative of theoretical development, focusing on the concepts measured and the assumptions of the scholars doing work in international news. The chapter's final section reviews foreign correspondency in the 21st century, exploring the impact of the Internet and broader forces of globalization on international news. Ultimately, this chapter seeks to place the rich international news literature within its primary theoretical approaches—gatekeeping, agenda setting and framing, and by doing so point to the possibilities of uniting or integrating the study of foreign correspondents with the broader study of international news.

Gatekeeping

Gatekeeping explains the process of how events become published as news. It explores how information passes through a system of "channels" before being published, and the decision makers at the channel "gates" determine which information is passed along (or rejected) and in what form (White, 1949). Shoemaker, who has studied gatekeeping for three decades, writes with her colleagues:

> The gatekeeping process is also thought of as consisting of more than just selection, to include how messages are shaped, timed for dissemination, and handled. In fact, gatekeeping in mass communication can be seen as the overall process through which the social reality transmitted by the news media is constructed, and is not just a series of 'in' and 'out' decisions. (Shoemaker et al., 2001, p. 233)

Although the gatekeeping phenomenon is easy to grasp, understanding the process of constructing and transmitting social reality has proven complex. Shoemaker and Reese (1996) define five concepts in the gatekeeping process: personal values, media routines, organizational influences, extramedia influences and ideology. They assert these factors create a "hierarchy of influences model," conceived as a continuum from micro (personal) to macro (ideological) factors, with the macro factors having the most influence on the gatekeeping process. The authors suggest that gatekeeping theory conceives media content as the dependent variable, and the five concepts are independent variables that predict and shape the published content.

The Shoemaker and Reese model was not articulated to explain international news per se; however, its relationship to the gatekeeping approaches employed to study international news are at times apparent. The authors assert the model provides the most comprehensive theoretical structure for understanding the concepts that determine media content. Reese (2001) contends these forces can be generalized to international news because globalization of media organizations has increased the focus on professionalism and associated standards of education, practice and performance. "More important than national differences may be the emergence of a transnational global professionalism, the shape of which will greatly affect how well the world's press meets the normative standards we would wish for it" (p. 173).

The model moves research beyond studying individual professionals, and accounts for the larger structures in which journalists function.

International News Flow

The first studies of international news were interested in gatekeeping questions: which stories got reported, by whom, and through which channels. Northern European scholars (Galtung & Ruge, 1965; Ostgaard, 1965) used content analyses to identify the types of international stories that survived the gatekeeping process, finding that Western journalists reported most news from around the globe and that an event's proximity to a Western news agency office or bureau was an important indicator of news coverage. This line of research was extended in the 1970s primarily by U.S. scholars who responded to UNESCO's call for the study of national images portrayed in the world press. Of particular concern to UNESCO was that developed Western nations (mainly the U.S. and Europe) were biased in their reporting of developing and newly independent nations. UNESCO supported the New World Information and Communication Order, asserting that coverage of developing nations was scant, and the stories that were reported misrepresented these countries by focusing on violence, deviance and conflict (Weaver & Wilhoit, 1981; Gozenbach et al., 1992; Wu, 1998). The study of international news flow quickly emerged in the 1970s as a primary focus of inquiry, with more than 150 studies executed by 1986 (Tsang et al., 1988). Wu (2000) noted that the flow of international news is one of the most highly researched areas of mass communication.

Ahern's (1984) attempt to synthesize the research suggested that influences on international news flow (into the U.S.) could be understood through two perspectives: gatekeeping and logistics. In general terms, the gatekeeping perspective identified international news flow as a matter of journalists' news judgment, and the logistics perspective identified national factors (e.g., economic factors and political stability) as predictors of news coverage. Wu (1998), in a meta-analysis, found these perspectives were the conceptual starting point for most of the international news flow literature.

However, Ahern's perspectives had several overlapping and ambiguous measures, most of which centered on the country where an event occurred. The gatekeeping factors considered the geographic and cultural proximity of the country in which the event takes place, while the logistics factors included government-press relations, trade between nations, distance between nations, geographic size, population, economic development, political stability, gross national product, and the cost of transmitting news from a country and whether wire service bureaus are located there.

Wu (1998) noted this conceptual confusion was reflected in international news flow scholarship, as his analysis identified inconsistent methods and definitions of key concepts. "As a result," he wrote, "few, if any, international communication theories have developed from this ample body of literature accumulated in the past few decades" (p. 508). Wu proposed to refine the conceptual definitions, stating that the gatekeeper perspective "predominantly centers on the social psychology of the news professionals and how these characteristics eventually affect news output" (p. 495). The logistics perspective, he continued, "examines the socio-economic components and physical logistics of news gathering, focusing on broad and systemic factors" (p. 495). The three most visible measures of the gatekeeping perspective are (1) wire services and news professionals, focusing on the relationship between what the wire services produced and what the news professionals sent through the news gates to the public, (2) deviance, the extent to which behaviors violate social norms, and (3) whether a story originates in the West versus non-West. He identified seven key measures of the logistics perspective (all involving national characteristics): trade, cultural affinity, political relations, communication resources (e.g., infrastructure and access), geographic proximity, regionalism, and national traits.

More recently, Wu (2007) studied how the Internet has impacted international news flow, noting that the medium redefines several of the important concepts that guided news flow research: space allocation for stories is no longer a factor; news reports are no longer bounded by geography; the number of information sources is virtually limitless; and hyperlinks provide audiences with the ability to go from one story to another instantly. He analyzed 1,258 international news stories in three media during two composite weeks in 2003: those printed in the *New York Times,* those broadcast on CNN, and stories found on the two news organizations' web sites. He found that online and traditional news flow were predicted by logistics factors, specifically economic interactivity between the U.S. and other countries and the presence of major news agencies. Also, news from "Middle Eastern countries, economic elites and military powers" (p. 549) received the most coverage by all three media. In essence, despite the potential for online media to impact international news flow, he concluded that the more things change, the more they stay the same. The similarities of coverage predictors in all three mediums, Wu wrote, "could be a great disappointment for those who ideally envisioned the web as a truly global medium that can break away from the structural, systematical barriers to deliver more—and more diverse—information to people around the world" (p. 549).

Related News Flow and Gatekeeping Measures

Several sub-genres of international news flow research emerged, most testing concepts identified in Ahern's (1984) gatekeeping and logistics perspectives. These merit closer attention because of their contributions to the literature and/or their refinement of existing concepts. The five approaches discussed below are listed roughly in the order they were introduced, an attempt to reflect the development of the approaches and concepts; to no surprise, some concepts and sub-genres emerged concurrently. These sub-genres consider concepts at the ideological, organizational and media routines levels (Shoemaker and Reese, 1996).

Context-oriented and Event-oriented news. Chang et al. (1987) suggested the splintered theoretical thinking about international news flow could be grouped into two categories, context-oriented and event-oriented, with context-oriented being the primary approach. The event-oriented approach recognizes that characteristics of international news, such as deviance and the negative nature of events, determine whether an international event makes news. These events, they contend, make news regardless of other (contextual) factors. The context-oriented perspective includes measures of economic relations, cultural similarity, political affiliation, social distance and geographic proximity. These scholars attempted to refine Ahern's model to address the conceptual overlap. However, they noted the difficulty of creating a valid model of international news flow, as measures in each perspective have produced inconsistent findings. "The results are mixed. No single factor is able to account for the variance of international news coverage. Some factors (e.g., hierarchy of nations) are useful in determining coverage of international events, whereas other factors (e.g., physical distance) are not" (p. 400).

Deviance. Shoemaker et al. (1987) noted that news reports often result from the media discovering ways in which social norms and expectations have been broken. Thus, news media fulfill a basic social function when they provide ways for society to understand and organize events by disseminating normative explanations of the events. U.S. journalists judge the news value of events by a set of criteria that they are taught in university journalism programs: timeliness, proximity, impact, conflict, prominence, novelty (Brooks et al., 2005). Included with these, Shoemaker et al. (1987) assert is sensationalism. Accordingly, at least four of the basic news criteria—novelty, conflict, prominence, and sensationalism—include some dimension of deviance.

In a study of 179 randomly selected international events of 1984 (that occurred outside the U.S.), Shoemaker et al. found that the *New York Times* covered 48 percent of the events, while the three major television networks at that time (ABC, CBS, NBC) covered only 16 percent. Three deviance constructs were created: statistical deviance, the extent to which an event is unusual; social change deviance, the extent to which the event threatens the status quo; and normative deviance, the extent to which the event, if it occurred in the U.S., would have broken U.S. norms. They found normative deviance was the strongest predictor of an international event becoming U.S. news, and social change deviance was a predictor for the *New York Times* coverage. They concluded that deviant events that provide opportunities for social change are newsworthy because they could impact the U.S. "The tendency of the U.S. media to cover deviant events disproportionately could therefore represent part of the overall process of identifying, evaluating, and controlling threatening changes from other countries" (p. 363).

Journalists as agents for the audience. Basic to the gatekeeping process is the notion that journalists and editors are acting in the interests of their audiences. In the simplest terms, this means that journalists base their news judgments on what they perceive to be the wants of the audience (e.g., similar to the relationship between suppliers and consumers), and the needs of the audience (e.g., what citizens need to know to function socially and politically) (Tai & Chang, 2002). Research in this area has taken three approaches: surveys of audience interest and preferred topics of international news, surveys and interviews of editors and foreign correspondents about the importance of international news to their audiences, and a comparison of the interests of editors and audiences.

In general, research spanning the past 30 years has shown that U.S. audiences are interested in international news, with some studies showing international news is of high audience interest (Shaw & Riffe, 1979; Burgoon et al., 1980), and other studies indicating it is a middle-of-the-pack interest when compared to other news topics (Weaver & Mauro, 1978; Nanney, 1993). In the most recent U.S. study, Hargrove and Stempel (2002) executed a national telephone survey asking respondents to rate their interest in 20 international story topics that also varied by geographic region or country.

They found that women were more interested in the stories than men, positive or good news stories were preferred more than negative stories, stories about "ordinary people" were the most popular, interest was highest in stories about the Middle East, and foreign stories that involved Americans were rated slightly more interesting than other stories. Hargrove and Stempel concluded that if newspapers want to increase reader interest in international news, then some conventional approaches (focus on governments and politics, negativity, and Western Europe) need to be re-examined.

Studies that have asked editors about the importance of international news and how they select it indicate a somewhat different perspective. Chang and Lee (1992) surveyed a probability sample of U.S. newspaper editors and found editors identified five factors as most important in their selection of international news: threat to the U.S., threat to world peace, anticipated reader interest, timeliness, and U.S. involvement. Just as important, the authors noted, is that measures of national characteristics (trade with the U.S., geographic distance from U.S., and economic development) were not factors the editors reported that they considered in selecting news.

Tai and Chang (2002) executed perhaps the most rigorous study in this area, exploring the triangular relationship over a five-year period (1995–99) among what editors said was the most important international news, what the audience prefers and what the U.S. and international media actually cover. The researchers found a significant relationship between what the editors perceived as important and what the audience preferred (Spearman's rho = .435), and between what editors perceived important and actual content (rho = .451); however, what the media actually covered and what the audience preferred resulted in nearly no relationship (rho = .031). The authors concluded "readers' interest in the events does not often translate into news that editors decide to publish. The opposite seems to be true" (p. 259).

Most recently, Hahn and Lönnendonker (2009) interviewed with 27 Europe-based American foreign correspondents about their coverage and perceptions of the U.S. audiences' interest in foreign news. They found that U. S. news media have fewer foreign correspondents providing less foreign coverage, and the perception was the U.S. public has little interest in European news unless the stories include U.S. interests. These journalists perceived that in a post-9/11 world the U.S. audience interest in international news was limited to a small number of terrorism-based topics and regions, including the American military effort in the Middle East and European countries' efforts to help the United States. They concluded that the focus of news geography toward the broader Islamic world since 9/11 has marginalized coverage of other regions of the world, including Europe. The correspondents said they increasingly report about Muslim communities in Europe.

Organizational resources and market factors. Lacy et al. (1989) wrote that an idea missing from the international news flow research was that news decisions are often made at the organizational level, and that international news can be understood as a product. The assumption is that U.S. media operate with a profit motive, and profit is increased by selling media products. The authors acknowledge that international news is more expensive to gather than local, state, regional or national news. They assert that the nature and extent of international news coverage is a function of attempts to control costs while meeting market demands.

Lacy et al. conducted a content analysis of 114 U.S. newspapers from 38 states, and they measured variables that had been in previous research (e.g., story source such as wire, news agency, staff, geographic location, and type of coverage including conflict or in-depth), and added several organizational measures, including paper circulation, staff size, and number of wire services in the content. They found that the strongest relationship was between international news coverage and circulation, followed by a dependence on wire service copy. Wire service content was highly conflict oriented, and 76 percent of all international news was conflict oriented. They also found that only six of the 114 newspapers in the study had any in-depth international news coverage, and most of these stories were produced by the wire services. The authors suggested that this finding reflects that newspapers with international staffs have so few journalists working overseas that conflict coverage takes precedence over more time-consuming in-depth coverage. The study also found that the percentage of non-U.S. born population in a market had no effect on the amount of international news coverage. The authors concluded that organizational variables influenced the amount of international news more than market variables.

Lowrey et al. (2003) studied organizational factors that determine a commitment to international news coverage. They conceived organizational commitment two ways: newspapers' information gathering resources and use of international news, and the expertise of the international editor. The study also considered the impact of community variables (size, international orientation) and organizational variables (size and resources) on the organization's commitment to international news.

They found that organizational size, more than community factors, was the dominant influence on the organization's commitment. However, community factors did matter, as communities with ethnic organizations and international corporations were more likely to have newspapers structured to cover international news. They also found international editors had relatively little influence in their organizations and low levels of international expertise. Nearly a quarter of the editors had no influence over the choice of wire services the paper used, and two-thirds said their papers did not reserve space for international news on a daily basis; 86.5 percent said their papers published staff-generated international news analysis less than once per month. In terms of expertise, more than 80 percent said they had received no postgraduate training in international issues. They concluded: "(international) editors are more likely to receive the knowledge they use to perform their jobs from the daily work process than from formal structures for training such as universities, job workshops, or work seminars" (p. 52).

Core Zones of the World System. Considering "globalization" as a key concept of social change, Chang (1998) proposed a model derived from world systems literature that identifies three zones of the world (determined by economic, political and social factors): the core, semi-peripheral and peripheral. The zones are predictors of coverage. Core countries include the U.S., European Union (treated as a single entity), Western European countries (United Kingdom, Germany and France), Japan and Canada. The semi-peripheral countries consist of the remaining Western European countries, China, Russia, and relatively advanced economies including S. Korea, Singapore and Malaysia in Asia, Argentina and Mexico in Latin America, and Egypt in Africa. The peripheral countries referred to most developing nations and nation states, including those in the former Soviet Union.

The model posits that core countries make news simply because they are core countries, but for the countries on the semi-periphery and periphery, there are several "filters" that determine whether these countries will be included in the news. These filters are conceptualized from previous news flow research, and include traditional definitions of newsworthiness, the context of the events (e.g., political affiliation, economic relations, geographical and cultural proximity) and the interaction among countries (e.g., if countries on the periphery and semi-periphery interact with the core nations, news flow and coverage increases, and vice versa).

Chang tested the model by studying Reuters stories about the World Trade Organization meetings in Singapore in 1996. His rationale for this approach was that because 162 countries were represented at the meetings and more than 1,000 journalists covered the meetings, the event provided a built in control for important gatekeeping issues—such as the nature of the event and media/organizational resources. He found the model predicted quite well. Generally, the few core nations were in the news the most. In contrast, he wrote, "the news appearances of most semi-peripheral countries are more likely to be determined by the company they keep, usually the core nations, whereas the peripheral nations may have to leave it to chance (e.g., natural disasters)" (p. 557).

Chang, Himelboim and Dong (2009) tested the world systems model of news flow on the Internet, studying which news sources were most likely to provide hyperlinks to other sites. They examined the hyperlinks from 1,259 stories posted by 28 media organizations in 15 countries equally divided between core (such as the United States and the United Kingdom), semi-peripheral (Brazil, South Africa) and peripheral (Kenya, Mexico) countries. More than two-thirds of all hyperlinks to foreign countries were sent to core nations. State-owned or -controlled media outlets (such as Turkey's TRT) never provided outgoing links to other sites, and publicly owned media outlets provided far more links to outside sites than privately owned outlets. They concluded, "The linkage between nations via outgoing hyperlinks to websites of other countries remains relatively closed . . . this configuration of online international communication flow closely resembles the landscape before the arrival of the Internet" (p. 155).

Gatekeeping Summary. Overall, the news flow and gatekeeping literature indicates the richness of the discipline as an area for study. International news is created by gatekeeping decisions, shaped by cultural values and ideologies, the organizations for which journalists work, professional norms of journalism, and individual journalists. Ideologies are reflected in nations' positions in the world system, and developing and smaller nations receive different international coverage than the core of developed Western nations. International news, especially about non-core nations, tends to focus on conflict and deviance. Logistical factors of cost and distance, and organizational resources for information gathering are also important in determining international news. These factors result in news media relying on a small number of news agencies and wire services for their international news. Although the Internet provides an international audience many more sources of news about the world, the potential of the Internet to create a more egalitarian and diverse flow of news throughout the world has, to date, been largely unrealized.

Agenda Setting and Framing

Agenda setting theory, as originally proposed, suggests that there is a transfer of salience from the agenda of objects (issues and topics) that media publish to the public's sense of importance of those objects (McCombs & Shaw, 1972). The theory shifts focus from the gatekeeping factors that influence the creation of news to the effects of that news on the audience. In the context of international news, Merrill (1983) writes, "The global press wields tremendous power as a purveyor of vital information. It has the potential to help erase erroneous impressions and stereotypes and to ease tensions; it can create fears and needlessly perpetuate anxieties. It can shake people from complacency, or it can lull them into an unthinking and dangerous sleep" (p. 3). The approach to measuring agenda setting involves an analysis of media content at a point in time to identify the media agenda, and a measure of public perceptions of the importance of the media agenda issues—or the attributes of those issues—at a later point in time (McCombs, 1981, 1992).

McCombs (1992) notes that the original agenda setting concept—that the media's agenda of issues influences the public's sense of issue salience—has expanded into broader areas of theoretical exploration and development. Two additional agenda setting approaches are important to understanding international news and will be addressed: (1) the idea that media create not only an agenda of issues, but they also focus or place salience on specific attributes of these issues, and (2) influences on media content, asking the question "Who sets the media's agenda?" The attributes of the media agenda issues extends the initial hypothesis to a second level, suggesting that the media are not only successful at telling the public what to think about, but also how to think about it. Second-level agenda setting is conceptually very close to what many scholars call framing (McCombs & Ghanem, 2001). In recent years, yet another offshoot of agenda setting research has included the media's ability to influence government policy; in other words, how the media's news agenda can influence the agenda and actions of governments.

Agenda Setting and International News

Although many studies have supported agenda setting in domestic U.S. settings, little research examined the agenda setting process in an international context prior to the late 1980s (Salwen & Matera, 1992; Semetko et al., 1992). Following the dissolution of the Soviet Union and tearing down of the Berlin Wall, researchers used the end of the Cold War as an opportunity to study how media coverage of international events influenced audience perceptions of the countries in the news.

Semetko, Brzinski, Weaver and Willnat (1992) analyzed the content of U.S. network television news and newspaper wire service coverage of nine countries (West Germany, East Germany, Soviet Union, Hungary, Poland, Great Britain, France, Japan, and Israel) over a six-month period in 1989 and 1990, then they surveyed a probability sample of 1,117 U.S. adults. The researchers were interested in a basic agenda setting question—the relationship between presence of foreign nations in U.S. news media and public opinion about those nations, and a second question: whether television and newspapers were equally important media for influencing public opinion. They found that television news coverage was more important than newspaper coverage in shaping opinions of countries, and that greater attention to international news on television was the best predictor of liking of a country, rather than simple exposure to television news or newspapers. The researchers also found that 29 percent of the audience had visited Europe. They concluded that television is particularly important as an agenda setting medium because relatively few U.S. citizens have direct experience outside the U.S. and television's visual images have influence in shaping public opinions.

Salwen and Matera (1992) assessed international coverage over a nine-week period on the U.S. network news broadcasts (613 stories on ABC, CBS, NBC), the national edition of the *New York Times*, and the *Miami Herald* (991 newspaper stories). The researchers then surveyed a random sample of 629 Miami-area residents. The stories were coded by country, frequency of coverage, and the extent to which coverage included conflict. The public was asked to rank nations in four ways: America's best friend, America's worst enemy, amount of media coverage, and the level of danger of living in a the nation. The public agenda revealed that Great Britain was perceived as the U.S.'s best friend with more votes than all other nations combined; the Soviet Union, Iran and Cuba were perceived as the greatest enemies; the Soviet Union, Israel and Nicaragua were perceived to receive the most media coverage, and Lebanon and Iran were perceived as most dangerous. When correlated to actual media coverage, there was a significant rank-order correlation between the public's perception of coverage of specific nations and actual coverage of those nations, supporting the basic agenda setting hypothesis. Other results revealed that as conflict coverage increased, so did the public's sense that the countries in which the conflicts occurred were enemies and dangerous. The authors concluded that nations reported in a conflictive context were more likely to be judged by the public as U.S. enemies and dangerous places; thus, the context of the coverage appeared to influence U.S. public evaluations of other nations.

Wanta, Golan and Lee (2004) were interested in whether the amount of media coverage about countries influences the U.S. public's perceptions of whether those countries are of vital interest to the U.S., and whether there was a relationship between the valance of coverage (positive, neutral or negative) and public perceptions. Their study analyzed international coverage by four network newscasts (ABC, CBS, NBC and CNN) in 1998. They surveyed 1,507 respondents immediately following the period of the content analyzed. The content analysis assessed the frequency of stories about 26 nations, and the valence (or frame) of the coverage. The survey asked the public to identify countries of vital interest to the U.S. and assessed public sentiments about the countries. In terms of coverage and vital interest, a significant correlation ($r = .568$) indicated that the more U.S. network coverage a country received, the more the public perceived that country was vital to U.S. interests. Results also showed that negative coverage was significantly correlated ($r = .578$) to negative feelings about the country. Positive and neutral coverage was not significantly related to the public's perceptions of countries. The results provided evidence of first- and second-level agenda setting; frequency of media coverage provides cues to the public about whether countries are vitally important to the United States (first-level), and story attributes (valence) can shape how countries should be viewed (second-level).

Framing International News: The Interdependence of Media and Government

Media systems operate within the broader political, social and economic frameworks of the countries in which they exist. The news media's role of reporting on the process and action of government makes media systems in all nations responsible to government to some degree (Merrill, 1974). At the same time, government officials understand the news media is an invaluable tool for communicating government policies and positions to the public. This interdependence of media and government is the focus of much research and debate. In a basic sense, scholars are asking about the extent to which the government sets the media's agenda and shapes media content, and, conversely, the extent to which media influence the actions of government.

The scholarship in this area is often interdisciplinary, and has drawn the interest of political scientists, public policy experts, sociologists, cultural studies and mass communication researchers. Although these scholars often use the term agenda setting in their work, their conception of agenda setting is quite different than what McCombs and Shaw meant about the relationship of media content to public opinion. Most of the research in this area relies on historical accounts of events, interviews and reflections of policy makers and journalists, and case studies.

Broadly speaking, two schools of thought shape most of this work. One approach assumes a somewhat independent media that is an important player in the creation of public policy because the media often pursue stories that (a) question or are critical of hegemonic interests, (b) air dissenting voices, and (c) convey powerful images of foreign places to the public, often forcing officials to respond to events or issues for which policy is undeveloped or unclear. The other school of thought assumes many of the sociological underpinnings associated with Marxism and critical theory. The media are seen as generally passive, accepting of and reliant upon the interests of government and powerful institutions. Accordingly, the media are a hegemonic tool, reflecting the interests of a powerful elite and acting to perpetuate these interests and maintain the status quo.

Herman and Chomsky's (1988) classic book *Manufacturing Consent* provides a contemporary starting point for much of the critical literature that assumes news reports reflect and serve the interests of powerful people and institutions. The basis for their "propaganda model" is rooted in assumptions that private media companies are large, profit-driven corporations that have similar interests as other political and business entities. Profit-driven media seek to maximize their audiences by pleasing (or not offending) advertisers and through organizational efficiency, which results in news content dominated by readily available official sources, usually from government, who expound on the actions and virtues of government and associated powerful institutions. Accordingly, news coverage is determined and framed by government, with a passive media having little influence over governance or public policy (the government sets the media's agenda). The model acknowledges that critical reporting does occur, and explains this as the result of conflicts among elites.

Several related models are rooted in similar assumptions. Hallin (1986), writing about the Vietnam War, asserted that U.S. media coverage of the war turned critical only after members of the Washington, D.C., political elite spoke out against the war. Although the news media have been blamed by U.S. government and military officials for contributing to a lack of support and ultimate failure in that war, Hallin asserts that the news media were merely reporting the division over policy among political elites. He poses a model of three spheres of reporting: consensus, legitimate controversy, and deviance. News reports most often reflect the consensus or legitimate controversy spheres. When there is a consensus among elites, the journalist's role is to be little more than to convey the consensus view; when there appears legitimate controversy among the elites, the journalist relies on the journalism values of objectivity and balance to accurately reflect the elite views. The deviance sphere includes ideas outside the mainstream, which are rarely covered. Hallin notes this sphere guides journalists because "it marks out and defends the limits of acceptable conflict" (p. 117).

At the other end of the spectrum, some policy makers have decried what has come to be called the "CNN Effect," which posits that media coverage—ubiquitous and often relayed around the world as it happens—drives public policy, often depriving government officials the time to reflect on important global crises before making pronouncements to reporters. The CNN Effect, which some call a theory, is largely the result of policymakers relating their experiences addressing global conflicts in the post-Cold War era (Seib, 2004), including Tiananmen Square (1989), the Gulf War (1990–91), the Russian coup attempt (1991), and civil strife and humanitarian interventions in Iraq (1991), Somalia (1992), Rwanda (1994), Bosnia (1992–95) and Kosovo (1999). The premise is that global television networks, by broadcasting powerful images of international events as they happen, arouse emotional public reactions that demand a prompt if not immediate response by governments. Gilboa (2002) asserts that the CNN Effect "constrains" more than controls policymakers. Global news network stories are generally short, headline-dominated, event-oriented, and repeated numerous times throughout the day. These formats create pressure on journalists, politicians and policy experts: "editors push reporters to broadcast new pictures, reporters push leaders to respond fast to unfolding events, and leaders push experts and diplomats to produce instant policy analysis and recommendations" (p. 6). Journalists are more likely to produce inaccurate stories or those that lack the context required for understanding.

Gilboa notes that an assumption of the CNN Effect is that the images of world events broadcast by global networks are given greater significance than what they have in reality. Seib (2004) suggests the term is treated too casually, especially by those who overstate the impact of news coverage.

The Manufacturing Consent-CNN Effect dichotomy can be seen as a theoretical continuum that has contributed to more complex, integrated models of media-government relations. Robinson (2001) proposes a "policy-media interaction model" that builds from the manufacturing consent idea that when a consensus exists among elite that there is little reason to expect the media to go beyond the views of the elite in the news coverage. However, he asserts, much like Hallin, that when a "dissensus" exists among elites, a variety of coverage ensues, some critical to existing government policy. He extends the work of others by considering the level of policy uncertainty in government. When there is elite dissensus on an issue and the government policy lacks certainty, then the media are most likely to frame messages critical of government. The media-state relationship changes in this scenario, and journalists become more active participants in framing the political debate, resulting in media having more influence on government policy.

Entman's "cascading network activation model" (2004) is an extension of earlier efforts to explain the relationship of media, government and other elites and how news frames are created, extended and revised. He contends that policy certainty has eroded since the end of the Cold War, leaving a greater likelihood for dissention among elites and less certainty that elites can control news frames. The model suggests that information frames usually begin with the Administration (in the U.S., the White House or State or Defense departments) and cascade down a series of steps, first to other elites, then to the media, which produce news frames in their reports that are passed down the public. The model includes upward feedback loops that account for the public's feedback to the media, the news frames' feedback to the elite, and the elite feedback to the Administration. The model assumes that information moves concurrently up and down among the Administration, elites and public, and media frames change based on feedback, but generally it is the elites who are most influential in creating the frames that shape public opinion.

Agenda Setting Summary. Agenda setting assumes that issues reported on by news media influence the public's sense of issue salience, and the attributes—or frames—of these issues impact how audiences interpret the news. The agenda setting research focusing on international news reflects the multi-disciplinary approaches of its scholars, and it is characterized by varying assumptions of passive and powerful media, resulting in findings of minimal to powerful media effects. Much of the international news scholarship extends the original agenda-setting hypothesis beyond the relationship between media content and public perceptions to include questions of who sets the media's agenda, how media content is shaped by powerful elites, and the impact of media content on government and public policy.

Foreign Correspondency and International News in the 21st Century

As the millennium began, foreign correspondent work was evolving primarily for economic and technical reasons. U.S. news organizations were reducing their numbers of international bureaus, relying increasingly on small reporting teams, foreign freelancers, and "backpack" journalists to deliver breaking international stories from locales that are hard to reach (Wu & Hamilton, 2004). The Internet was beginning to impact how foreign correspondents determined and gathered news, as they were able to keep an eye on competitors, find sources and retrieve background information. All these factors influence the gatekeeping process that foreign correspondents use as they consider what makes news and how to report it.

In the past few years, as the Internet's presence and impact has emerged, some significant changes in international news have occurred, and the potential for even greater changes appears on the horizon. Today's media environment has more media competitors, including the growth of regional media (e.g., Al Jazeera) and national media in developing nations. The availability of these additional choices for international news can reduce the supremacy that Western news agencies and organizations have long held over international news flow (Boyd-Barrett & Rantanen, 2004), although the few recent studies have shown the agencies remain the prominent sources of international news (Paterson, 2006; Wu, 2007; Chang, Himelboim & Dong, 2009).

Perhaps more apparent is the emphasis on timeliness that global broadcast networks, satellite and the Internet have placed on journalists. The Internet is a 24/7 medium that is always on deadline, and journalists find themselves expected to publish and update information, often using information from other online sources. This makes the task of verification and authenticity more daunting, while providing less time for original information gathering and reporting (Gilboa, 2002; Philips et. al, 2009).

Mobile media and simple ways of sending and sharing content have changed how journalists work, but because these tools are shared by journalists and non-journalists alike they also reflect that journalists are no longer the sole creators of news and have ceded some control of the flow of information to citizens and amateurs. Dramatic footage shot by cell phones, as well as messages sent from one person to another, were found by Gordon (2007) to both bolster news reports and circumvent lax or inaccurate government information during disasters that received worldwide attention (e.g., Hurricane Katrina and the London bus and train bombings in 2005 and the 2003 Severe Acute Respiratory Syndrome (SARS) outbreak in China). Cell phone activity increased dramatically during these crises, with messages a mix of accurate information, rumor, and video. Although citizens sent news media many cell phone images of these crises, Gordon found news organizations subjected these amateur images to the same editorial decisions as other stories. However, Robinson (2009) found that citizen coverage of Hurricane Katrina demonstrated citizens' ability to "occupy a dominant place in the tiers of the information hierarchy as co-producers of a collective memory" (p. 809).

Blogs have become an influence in news because journalists spend considerable time paying attention to them (Woodly, 2008). They also offer a popular alternative to mainstream media, and this became apparent during the Iraq War (Wall, 2005). Blogs draw much of their initial content from mainstream media (Picard, 2009); however, they offer a postmodern option that fits well with a broader rejection of objectivity and sense that media fail to provide accurate representations of reality. Blogs' credibility as sources of news is due in part to their give-and-take with readers, which circumvents the traditional gatekeeping roles and norms of professional journalists. Blogs also create the reality that anyone can publish as an amateur foreign correspondent.

And, finally, the foreign correspondents themselves—at least those working for U.S. media—are changing. Wu and Hamilton (2004) surveyed 354 foreign correspondents working for U.S. media, finding that only about one-third were U.S. citizens. This is considerably less than previous studies, including two from the 1990s that found 66 percent (Kliesch, 1991) and 77 percent (Hess, 1996) of foreign correspondents were U.S. citizens. Although the U.S. and non-U.S. correspondents were found to have similar news values, Wu and Hamilton suggested cultural differences will likely produce subtle differences in reporting and news content, including news angles, sourcing and context.

Taken together, the 21st century has brought more sources of international news that are less bound by geography and Western ideology. Journalists have new ways of accessing and gathering information, but they have endless deadlines, which impacts the time they have for verification and original reporting. They are monitoring and using citizen-created content. And, at least in regard to foreign correspondents working for U.S. media, the correspondents themselves reflect a changing demographic cohort, with a greater number of "foreign" foreign correspondents reporting international news for U.S. audiences. All these developments have implications for international news gatekeeping decisions.

These changes in foreign correspondency work and their potential for impact on content and the flow of news also have implications for the agenda setting function of international news. Although so far the evidence suggests that Western news agencies and organizations have maintained their influence in the production and dissemination of international news, what is not so clear is how the gatekeeping changes described above have impacted news content (Wu & Hamilton, 2004). The news agenda of the major agencies may, over time, become less reliant on Western sources, Western journalists and original reporting. Scholars seem to agree that these changes could improve international news, making it more diverse and inclusive of more cultural perspectives and ideologies. These same scholars also acknowledge this potential remains largely unfulfilled (Paterson, 2006; Wu, 2007; Berglez, 2008; Berger, 2009; Chang, Himelboim & Dong, 2009).

Berglez (2008) asserts that the ability of journalists to provide a more nuanced, global perspective has not kept pace with the global technology that instantly links people and news events in different countries. He urges a greater emphasis on a "global outlook," an epistemology that moves away from the traditional nation-based perspectives on space, power and identity and "instead seeks to understand and explain how economic, political, social and ecological practices, processes and problems in different parts of the world affect each other, are interlocked, or share commonalities" (p. 847).

Berger (2009) noted another paradox between the promises and realities of international news on the Internet: Most online news sites provide more local and national news than international news. At the same time, more Third World audience members are going to First World news sites. "The irony therefore seems to be that online news, in the U.S. at least, has mainly a national character, though there is also a sizeable global audience. While such websites do not aim at a global audience, foreigners come anyway. The result suggests an information universe in which the U.S. news agenda and perspectives are disproportionally large" (p. 365).

For U.S. audiences, there has been a surge of traffic to non-U.S. media that offer alternative viewpoints to the pro-war/pro-America perspectives prevalent in the U.S. media (Allen, 2004). These included web sites connected with major British newspapers, such as the *Manchester Guardian*, as well as Al-Jazeera, which broadcast news and images that often sharply contrasted with American news sites. This recent, if steady, shift toward foreign (and particularly British) web sites by American readers is facilitated in large part by such aggregate sites as Google News and Drudgereport.com (Thurman, 2007).

The additional sources of international news available online and the fragmenting of the audience that occurs when people get their news from different media sources would logically diminish traditional notions of agenda setting effects. The media agenda is more diverse and the public's consumption of international news is a less common (or shared) experience. However, recent studies have indicated that the additional number of media and increased citizen control over the media they consume can contribute to citizens' better understanding of the world around them. Kwak, Poor and Skoric (2006) surveyed 389 Michigan adults and found that the Internet was important in helping people understand and engage in countries beyond the United States; this was done "by helping them increase their knowledge of the world, facilitating their sense of belonging to the greater world, and motivating them to participate in international events and foreign volunteer opportunities" (p. 207). Moreover, the Internet can contribute to understanding the world more than other mediums, in part because it is more diverse and allows for more interaction. Beaudoin (2008), in a national survey of U.S. citizens, found that the combination of the Internet and network TV (as opposed to newspapers or cable TV) was the most important synergy of mediums in terms of international knowledge. But whether alone or paired with any of other medium, Internet use was the most important predictor of international knowledge. "This suggests that the Internet, with its powerful interactivity, control, organization and multi-channel attributes, is poised to help Americans address their historically low levels of understanding of foreign affairs, countries, and people" (p. 469).

Conclusion

Emerging from this theoretical overview of the study of international news is the diversity of its approaches, assumptions and findings. Yet, the theoretical threads that bind most of the conceptual thinking are rooted in gatekeeping or agenda setting. These theories, and their sub-disciplines reviewed in this chapter, provide excellent—although largely underutilized—frameworks for studying foreign correspondents and their work.

Connecting the largely descriptive body of research on foreign correspondents to the existing theories of mass communication and international news is a logical goal for future research.

Gatekeeping theory suggests that the study of foreign correspondents can be extended conceptually by focusing on the social processes that influence the creation of news. These transcend individual correspondents and include influences on correspondents at media, organizational, external, and cultural levels. Relative questions include: studying whether news judgments and stories differ when they are reported by nationals or "foreign" foreign correspondents; exploring the influence of organizations on correspondents' news content (e.g., to what extent do editors or a medium's political leaning impact the foreign correspondents choices of stories and story frames); exploring the external forces (e.g., access to sources, economic resources, and media in the region) and their impact on news; and studying how cultural values and ideologies shape news content in national, regional and online media. Perhaps most important is seeking relationships among these concepts as predictors of news coverage and frames, so an integrated theory of international gatekeeping and news flow can be developed. It is in this capacity that Shoemaker and Reese's (1996) hierarchy of influences model has provided useful guidance, and some scholars are incorporating the model into their study of international news. It is a small leap to extend this theoretical thinking to the study of foreign correspondents.

Agenda setting research provides mechanisms to understand how the stories reported by foreign correspondents translate to the "pictures"—or perceptions of other countries and cultures—in the minds of readers and viewers. Much of the research in this realm begins with assumptions about the media (passive or active) and media effects (minimal or powerful), and fails to actually study the content produced in relation to the perceptions and attitudes of the audience. It appears important to study the objects of the stories (and their frames) produced by foreign correspondents and test the extent to which foreign correspondents' reporting of issues and their attributes (frames) transfers to the public. In an era when global media and the Internet provide more sources of information for citizens throughout the world, the influence and importance of foreign correspondents and alternative online media sources as agenda setters in their home countries deserves scrutiny. Beyond this basic agenda setting question, the interdependence of governments, media and important societal institutions and their relative struggle in shaping the news is an ongoing, unresolved debate among scholars and policy experts. Questions of who sets the media's agenda or to what extent do media set government agendas (questions that are at the nexus of gatekeeping and agenda setting) appear increasingly relevant. Many developing nations are transitioning from authoritarian societies, creating their own increasingly sophisticated national and regional media systems, and experimenting with expanded forms of free expression. The Internet puts more voices and perspectives in media content. These changes are likely to impact the agenda setting dominance of Western media and wire services, and the creation and flow of international news.

The 21st century has in its first decade already seen considerable shifts in the international news landscape. These changes don't reduce the value of the work of two generations of scholars. As this chapter has attempted to show, rich and multiple conceptual approaches have provided excellent frameworks for studying international news, although these theoretical frameworks have been seldom and inconsistently applied to the study of foreign correspondents. The shifting landscape adds complexity and provides new challenges for scholars studying foreign correspondents and international news. A key challenge for future study is integrating the study of foreign correspondency with theoretical frameworks that have guided the study of international news. Accounting for the shifting landscape through these theoretical frameworks creates numerous opportunities and incentives for advancing the study of foreign correspondents.

References

Ahern, T. (1984). Determinants of Foreign Coverage in U.S. Newspapers. In R. Stevenson and D. Shaw, *Foreign News and the New World Information Order* (pp. 217–236). Ames, IA: Iowa State University Press.

Allan, S. (2004). Conflicting Truths: Online News and the War in Iraq. In C. Paterson and A. Sreberny, *International News in the 21ˢᵗ Century* (pp. 285–299). Eastleigh, England: John Libbey Publishing.

Beaudoin, C.E. (2008). The Internet's Impact on International Knowledge. *New Media & Society*, 10(3), 455–474.

Berger, G. (2009). How the Internet Impacts on International News. *The International Communication Gazette*, 71(5), 355–371.

Berglez, P. (2008). What Is Global Journalism? Theoretical and Empirical Conceptualizations. *Journalism Studies*, 9, 845–848.

Boyd-Barrett, O., and Rantanen, T. (2004). News Agencies as News Sources: A Re-Evaluation. In C. Paterson and A. Sreberny, *International News in the 21ˢᵗ Century* (pp. 31–45). Eastleigh, England: John Libbey Publishing.

Brooks, B., Kennedy, G., Moen, D., and Ranly, D. (2005). *News Writing and Reporting*. New York: Bedford/St. Martin's Press.

Burgoon, M., Burgoon, J., and Wilkinson, M. (1980). Dimensions and Readership of Newspaper Content. *Newspaper Research Journal*, 3, 74–93.

Chang, T.K. (1998). All Countries Not Created Equal to Be News. *Communication Research*, 25(5), 528–563.

Chang, T., Himelboim, I., and Dong, D. (2009). Open Global Networks, Closed International Flows: World System and Political Economy of Hyperlinks in Cyberspace. *The International Communication Gazette*, 71(3), 137–159.

Chang, T.K. and Lee, J.W. (1992). Factors Affecting Gatekeepers' Selection of Foreign News: A National Survey of Newspaper Editors. *Journalism Quarterly*, 69(3), 554–561.

Chang, T.K., Shoemaker, P., and Brendlinger, N. (1987). Determinants of International News Coverage in the U.S. Media. *Communication Research*, 14(4), 396–414.

Cohen, B. (1963). *The Press and Foreign Policy*. Princeton, NJ: Princeton University Press.

Entman, R. (1993). Framing: Toward Clarification of a Fractured Paradigm. *Journal of Communication*, 43(4), 51–58.

Entman, R. (2004). *Projections of Power: Framing News, Public Opinion and Foreign Policy*. Chicago, IL: University of Chicago Press.

Friedman, T. (2007). *The World Is Flat: A Brief History of the 21ˢᵗ Century*. New York: Picador.

Galtung, J., and Ruge, M. (1965). The Structure of Foreign News. *Journal of Peace Research*, 2, 64–91.

Gilboa, E. (2002). The Global News Networks and U.S. Policymaking in Defense and Foreign Affairs. Cambridge, MA: Shorenstein Center for Press, Politics and Public Policy, Harvard University.

Gordon, J. (2007). The Mobile Phone and the Public Sphere: Mobile Phone Usage in Three Critical Situations. *Convergence: The International Journal of Research into New Media Technologies,* 13(3), 307–319.

Gozenbach, W., Arant, M.D., and Stevenson, R. (1992). The World of U.S. Television News: Eighteen Years of International and Foreign News Coverage. *Gazette*, 50, 53–72.

Hahn, O., and Lönnendonker, J. (2009). Transatlantic Foreign Reporting and Foreign Correspondents after 9/11: Trends in Reporting Europe in the United States. *International Journal of Press/Politics*, 14, 497–515.

Hallin, D. (1986). *The Uncensored War: The Media and Vietnam*. Berkeley, CA: University of California Press.

Hamilton, J.M., and Jenner, E. (2003). The New Foreign Correspondence. *Foreign Affairs*, 82(5), 131–138.

Hamilton, J.M., and Jenner, E. (2004). Redefining Foreign Correspondence. *Journalism*, 5(3), 301–321.

Hargrove, T., and Stempel, G. (2002). Exploring Reader Interest in International News. *Newspaper Research Journal*, 23(4), 46–51.

Herman, E., and Chomsky, N. (1988). *Manufacturing Consent: The Political Economy of the Mass Media*. New York: Pantheon Books.

Hess, S. (1996). *International News and Foreign Correspondents*. Washington, DC: The Brookings Institute.

Kliesch, R.E. (1991). The U.S. Press Corps Abroad Rebounds: A 7th World Survey of Foreign Correspondents. *Newspaper Research Journal*, 12(1), 24–33.

Kwak, N., Poor, N., and Skoric, M.M. (2006). Honey, I Shrunk the World! The Relation between Internet Use and International Engagement. *Mass Communication & Society*, 9(2), 189–213.

Lacy, S., Chang, T.K., and Lau, T.Y., (1989, Fall). Impact of Allocation Decisions and Market Factors on Foreign News Coverage. *Newspaper Research Journal*, 23–32.

Lippmann, W. (1922). *Public Opinion*. New York: Harcourt Brace.

Lowrey, W., Becker, L., and Punathambekar, A. (2003). Determinants of Newsroom Use of Staff Expertise: The Case of International News. *Gazette*, 65(1), 41–63.

McCombs, M. (1981). The Agenda-Setting Approach. In Nimmo, D., and Sanders, K. (eds.), *Handbook of Political Communication*, 121–140. Beverly Hills, CA: Sage.

McCombs, M. (1992). Explorers and Surveyers: Expanding Strategies for Agenda Setting Research. *Journalism & Mass Communication Quarterly*, 69 (4), 813–824.

McCombs, M., and Ghanem, S. The Convergence of Agenda Setting and Framing. In Reese, S., Gandy, Jr., O, & Grant, A. (2001), *Framing Public Life*, 67–80. Mahwah, NJ: Lawrence Erlbaum Associates.

McCombs, M., and Shaw, D. (1972). The Agenda Setting Function of the Mass Media. *Public Opinion Quarterly*, 36, 176–187.

Merrill, J.C (1974). *The Imperative of Freedom*. New York: Hastings House.

Merrill, J.C. (1983). *Global Journalism: A Survey of the World's Mass Media*. New York: Longman.

Nanney, R. (1993). *Do Community Editors Lead or Follow Their Audiences?* Unpublished Ph.D. dissertation, Ohio University.

Ostgaard, E. (1965). Factors Influencing the Flow of News. *Journal of Peace Research*, 2, 38–63.

Paterson, C. (2006). News Agency Dominance in International News on the Internet. *Papers in International and Global Communication*, 1(6), 1–23.

Phillips, A., Singer, J., Vlad, T., and Becker, L. (2009). Implications of Technological Change for Journalists' Tasks and Skills. *Journal of Media Business Studies*, 6(1), 61–86.

Picard, R. (2009). Changing Structures and Organization of Newsrooms. *Journal of Media Business Studies*, 6(1), 1–6.

Reese, S. (2001). Understanding the Global Journalist: A Hierarchy-of-Influences Approach. *Journalism Studies*, 2(2), 173–187.

Robinson, P. (2001). Theorizing the Influence of Media on World Politics: Models of Media Influence on Foreign Policy. *European Journal of Communication*, 16(4), 523–544.

Robinson, S. (2009). 'If You Had Been with Us': Mainstream Press and Citizen Journalists Jocket for Authority over the Collective Memory of Hurricane Katrina. *New Media & Society*, 11(5), 795–814.

Salwen, M., and Matera, F. (1992). Public Salience of Foreign Nations. *Journalism Quarterly*, 69(3), 623–632.

Seib, P. (2004). *Beyond the Front Lines: How the News Media Cover a World Shaped by War*. New York: Palgrave/Macmillan.

Semetko, H., Brzinski, J., Weaver, D., and Willnat, L. (1992). TV News and U.S. Public Opinion about Foreign Countries: The Impact of Exposure and Attention. *Journal of Public Opinion Research*, 4(1), 18–36.

Shaw, D., and Riffe, D. (1979). Newspaper Reading in Two Towns. *Journalism Quarterly*, 54, 477–487.

Shoemaker, P., Chang, T.K., and Brendlinger, N. (1987). Deviance as a Predictor of Newsworthiness: Coverage of International Events in the U.S. Media. *Communication Yearbook 10*, 348–365.

Shoemaker, P., Eicholz, M., Kim, E., and Wrigley, B. (2001). Individual and Routines Forces in Gatekeeping. *Journalism & Mass Communication Quarterly*, 78(2), 233–246.

Shoemaker, P., and Reese, S. (1996). *Mediating the Message: Theories of Influence on Mass Media Content* (2nd edition). White Plains, NY: Longman.

Tai, Z., and Chang, T.K. (2002). The Global News and the Pictures in Their Heads: A Comparative Analysis of Audience Interest, Editor Perceptions, and Newspaper Coverage. *Gazette*, 64(3), 251–264.

Thurman, N. (2007). The Globalization of Journalism: A Transatlantic Study of News Websites and Their International Readers. *Journalism*, 8(3), 285–307.

Tsang, K.J., Tsai, Y., and Liu, S. (1988). Geographic Emphasis of International News Studies. *Journalism Quarterly*, 65, 191–194.

Wall, M. (2005). 'Blogs of War': Weblogs as News. *Journalism*, 6(2), 153–172.

Wanta, W., Golan, G., and Lee, C. (2004). Agenda Setting and International News: Media Influence on Public Perceptions of Foreign Nations. *Journalism & Mass Communication Quarterly*, 81(2), 364–377.

Weaver, D., and Mauro, J. (1979). Newspaper Readership Patterns. *Journalism Quarterly*, 55, 85–91.

Weaver, D., and Wilhoit, G. C. (1981). Foreign News Coverage in Two U.S. Wire Services. *Journal of Communication*, 31(2), 55–63.

White, D.M. (1949). The "Gatekeeper": A Case Study in the Selection of News. *Journalism Quarterly*, 27, 383–390.

Woodly, D. (2008). New Competencies in Democratic Communication? Blogs, Agenda Setting and Political Participation. *Public Choice*, 134, 109–123.

Wu, H.D. (1998). Investigating the Determinants of International News Flow: A Meta-Analysis. *Gazette*, 60(6), 493–512.

Wu, H.D., (2000). Systematic Determinants of International News Coverage: A Comparison of 38 Countries. *Journal of Communication*, 50(2), 110–130.

Wu, H. D. (2007). A Brave New World For International News? Exploring the Determinants of the Coverage of Foreign Nations on US Websites. *The International Communication Gazette,* 69(6), 539–551.

Wu, H.D., and Hamilton, J. M. (2004). US Foreign Correspondents: Changes and Continuity at the Turn of the Century. *Gazette: The International Journal of Communication Studies*, 66(6), 517–532.

Wu, W., Weaver, D., and Johnson, O. (1996). Professional Roles of Russian and U.S. Journalists: A Comparative Study. *Journalism & Mass Communication Quarterly*, 73(3), 534–548.

CHAPTER 6

Foreign Correspondents: Necessary Mythmakers

Meta G. Carstarphen & Mihai Coman

Introduction

Imagine the milieu of foreign correspondents. For most, the image may be shrouded in mystery and intrigue. For others, the travails of these transported journalists only become evident when tragedy strikes, as when headlines announce their disappearances, injuries and even deaths. The changing parameters of foreign news coverage, taking into consideration the shrinking resources of traditional media and the proliferation of new media, call into question the roles of journalists and their real, as well as perceived, influence upon foreign policy (Hamilton, 2004).

However, perhaps the essence of their work is not grounded in folklore, but instead, in the most profound, intrinsic parts of the human experience—the ability to create and sustain myth.

Why Myth? Why Now?

Owing to the place they hold within the mass media system, foreign correspondents seem to be pre-destined to mythological development. The first level is self-referential—it appears in and through the symbolic constructs that emerge from within the professional area/guild. The professional imagery has built a symbolic aureola centered on the ideas of adventure, borderline experiences, direct confessions/witnessing at the moment when history is being written, self-sacrifice, etc. This system has been manufactured both by the foreign correspondents narratives (that equally tell about the events and their main characters and the personal merits and experience of the journalists), and by the "professional folklore."

The stories about their work that the foreign correspondents produce and broadcast, have a standard structure, with few connections to the reality of the field, as a foreign correspondents ethnographer noticed, they "usually begin with the reporter-protagonist choosing to enter a dangerous situation, followed by the intervention of authority and/or sudden violence, and serious threats to the reporter-protagonist life. Traditionally, an act of unusual intelligence and/or bravery on the part of reporter-protagonist leads to a narrow escape in the end" (Pedelty, 1995:129).

This ensemble of epic structures and heroic stereotypes crosses the 'borders' of the guild in order to become a system of representations shared by the society as a whole, by means of the folk culture products, especially by means of the consumer film/movie or novel (or romantic autobiographies)—which does not mean that some masterpieces belonging to the genre, like "Killing Fields" and "Salvador" are not anchored in the same symbolic patterns.

The second level is that of the various non-referential or partially referential symbolic constructs that pervade the public area through the narratives that the foreign correspondents pass on for broadcasting from various crisis areas or moments/events. Obviously, not all that the foreign correspondents pass on for broadcasting is subject to, nor charged with symbolic, non-accurate values.

The foreign correspondent's system is actually determined by two series of parameters: One is the type of event (routine or crisis) and second is the geo-symbolic "distance" between the event and the foreign correspondent's country and culture of the broadcasting areas. Such areas are perceived as *political interest centers* that are said to be rather *exotic*. This system of representations may appear in the following patterning:

Centers

Certain information	Uncertain verifiable information
Dominant role of the PR types of sources	Dominant role of the PR types of sources
Routine Events	Disruptive/Crisis Events
Certain information	Uncertain information, hard to verify
Direct sources	Uncertain sources

Exotic Areas

The symbolic constructs are produced mostly in the *fourth corner* situations where the convergence of the following factors can be encountered: a) "exotic" areas that are charged with symbolic connotations;

b) emergence of social and political crisis situations, or chaos brought about by natural catastrophes; and c) lack of information production and distribution systems. Owing to such circumstances, foreign correspondents are subject to public pressure that await secured versions; that is, those versons that are easy to grasp and to accept from the viewpoint of the cultural categories and personal values. Consequently, foreign journalists produce narratives that are enriched in their symbolic content, and therein acquire mythological traits.

This does not set them apart from the possibility that in other routine, work specific situations, the foreign correspondents use numerous cultural stereotypes; these are scattered within the most diverse factual narratives that are accurate according to professional norms, and hence more difficult to notice.

Sociologists long ago defined stereotypes as a conceptual shorthand system for classifying ideas about people. Social stereotyping concepts have been used to predict, for instance, white bias against African Americans in the political sphere (Peffley et al., 1997) even when faced with information about individuals that contradicts a negative stereotype. Mass media collectively offer powerful channels through which racial myths accumulate in time and intensity, offering a portal through which stereotypes are amplified to the status of myth (Gorham, 1999: 240). Such is the power of a stereotype. Although crafted with the selective use of partial facts and misrepresentations, stereotypes nevertheless function as incomplete narratives in a larger discourse. Fostering the efficacy of racial stereotypes, for instance, is an underlying racist ideology, or system or beliefs, that promote inherent and intractable differences among populations. While historically such arguments were embedded in pseudo-scientific beliefs that privileged biological determinism, modern racism uses "cultural pathology" (Shelby, 2003:169).

Race and Stereotypes in Theory and Practice

A number of scholars over the years (Gates, 1986; Hartley, 1982; Montagu, 1985; van Dyck, 1987) have argued that race is a „socially constructed" idea, having little to do with biological or scientific fact. Gandy (2000) acknowledges also the influence of race as a socially, or contextually driven idea, but introduces the concept articulated by Hall (1993) and others about ethnicity as a new identifier that is both socially and individually constructed (Gandy, 2000: 65). In this view, cultural experience becomes the conduit of racial and ethnic identity, so long as the individual makes conscious choices through the selection of such things as food, ritual, culture and self-identity. Thus, Gandy's challenge to communication theorists is to examine how structural influences of racism become maintained and supported through communication practices.

By structural, Gandy refers to two kinds of influences. One is external, which imposes itself on individuals and limits choice. The second presents structure as outcome or product. Thus, in the context of journalism product generated by foreign correspondents, the *external* influence anticipates socially constructed views of race that might become transmitted without question as a common knolwedge base or societally shared information. The *product* side of the influence characterizes limited discourse among colleagues as well as the race narratives generated from their own work.

Underlying this is a basic notion: that race has fluidity as a socially constructed idea, instead of as a fixed marker of identity. Even within the seemingly fluid contexts of the Internet, racial construction plays a factor in cyberspace communication (Carstarphen & Lambiase, 1998).

One of the more subtle challenges facing European correspondents assigned to report within American communities would be their ability to read their substructures and social relationships, and the historical frameworks informing them. Given the expansive variety of geography, ethnicity and even language idiom within the United States, the notion of being able to ascertain the views of "the American people" presents a formidable task. Examining the impact of myth and society over the millennia of human history shows how critical its presence is in enabling humans to make sense of their world. Within the U.S. context, cultural myths that reverberate as part of the American saga are intimately intertwined with narratives about race, identity and a colonial past. Such experiences occurring within relatively recent historical periods reflect the dominant codification of Euro-American influences and the colonial prerogatives of the victors. From such a framework, key mythological components become embedded, such as the creation of heroes, holidays and symbols to commemorate heroic acts, and the submersion of minority histories and cultures (Heidenreich, 2005:41).

For the foreign correspondent, thus, the fullest interpretation of U.S. news events may seem to be elusive without the context of the "mythic paradigm"—a construct that analyzes the dynamic interplay of myth, ritual and philosophy (Allender, 2002:54) in order to excavate hidden narrative connections. In recent journalism practice, one of the more salient strategies used to broaden journalists' coverage in the U.S. is the "fault lines" framework that the late Robert C. Maynard developed (Maynard). This argument for examining news around the five "fault lines" of race, class, gender, geography and gender, may establish a structure for excavating mythic paradigmatic themes by pointing correspondents to areas of inquiry that might not naturally occur to them. Without such an intentional set of strategies, the recognition of myth could easily merge into the codification of stereotypes.

Stereotypes and News

In the United States, the majority press followed an unstated policy for decades of omitting coverage of minorities from its news pages as an industry-wide practice of absence. This hegemonic construct transcended the prejudices within individual reporters (Martindale, 1986). The print media were not alone, however. Persistent stereotyping of people of color has influenced content in all mass media arenas, generating over time patterns of *negative stereotyping* (Wilson and Gutierrez, 1995).

Tracing an evolution of what he calls *modern racism*, Entman (1992) assessed local Chicago newscasts, concluding that patterns of persistent and negative crime reporting about African Americans fueled a continuation of modern racism in a television studio. Later, he argued that, despite even a greater visibility of African Americans on televised newscasts (1994), the shows constructed a meta-narrative that actively contributed to stereotyping. This race-based continuum reflected a hegemonic policy that other scholars found evident in other media outside of Chicago.

For example, Christopher Campbell's content analysis of 39 local television news programs from across the country found persistent racial stereotyping, done so in a more aggressive fashion than even fictional television (1995). Don Heider found similar, disturbing patterns in his ethnographic study of two newsrooms in diverse communities, an approach that enabled him to examine constructs of television personnel from the inside out. Among the most prevalent of the persistent schemas found of traditional stereotypes was the propensity to frame minorities as "curiosities" who operate outside of a social norm (2000).

If studies on the field work of foreign correspondents are extremely rare (Hanerz, 2003; Hess, 1996; Pedelty, 1995), those covering cultural frameworks and those focused on symbolic elements in such narratives, are almost nonexistent. A survey on the elements that entail the emergence of symbolic constructs in foreign correspondent coverage should refer to the following elements:

- Professional constraints specific to foreign correspondents work (domain within the sociology of the mass media organisations and of the ethnography of journalism);
- Text writing constraints specific to the production of narratives covered by the foreign correspondents (domain within the discourse analysis);
- Symbolic constraints specific to the manufacturing of representations about certain events (domain within cultural studies and cultural anthropology).

Thus, foreign correspondents play dual roles heightened by the symbiotic nature of their places as both *stranger-citizens* and *expert-journalists*. The danger is that they can be erroneously influenced by biased mythmaking, while guarding against the real possibility that their work could contribute to erroneous narratives in an ever smaller mediated world.

The Professional Field: Behavior and Context

The sociology of the newsroom—in the Michael Schudson formula—included research on the behavior of journalists (but not on that of foreign correspondents) in times of crisis. In a classic study, Dan Berkowitz (1997: 362–375), shows that the journalists' first reaction when they find out about a crisis is surprise and then, an enthusiastic cry "What a story!" Only afterwards do they decide "to give non-routine news better play than most routine stories" (1997: 364), changing the structure of the product. As the crisis unfolds, journalists start searching for further resources—such as available personnel, travel funds, reliable sources, background material—in order to gather as much information as possible regarding the respective events. Last but not least, journalists select those data that supply the public with a 'securing' version; that is, a version that meets the public's expectations. The journalists accomplish this by using and employing metaphors, cultural clichés acknowledged by the public, sensational details, and dramatic but stereotyped elements. In other words, they routinize the unexpected.

Another study focusing on the journalists' behavior in situations of crisis (Sood et al., 1987) identifies the following types of action:

- change in the normal structure of the media product;

- involving all the available personnel in covering the event;
- a reduction of the editors' role ("gate-keepers") in selecting and distributing news;
- an increase in the supply of information by institutions and persons that usually do not work in this field;
- extensive use of unverified information;
- insistent pressure on official sources or high-status persons to confirm or comment on the event.

Doris Graber (1997:139–142) points out that during the initial stage of the crisis, when "a flood of uncoordinated messages is transmitted," the media turns into "an information collection center," which works "to coordinate public activities and to calm the audience" by rapidly disseminating the news. During the subsequent stages of the crisis, mass media "try to correct past errors and put the situation into its proper perspective" and to prepare the public to face the consequences of the crisis. Analyzing the behavior of the media in situations of technological crisis, M.N. Sicard (1998:66) sets apart the following roles (and types of action) of the media: 1. observers of the event; 2. producers of information; 3. social actors in the crisis; 4. witnesses to the event; 5. fear-increasing narrators; 6. organizers of public space and public debate; and 7. creators of a 'memory' of the crisis.

Several previous studies (Altheide, Snow, 1979; Halliday et al., 1992; Howitt, 1982; Smit, 1992; Singer, Endreny, 1993; Veron, 1981; & Zelizer, 1992; etc.) confirm that in situations of crisis, journalists act according to typical strategies created both by organizational pressures and by their assumptions about the public's interests and cultural knowledge. Generally speaking, "even when they were faced with non-routine news, news workers were able to accomplish their work in a more or less routine fashion" (Berkowitz, 1997: 373). The same author emphasizes that journalists employ two means of typecasting. One is organizational, based on the attempt to use the same working procedures as in routine periods. The other is thematic, based on identifying the respective event with one of the narrative stereotypes present in the professional data. When one considers the tension between society's cultural influences upon journalists, vs. the culture of journalism that can form its own interpretative community, then the forces of these two polarities can create what one study calls 'contradicting allegiances" (Zandberg & Neiger: 133).

What these studies neglect is that before routinizing the coverage of such events, journalists produce a whole host of versions of the facts that are contradictory, incomplete and biased. These versions are narratives that have little in common with the real evolution of the events; yet, the public accepts them without much argument or scrutiny. This means that, although these stories are inaccurate when compared to reality, they are 'true' if related to the public's expectations, and to the cultural framework within which the public confer meaning to the world. It also means that such stories are "true" to the narrative principles and rules of signification that bring together all of the other truths popular universe and the system of representations employed by the media.

Additionally, in these versions, journalists and mass media organizations appear in atypical stances: They do not present themselves as mere observers of the events, but as leading actors who control the evolution of history. In the process, journalists abandon routine procedures, a change that accompanies a shift in their roles leading to their promotion to a new and much more prestigious social status. In such crises, the erroneous presentation of events becomes, on the one hand, the result of a combination between the incoherent stream of information and the pressure of production. This creates a tenuous relationship between such *incoherency* factors, such as a lack of data or a surplus of uncertain and contradictory information, with *production* influences, such as a lack of time, increased competition, editing desk pressure, the lure of stardom, and so forth. At the same time, it also stems from journalists using self-promoting strategies that cast them as leading actors in the events and, implicitly, as makers of history. In order to gain control over this process, journalists begin to use symbolical logic and elements, creating narratives capable of validating the control they exert in the complex process of building a particular social image of reality.

Narrative, Reality and Journalistic Discourse

We have already shown (Coman, 1994) that reporters are the only modern category of the intellectual elite that provides the public with narrative definitions of the immediate world. There are numerous ways in which they accomplish this, including press editorials and commentaries, political analyses, scientific explanations ranging from those in leaflets to those in the most elaborate treatises, practical instructions such as those regarding health, to those referring to the use of mobile phones. All these discourses addressing the public are based on cause-effect patterns, on more or less complex syllogistic structures, and on a discursive representation of the surrounding universe. The mainly narrative views of the world, which act as constructs based on ordering elements according to a logic founded on 'emplotting,' are used only by historians and writers. However, there are clear distinctions. Historians refer to a reality that has already been consumed and saved in a particular socially accepted memory (i.e., manner of interpretation); writers build a potential reality, acknowledged as 'real' only within the frameworks supplied by artistic conventions. Yet, only journalists deal with concrete reality. Only they act under time pressure. And only they have to provide a narrative version of reality capable of meeting both the people's expectations and the definitions of reality that they employ.

The fact that the media employs narrative forms to give meaning to the surrounding world (while writers and historians speak about a reality that is either fictitious or distant in time) is explained by the journalists' dependence on the popular public that has never ceased to tell and to believe in the power of the story to possess and signify the world. Thus, it should answer the need for ontological security (Silverstone, 1984) and confirm the symbolical frameworks for interpreting the existing reality. Thus, it should answer the need for ontological security (Silverstone, 1984) and confirm the symbolical frameworks for interpreting the existing reality.

The system that binds events, journalistic methods and mechanisms of structuring versions of reality according to public expectation is *the story*, or, to be more precise, the *narrative*. It has to be conceived of not so much as a (more or less literary) genre than as a category of thought. Narratives are organizations of experience. They bring order to events by making them something that can be recounted; they have power because they make the world make sense. The sense they make, however, is conventional. No story is the inevitable product of the events it reports; no event dictates its own narrative form.

News occurs at the conjunction of events and texts, and while events create their story, the story also creates the event. The narrative choices made by the journalists are therefore not free choices. Instead, journalists make choices guided by the appearance reality has assumed for them, by institutions and routines, and by conventions that shape its perceptions and that provide the formal repertory for presenting them (Manoff, 1986:228–229). Anderson et al. (1994: 154) also invokes the capacity of ordering events: "Narrative constructs order out of disorder and meaning from meaningless."

Adopting the same view, S.E. Bird and W. Dardenne emphasize the power of journalistic stories to give meaning to the surrounding world: "For news, too, is a way in which people create order out of disorder, transforming knowing into telling. News offers more than facts—it offers reassurance and familiarity in shared community experience" (1988:70–71).

As symbolic systems, myths and news act both as models of and as models for culture." C. Geertz's formula ('model of'—'model for') is cited as universal key to explaining the double function (as discourse and metadiscourse) of news and myths. Hence, their status as instruments by means of which human knowledge controls the surrounding world offer templates for interpreting future accounts.

In all the above-mentioned approaches, narrative is conceived of as a mental mechanism that subsumes numerous forms of manifestation: myths and legends, novels, films, news, accounts of everyday conversations. Thus, the term 'narrative' no longer designates a particular genre or a particular text, but the ability of human knowledge, whether modern or non-modern, to order events using epic schemata and conventions. Instead, narrative transcends genre and so does myth—it not just the province of fictional literature.

Narrative Influences on Journalism

Numerous studies that make reference to the narrative consider that it has a double power to influence the journalistic world. The story operates simultaneously as category through which mankind makes sense of the surrounding world (Anderson et al., 1994; Bennett, 1997; Dahlgren, 1992; Davis, 1995; Hichman & Hinchman, 1997; Lits, 1996; Turow, 1991) and as particular professional category: journalists conceive, interpret and describe events within the narrative categories of journalistic genres (Bird, 1992; Cornfield, 1992; Dobkin, 1992; Jacobs, 1996; Manoff, 1986; Quere, 1982; Schudson, 1995; Tuchman, 1976; Zelizer, 1990; Zandberg & Neiger, 2005).

Various applied studies and theoretical debates have been aimed at revealing the manner in which narrative schemata influence the journalists' work. They have mostly emphasized that in media texts the intelligibility of events derives from the intelligibility proposed by the story about the events. In other words, the narrative coherence is based on chronological sequences and credibility of characters; it replaces the chaotic flow of events and the sum of contradictory and obscure human interests by a narrative coherence, which relies on the temporal order of sequences and on the 'truth' of standardized psychological motivation. "Journalism officially aims to inform about events in the world—an analytic mode—and does this most often in the story mode. One of the key features of stories is that they generate their 'own' worlds. It could be suggested that the more intense the narrative coherence, the less imperative is the referential function to an external reality for meaning to be conveyed.

In other words, facts give way to a good story. And, good stories can become in a sense independent of an outer-reality and can be more readily lifted from their original context and 'transplanted' into another, i.e. put to other psychological uses and given other "meanings" (Dahlgren, 1992:14). From this point of view, the professional thinking and the discourse through which journalists describe the world are narrative, or, as according to R. N. Jacobs (1996:381): "It is not merely that news workers tell stories, but that they receive the world in a storied way."

The narrative conception of events presupposes their ordering according to the logic of a plotted story, that is, according to a configuration in which the chaos of occurrences is structured by two simultaneous operations: a) a particular event becomes conflict; as a result its newsworthiness potential is directly proportional to its capacity of generating dramatic questions and climax; b) the order that secures the passage from conflict to climax is sequential in nature: it presupposes the addition of episodes one after the other, the previous explaining the following. By means of these two operations that organize information, disparate events that did not have any purposefulness or finality come to be structured into an order generated by the various actors' intentions and by the finality of the denouement towards which those events are heading. The process of emplotting allows journalists to propose to the public a closed version (which offers by itself a principle of coherence and a specific meaning) and to transform an ambiguous amount of events into one coherent story and by this, into a meaningful version of reality.

Journalism: An Antidote to the Crisis of Cultural Mythmaking

We might consider that in a situation of crisis journalists are confronted with the same challenge mythmakers other cultures face. They have to confer meaning to events that are often threatening, absurd and meaningless, with the help of stories built on available cultural units. As already pointed out, the crisis affects society and questions its values and norms. Coming out of this crisis means not only solving a situation, but also re-building (sometimes for real, other times only symbolically) the social edifice. Therefore, the discourse on crisis must simultaneously deal with two realities: that of the ongoing events and that of the society on trial.

Mythologization is an instrument perfectly adapted to the double challenge and double discourse. It uses a story (actually, the relevant facts) to raise questions about the values, institutions, expectations and fears of a society by symbolically 're-constructing' these facts. The story thus built offers a frame of interpretation for the respective crisis (a meaning that can be accepted within the code system specific to a collective). Usually, this story is unlikely, exaggerated, dramatic and contradictory. When analyzed later, both journalists and observers will label it a media bias, and the professional group will employ a complex ideological machinery to restore the journalists' reputation and to place the causes of the errors outside the profession. They will invoke the difficult access to the events, the scarcity of sources, the impossibility of verifying them, the risk factors, the manipulative intentions of the spin-doctors, etc. And then, when they are confronted with the next crisis, the same exaggerated, incomplete, dramatic and distortive stories will reappear in spite of the warnings and the acquired 'experience.'.

This phenomenon is not an accident caused by the journalists' lack of ability or the great prowess of some evil 'spin-doctors.' On the contrary, this phenomenon represents a structural constant deriving from the double function of journalistic discourse during crisis (it describes events and it preserves social order).

Therefore, journalists resemble mythmakers, that is, they act as 'bricoleurs'; they employ the narrative elements (action patterns, characters, systems of signification) present within the respective cultural inventory which they share with the public. They build numerous stories about concrete events by combining the various narrative units and codes available in the cultural repertoire. As in the case of myths, these stories offer 'an intelligibility matrix' and a coherent manner of representation of the surrounding world.

Although structures of media may change over time, the power of myth and narrative will not alter. Within the frame established by the symbolical definitions of reality, the various versions of the same 'narrative' oppose one another or turn from one into the other, all contained by 'this giant combinatorial machine,' which offers 'a table with the possible variants in which social groups find adequate formula to solve their own problems' (C. Levi-Strauss, 1983:232).

References

Altheide, D. and Snow, R. (1979). *Media Logic*. Beverly Hills: Sage.

Anderson, B., Dardenne, R., & Killenberg, G. (1994). *The conversation of journalism: Communication, community and news.* Westport, CT: Praeger.

Allender, D. (2002). "The Myth Ritual Theory and the Teaching of Multicultural Literature." *The English Journal,* 91(5): 3.

Bennett, A. (1997). Changing media in an aging society: Forum report 10–11 October 1997. Utrecht: Netherlands Platform Older People and Europe.

Berkowitz, D. (1997). Non-routine news and network: Exploring a "what-a-story". In D. Berkowitz (Ed.), *Social meaning of news* (pp. 362–375). London: Sage.

Bird, E. S. (1992) *For enquiring minds: A cultural study of supermarket tabloids.* Knoxville: The University of Tennessee Press.

Bird, E. S., & Dardenne, R. W. (1988). Myth, cronicle and story. In J. Carey (Ed.), *Media, myth and narratives* (pp. 67–85). London: Sage.

Campbell, C. P. (1995). *Race, myth and news.* Thousand Oaks, CA: Sage.

Carstarphen, M.G. & Lambiase, J. J. (1998). Domination and democracy in cyberspace: Reports from the majority media and ethnic/gender margins. In B. Ebo (Ed.), *Cyberspace or cybertopia? Race, class, and gender on the Internet* (pp. 121–135). Westport, CT: Praeger.

Coman, M. (2003). *Pour une anthropologie des medias.* Grenoble, France: Presses Universitaires de Grenoble.

Coman, M. (2005). Cultural anthropology and mass media: A processual approach. In E. Rothenbuhler & M. Coman (Eds.), *Media anthropology* (pp. 46–55). Thousand Oaks, CA: Sage.

Coman, M. (2008). A media anthropological view: Myths, legends, stereotypes and multiple symbolic identities of journalists. In O. Hahn & R. Schroeder (Eds.), *Jurnalistiche Kulturen: Internationale und interdisziplinare Theoriebaunsteine* (pp. 111–124). Köln. Germany: Halem Verlag.

Cornfield, M. B. (1992). The press and political controversy: The case for narrative analysis. *Political Communication,* 9(1), pp. 47–59.

Dahlgren, P. (1992). Introduction. In P. Dahlgren & C. Sparks (Eds.), *Journalism and popular culture* (pp. 1–24). London: Sage.

Dates, J. L., & Barlow, W. (Eds.). (1990). *Split image: African Americans in mass media.* Washington, DC: Howard University Press.

Davis, M. (1995). *Public Journalism and Public Life: Why Telling the News Is Not Enough.* Hillsdale, N.J.: Lawrence Erlbaum.

Dobkin, B. A. (1992). *Tales of terror: Television news and the construction of the terrorist threat.* New York: Praeger.

Entman, R. M. (1990). Modern racism and the images of Blacks in local television news. *Critical Studies in Mass Communication,* 7, 332–345.

Foerstel, H. N. (2006). *Killing the messenger: Journalists at risk in modern warfare.* Westport, CT: Praeger.

Gandy, O. H. Jr. (1986). *'Race,' writing and difference.* Chicago: Chicago University Press.

Gorham, B. W. (1999). Stereotypes in the media: So what? *The Howard Journal of Communication,* 10, 229–247.

Graber, D. (1997). *Mass media and American politics.* Washington, DC: Congressional Quarterly.

Halliday, J., Jansen, S. C., & Schneider, J. (1992). Framing the crisis in Eastern Europe. In M. Raboy & B. Dagenais (Eds.), *Media, crisis and democracy* (pp. 63–78). London: Sage.

Hamilton, J. M. (2004). "Redefining Foreign Correspondence." *Journalism,* 5(3) 20.

Hannerz, U. (2004). *Foreign news: Exploring the world of foreign correspondents*. Chicago: University of Chicago Press.

Heidenreich, L. (2004). "Mobilizing linear histories: Violence, the printed word, and the construction of Euro-American identities in an American county." *Journal of American Ethnic History*, 23(3) 36.

Hess, S. (1996). *International news and foreign correspondents*. Washington, DC: The Brookings Institution.

Hinchman, L., & Hinchman, S. (Eds.). (1997). *Memory, identity, community: The idea of narrative in human sciences*. Albany: State University of New York Press.

Howitt, D. (1982) *The Mass Media and Social Problems*. Oxford: Pergamon Press.

Jacobs, R. N. (1996). Producing the news, producing the crisis: Narrativity, television and news work. *Media Culture and Society*, 18(3).

Kunelius, R. (1994). Order and interpretation: A narrative perspective on journalistic discourse. *European Journal of Communication*, 9(2), 249–270.

Levi-Strauss, C. (1983). *Le regard éloigné*. Paris: Plon.

Lits, M. (1996). *Récit, médias et societé*. Louvain la Neuve, Belgium: Bruylant Academia.

Manoff, R. K. (1986). Reading the news: By telling the story. In, R. K. Manoff & M. Schudson (Eds.), *Reading the news* (pp. 197–229). New York: Pantheon Books.

Maynard, D. J. (1999). Facing the Truth. *American Journalism Review*. 21: 2.

Pedelty, M. (1995). *War stories: The culture of foreign correspondents*. New York: Routledge.

Peffley, M., Hurwitz, J., & Sniderman, P. M. (1997). Racial stereotypes and Whites' political views of Blacks in the context of welfare and crime. *Journal of Political Science*, 41(1), 30–60.

Quere, L. (1982). *Des miroirs equivoques: Aux origins de la communication moderne*. Paris: Aubier-Montaigne.

Schudson, M. (1995). *The power of news*. Cambridge, MA: Harvard University Press.

Shelby, T. (2003). Ideology, racism and critical social theory. *The Philosophical Forum*, 34(2), 153–188.

Sicard, M. N. (1998). *Entre médias et crises technologiques*. Paris: Presses Universitaires de Septrin.

Silverstone, R. (1994). *Television and everyday life*. London: Routledge.

Singer, E., & Endreny, P. (1993). *Reporting on risk: How mass media portray accidents, diseases, disasters and other hazards*. New York: Russell Sage Foundation.

Skinner, J. (2010). Mount Chance, Montserrat and the media: Global British journalism under fire. In E. Bird (Ed.), *The anthropology of news and journalism: Global perspectives*. Bloomington: Indiana University Press.

Smith, C. (1992). *Media and apocalypse: News coverage of Yellowstone forest fires, Exxon Valdez oil spill and Loma Prieta earthquake*. London: Greenwood Press.

Sood, R., Stockdale, G., & Rogers, E. (1987). How the news media operate in natural disaster. *Journal of Communication*, 37(3).

Tuchman, G. Mass media values. *Society*, 14(1), pp.51–54.

Turow, J. (1991). *Media Systems in Society: Understanding Industries, Strategies and Power*. New York: Longman.

Veron, E. (1981) *Comprendre l'événement: les médias et l'accident de Three Miles Island*, Paris, Les éditions de minuit.

Zandberg, E., and M. Neiger (2005). "Between the nation and the profession: Journalists as members of contradicting communities." *Media, Culture & Society*, 27(1) 10.

Zelizer, B. (1992). *Covering the body: The Kennedy assassination, the media and the shaping of collective memory*. Chicago: University of Chicago Press.

CHAPTER 7

Foreign Correspondents as Mediators and Translators Between Cultures: Perspectives From Intercultural Communication Research in Anthropology, Semiotics, and Cultural Studies

Ralph Beliveau, Oliver Hahn, and Guido Ipsen

1. Introduction

Foreign correspondents play an important role in mediated image-building of foreign countries and in translating foreign cultures to their home countries. But in spite of their importance in international (mass) media communication and their impact on international relations, research literature on the work, work routines and conditions, structures and processes, functions, roles, and tasks, effects and perspectives of foreign correspondents under actual and nominal conditions is still rare (e.g., Hahn & Lönnendonker, 2005, 2009; Hahn, Lönnendonker & Schröder, 2008a; Kopper, 2006; see also AIM Research Consortium, 2007a, b, c[1]). Earlier definitions of who is a foreign correspondent and what a foreign correspondent does are rather basic. Sange (1989, p. 68) equates the definition of foreign correspondents to the first article of the 1949 United Nation convention on information exchange, e.g., the activities of foreign correspondents in countries different from their home country. Sange states that their on-site presence adds credibility and authenticity to the media coverage. Another definition by Theodor Marx (1970, p.

---

1 From a European Union's political inside perspective, it is still controversial whether particularly Brussels–based correspondents hailing from EU member–states should be considered as *foreign* correspondents or *domestic* ones.

56) also names the attribute of "cross-border information-mediation"[2] as central to the work of foreign correspondents: "The foreign correspondent is a journalist who works in a state different from the one in which his information-medium is located; it is irrelevant whether he is salaried or a freelancer, whether he mediates his news in words or pictures, whether he works for a news agency or for the media, and whether he is a constant or a special correspondent." Hafez (2002 I, p. 24) describes foreign correspondence/foreign news coverage, in accordance to Theodor Marx's definition, as a "system of the journalistic information mediation, in which course information and news cross state-borders."

Discussions of the functions, roles, and tasks of foreign correspondents need to consider their effect on diplomacy and foreign policy. Foreign correspondents have to continuously inform media consumers in their home countries about current affairs and events from abroad. Local events give consumers direct experience, and allow them to apply critical correctives through either their own experiences or through alternate sources. This cannot happen with foreign news. Media audiences need the information provided by foreign correspondents in order to perceive and to build up images of foreign countries. This, in turn, also means that foreign correspondents create and transfer images of foreign countries. This fact potentially leads to stronger effects on the societal image formation of foreign countries. Consequently, being central relays in international information transfers, foreign correspondents have to minimize "geopolitical and geocultural distance" (Hafez, 2002, pp. 12, 42, 50). This task emphasizes the crucial importance of the foreign correspondents' interpretation function (Koschwitz, 1979, p. 466). They have to frame and contextualize current affairs and events happening abroad in order to help media consumers at home evaluate and order them in a particular context to avoid misunderstandings and misperceptions.

The position of foreign correspondents in the fields of diplomacy and foreign policy is controversial. In this context, political scientists differentiate between two rival schools of thought: the realistic approach (Morgenthau, 1978) and the perception-theoretical approach (Chase, 1951). The latter considers international relations to depend on and to be conditioned by international (mass) media communication. In fact, combined approaches describing the interdependences between realist and (mass) mediated international relations seem to be more appropriate (Rosecrance, 1973). However,

---

2   All non–English quotes have been translated by the authors.

diplomats and political actors on the international scene use foreign correspondent's work to inform themselves about current affairs and events in foreign countries, to contact governments of foreign nations, and to exchange viewpoints with them (Koschwitz, 1979, p. 471). Two sub-functions directly related to the diplomatic and foreign policy-related function of foreign correspondents are the following: (a) to be an early-warning system by observing, recording, and transferring international political decisions (Schenk, 1987, p. 39) and (b) to be a promoter of international understanding and peacekeeping (Koschwitz, 1979, p. 467). Different ideals of foreign correspondents arise from the discussion on their diplomatic and foreign policy-related function. First, the assumption of foreign correspondents to be "neutral informant[s]" is strongly connected to the so-called objectivity norm in democratic journalism. Second, and by contrast, foreign correspondents are conceptualized as "co-author[s] or co-actor[s] of foreign policy." The latter model differentiates between (a) "representative[s] of the public"; (b) "critic[s] of foreign policy," fulfilling the media's control function—also known as the so-called fourth power—in the field of national foreign policy; and (c) "advocate[s] of foreign policy" (Cohen, 1963, pp. 22–47; Hafez, 2002 I, pp. 79–80). This paradigm, today, has replaced the older assumption of foreign correspondents as "ambassador[s] of a country" (Hafez, 2002, p. 181).

In the following, analytical perspectives for future research on foreign correspondents and for adequate theory building are drawn from intercultural communication research in anthropology, semiotics, and Cultural Studies. These perspectives propose interdisciplinary approaches to the study of foreign correspondents and their work.

2. Intercultural Communication Research in Cultural Anthropology and Foreign Correspondence

Although the former assumption of foreign correspondents as ambassadors of their home countries abroad seems to be obsolete, the early seminal findings of intercultural communication research in cultural anthropology used to educate and train diplomats may be useful. In 1946, the U.S. Congress approved the Foreign Service Act to reform diplomacy. According to Kleinsteuber (2003, pp. 151–152) this might be seen as a step taken as a reaction against criticism and complaints from abroad about an alleged ignorance shown by U.S. diplomats towards their host countries. As part of this reform a school for diplomats, called the Foreign Service Institute (FSI), was started by the U.S. State Department in Washington, D.C. One of the FSI's first teachers in the 1950s was U.S. cultural anthropologist Edward T. Hall. To counter this criticism and these complaints, he taught diplomats how to properly act and behave abroad according to different mentalities in the host countries. Hall did so by applying his fundamental research findings on cultural aspects of interpersonal communication in international comparison (Hall, 1959, 1963a, b, 1964, 1966, 1976, 1983). He also translated his findings to popular-scientific books and practical manuals on dealing with intercultural communication issues, particularly relevant for international management and business people (Hall, 1960; Hall & Reed Hall, 1984a, b, 1987, 1990; Hall & Trager, 1953; Hall & Whyte, 1960).

Hall argued that culture is communication and communication is culture.[3] He worked in a tradition of cultural relativism rather than essentialism. Hall argued that cultures or civilizations across the world tend to differ in their communication systems despite the fact that they are constantly in contact with each other. Thus, cultures across the world can be discussed between two tendency poles on an open continuum-scale, with regard to their

---

3   Kleinsteuber (2003) reminds us that Hall has introduced the concept of intercultural communication—as a variant of global communication—in the context of the understanding of culture which prevailed at that time, and which was congruent with the concept of nation. [Besides intercultural communication, there are two other variants of global communication: transcultural communication (crossing national borders) and glocal communication. The neologism glocalization, although combining two seeming opposites, globalization and localization, is only superficially contradictory. It is in fact translated from the Japanese word dochaduka, meaning global localization. Robertson (1992, pp. 173–174) defines glocalization as "a term which was developed in particular reference to marketing issues, as Japan became more concerned with and successful in the global economy, against the background, [...] of much experience with the general problem of the relationship between the universal and the particular".] However, one has to concede that the concept of culture itself is notoriously ambiguous and can be defined, in a broad sense, as the "totality of living appearances and living conditions" (Weber, 1982, p. 217). But, such a broad definition of culture does not meet the criteria of scientific operationalization. To counter this and in order to analyze cultural aspects of communication, media, and journalism in international comparison, Löffelholz (2002, p. 191), for instance, proposes four aspects in a modern understanding of culture: "(1) Culture evolves by communication as a social process. (2) Culture clots in forms of social standardizations and cognitive schemes. (3) Culture stabilizes orientations and consequently leads to building models of interpretation and behavior relatively long existing. (4) Culture is not a static fact, but remains a dynamic process which is time–dependent and may be generated and changed."

respective typical information context as well as to their respective typical senses of time and space (chronemics and proxemics). He refers to the two tendency poles as Low-Context Cultures (LCCs) and High-Context Cultures (HCCs). LCCs are informational extensive, monochronic, and contact distance keeping. HCCs, on the other hand, are informational intensive, polychronic, and contact proximity admitting. The communication style or logic in LCCs is rather 'digital'; while in HCCs it is rather 'analogic' (Watzlawick, Beavin & Jackson, 1967). In LCCs, "[t]he instrumental verbal style is sender-oriented language usage and [...] goal-oriented in verbal exchange [...]. The instrumental style relies heavily on the digital level to accomplish goal objective [...]." In HCCs, "[t]he affective verbal style is receiver-oriented language usage [...] and [...] is process-oriented in verbal exchange [...] and the affective style relies heavily on the analogic level to negotiate relational definition and approval" (Gudykunst & Ting-Toomey, 1988, p. 112). The communication style or logic in LCCs is rather direct, mediating, pragmatic, rational, and abstract; while in HCCs it is rather indirect, narrative, ludic, emotional, and personalized.

If we say that media and journalism always reflect typical patterns of interpersonal communication within a specific culture, it is interesting to see that Hall's findings from interpersonal intercultural communication research across the world are also applicable to (mass) mediated intercultural communication, especially when we engage in international comparative studies operating with Hall's prominent differences between (territorial) cultures.[4] In Europe, for example, Schroeder (1993, 1994) analyzes preponderantly print media in different countries. He discusses so-called transfer titles that appear in different countries and are adapted to different national contexts, as they appear against the backdrop of interpersonal intercultural communication research in cultural anthropology. Hahn (1997a, b, 2008), in discussing how French and German (broadcast) journalism(s) differ from each other, but nonetheless they formed a Franco-German public service cultural television channel ARTE, found that the fundamental research of interpersonal intercultural communication conducted in cultural anthropology is applicable to broadcasting media. Both authors differentiate between LCC media outlets found more in Protestant Northern (European) territories and HCC media

---

4   Interestingly, these findings are implicitly in line with others drawn from systemic modeling comparative conceptualization approaches to media and politics (Hallin & Mancini, 2004).

outlets which are more often located in the predominantly Catholic Southern (European) territories as well as in the Mediterranean region.

In somehow similar to Edward T. Hall's model another one has been developed in intercultural/international management research conducted by Dutch social and organizational anthropologist Geert Hofstede (1980, 2005) who differentiates between cultures against the backdrop of five dimensions, four of which, namely: (a) gender (masculinity/femininity), (b) individualism/collectivism, (c) power distance, and (d) uncertainty avoidance were developed as a first set, later to be added by (e) long-term/short-term orientation.

These findings of both interpersonal and (mass) mediated intercultural communication research in cultural anthropology as well as in intercultural/international management studies[5] stress the fact that any item of information, whether found in interpersonal or (mass) media organizational/ institutional communication is culturally conditioned and coded. An information item is not unequivocal per se; it acquires meaning only within its cultural context. Thus, the same information item can be extremely different in meaning and its significance can vary from one cultural context to another. Different cultural contexts and communication systems lay down different sets of parameters within which their respective (mass) media operate. They do not operate within hermetically sealed cultural spaces but within their respective cultural contexts and with the communication systems of their respective target recipients.

These findings also underline the fact that in international and interpersonal and (mass) mediated intercultural communication (Maletzke, 1981) just (sometimes fictive) interactions/relations (McLeod & Chaffee, 1972) and, at worst, collisions between different cultural contexts and communication systems, can lead to intercultural frictions.[6] In order to emit and receive, to understand and explain and make sense of an information item coming from foreign cultural and linguistic systems and contexts, one has to know the latter exactly. Only thorough knowledge of culturally conditioned and coded as well as of specific mentality-'coining' differences in communica-

---

5   See also Trompenaars & Hampden–Turner (1998).

6   The notion of intercultural frictions does not explicitly refer to self–fulfilling prophecies such as the "Clash of Civilizations" predicted by Huntington (1993, 1996). Arguing against Huntington, Said (2001) puts it as a "Clash of Ignorance."

tion assures an 'undisturbed' (Watzlawick, Beavin & Jackson, 1967) process of interpersonal and (mass) mediated intercultural communication.

As Stuart Hall (1980) discussed in his model of encoding and decoding information, both, the encoder (or re-encoder) and the decoder negotiate the meaning of cultural signs: their mediated meaning is not immediately clear due to the polysemy of signs, but nonetheless it depends on the code symmetry shared by the participants in the communication process.

Intercultural frictions may result from inexact translation equivalents from one language to another or from one culture to another (Bassnett, 2002; Koller, 2004). Also, intercultural frictions result from communication interferences within political and cultural power relations in international relations and their implications for communication (Bartholy, 1992).

In this context, one dilemma relates to the controversial issue of who or which collective cultural identity holds the political and cultural power of definition. So far, the so-called West, due to its political and economic hegemony, has held the political and cultural power of definition; it has been able to dominate 'imperialistically' the 'non-Western hemisphere' leading to a dichotomization of the world into two sharply different categories: civilization (the 'West') versus barbarism (the 'non-Western rest') (Stuart Hall, 1996; Said, 1978, 1993).

Furthermore, all foreign correspondents—like journalism researchers—are members of at least one culture and native speakers of at least one natural verbal language, a fact that both influences their intellectual work and communication patterns continually. Since they are unable to free themselves from their own cultural and linguistic baggage (Hall & Reed Hall, 1990, pp. xx–xxi; Kleinsteuber, 1993, p. 322; Esser, 1998, p. 19) or risk going native in their host culture, the journalistic 'objectivity' demanded from them can only be evaluated against the backdrop of their respective cultural context.

Therefore, El-Nawawy & Iskandar (2002, pp. 27, 54, 202) suggest that news values and selection criteria are conditioned by "contextual objectivity." They describe their perhaps somewhat controversial theory as follows: "The journalistic standard applied here require[s] some form of contextual objectivity, because the medium should reflect all sides of any story while retaining the values, beliefs, and sentiments of the target audience. [...] This dual relationship underscores the conundrum of modern media. [...] It would seem that the theory of contextual objectivity—the necessity of television and media to present stories in a fashion that is both somewhat impartial yet sensitive to local sensibilities—is at work. [...] Although this appears to be an oxymoron, it is not. It expresses the inherent contradiction between attaining objectivity in news coverage and appealing to a specific audience."

In order to better understand foreign correspondents and foreign correspondence the research findings about interactions among different cultural contexts and communication systems have to be taken into consideration. Foreign correspondents themselves should reflect on the process because they always adapt the information from their work place abroad to the cultural context and communication system of their home countries. Often they have to negotiate information gaps between different cultural contexts and communication systems. Thus, foreign correspondents can be considered as mediators and translators[7] between cultures (Hahn, Lönnendonker & Schröder, 2008b), being positioned *in-between* them.

3. Cultural Semiotics of Foreign Correspondence: The Competences of Sign Transfer

To the present day, no comprehensive semiotic theory of journalism or foreign correspondence has been developed. However, since foreign correspondence may be understood as a prototypical act of communication, a semiotic approach towards its mechanics and problems may well be useful. For semiotics,[8] the phenomenon of foreign correspondence may be defined as a specialized form of sign transfer (Ipsen, 2008). Foreign correspondents have the task of collecting and transferring signs from one cultural sphere to another, thus employing competences of encoding and decoding signs in order to successfully resolve the transfer process. But in order to understand the process as a whole and to gain access to the semiotic approach, it is useful to have a

---

7   Looking at transcultural communication, Hafez (2002 I, p. 163) describes "the journalist as 'sense–translator' between the cultures."

8   Semiotics, the science of signs, or doctrine of signs, as it is also sometimes called, is a discipline that investigates the meaningful elements, or signs, of cognition and communication in nature and culture. As such, the sign is considered as 'something that stands for something else' in the traditional definition 'aliquid stat pro aliquot.' In this sense, perceptions and communications are always composed of signs. Modernity has seen two major branches of the study of signs: (a) structuralist semiology as founded by Swiss philologist Ferdinand de Saussure and (b) pragmatist semiotics in the tradition of U.S. philosopher and polymath Charles Sanders Peirce. Whereas semiology is almost exclusively concerned with the structure of signs and sign systems, semiotics focuses on sign processes of understanding and sign production. These considerations combine models from both traditions; however, in its orientation it should be seen as pragmatist.

look at relevant semiotic and communicational models. From this basis, these considerations proceed into the semiotic practice of foreign correspondents, and finally have a view on the transcultural pragmatics of the sign transfer process. This forms the interdisciplinary bridge between semiotics and linguistics as the science of natural verbal language signs.

3.1 The Peircean Model of the Sign and Foreign Correspondence

The sign, as conceived by the U.S. pragmatist Charles Sanders Peirce, is a dynamic relation of three elements (Deely, 2001) and is therefore also called a *triadic* concept (Peirce, 1931–58 I, § 345[9]). These considerations concentrate on the immediate meaning of the three apices of the Peircean sign for foreign correspondents as sign users (fig. 1):

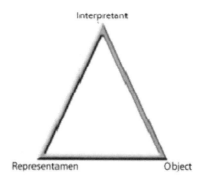

Fig. 1 Peircean sign

Every sign requires as a first correlate a *representamen*. This is the correlate Peirce (1931–58 I, §§ 540, 564) refers to as the *perceptible sign*. "Perceptible" in this context refers to physical as well as mental perception. Since everything may serve as a sign, visual or tactile representations of bodies are perceptible in the same manner as thoughts. The latter are not perceived by a sensory channel, but emerge in the mind. The *representamen* furthermore mediates between the other two correlates of the sign, as every perception *stands for* a certain meaning and causes a *mental effect*.

Foreign correspondents are confronted with the signs they are to gather, i.e., the data they find relevant and decide to send home. These perceptible

---

9   References to Charles Sanders Peirce (1931–58) are indicated by volume number followed by paragraph number.

signs are of various natures like visual signs of buildings or natural occurrences such as storms or earthquakes or like oral signs such as linguistic
signs produced by interview partners, sounds produced by artifacts, or again
by natural effects. Within these two large classes of signs are hybrid signs
and composed signs (e.g., a noisy crowd, a rainforest boasting with life), and
these sub-classes are characterized by traits of behavior and expression
found, in mimics, gestures, and body language. Here, signs of spatial behavior appear which can be analyzed by proxemics, like the social distance, the
number of people present in one place, the publicity of events, etc. Foreign
correspondents, however, are not restricted to perceiving and interpreting
signs. They will also produce new signs in the collection and transformation
process; for example, they are not merely relay nodes for sign transportation.
Their interpretation of signs will influence the transfer of signs they are to
initiate. Finally, foreign correspondents themselves may serve as *represen-
tamina* within the composition of signs of their report.

In order to better understand how foreign correspondents' interpretations
influence their own sign production, it is useful to have a look at the correlate
of the sign named the *object*. The object of the sign is equal to the experience, or knowledge about a sign the individual has; in Peirce's (1931–58 II, §
330) words, "perceptual acquaintance." The object can be understood as the
relative perspective on the sign as a whole. The learning process is a good
example of how experience of the sign is never absolute, but relative. Begin-
ners evince a limited amount of knowledge of a subject; their experience horizon is relatively narrow. While proceeding in acquiring knowledge, the
perspective on the subject matter will change: the object of learners is enriched. Peirce (1931–58 VIII, § 314) furthermore distinguishes between the
immediate and the dynamic object: "We must distinguish between the Immediate Object,—i.e. the Object as represented in the sign,—and the [...]
Dynamical Object, which, from the nature of things, the Sign cannot express,
which it can only indicate and leave the interpreter to find out by collateral
experience."

The two dimensions of the object identify two levels of experience. The
group experience, which forms a consensus of meaning, is added by the personal experience of the interpreter who is also part of the group. The immediate object is therefore bound to the societal agreement of what a sign
means. A sign that represents a specific person, such as a photograph of
George W. Bush, will have an immediate object that contains the meanings
of human, male, and other generally stable meanings. However, in order to

understand that it is a photograph of a former U.S. President, one needs to have collateral experience that is not directly indicated by the sign. Thus, somebody from Europe will have collateral experience that a person from Central Asia may not share. In the course of cognizing signs, both aspects of the object inevitably change, but naturally at different speeds. For the task of foreign correspondents, their personal collateral experience, but also the experience of the culture they stem from, is of utmost importance, as it affects the ways in which they themselves perceive the foreign culture that they are supposed to report on.

The third correlate of the sign is the *interpretant*, or, as Peirce (1931–58 V, §§ 474, 475) paraphrases it, the *effect of the sign*. The effects of the cognition of a sign may be varied. Upon perceiving a *representamen* and identifying it as standing for a specific object, one may feel affirmed in own experiences, for example: 'This is a tree. I have seen trees before. Hence, I recognize it.' This is one of the most common sign effects, which is also the basis for the recognition of the world. A sign may, however, also have the effect of changing the perspective, for example, if the perceived sign has not been perceived formerly, or it triggers collateral experience that is in opposition to former creeds.

For Peirce, the process of perceiving and interpreting signs is by principle endless, it also happens continuously. He calls this process *semiosis*. In the context of foreign correspondence, two acts of *semiosis* require further investigation. The first is the *semiosis* of foreign correspondents within the supposedly alien cultural sphere from which the signs to be reported originate. The second act of *semiosis* being set in the foreign correspondents' audience. In order to integrate the theory of *semiosis* into a pattern of intercultural contact, these considerations now take a look on another elaborated semiotic theory, namely the concept of the semiosphere.

3.2 Semiospheres, Contact between Semiospheres, and Foreign Correspondence

The Estonian semiotician Juri Lotman devises the model of the semiosphere for reasons of mapping the structures and dynamics of cultural signs. The model originally has served to illustrate both cultural contact and the differences between the realms of culture and nature. In the context of foreign correspondence, the model illustrates well the integrity of signs within an interpretive community and the effects of sign transport to another semiotic sphere.

The space of culture in Lotman's (1990, pp. 124–125) theory is called the *semiosphere*, contrasting the *biosphere* of biological life. The important features of culture are communication, language, and the intricate means of using these to trade culture to following generations. As this dynamic communicative definition shows, the semiosphere is by no means static or delimited. This author perceives the world of cultures as composed of semiospheres that may come into contact and influence one another. To the end of illustrating these mechanisms, he devises the following model of the semiosphere (fig. 2):

Fig. 2 Lotman's model of the semiosphere

Internally, the semiosphere is divided in center and periphery. These areas are not to be misunderstood as regional geographical centers; rather, this author uses the terms as metaphors for areas of stability and change within a culture. The center of the semiosphere is the location of stability, rule, and law. Here, the meanings of signs are fixed by convention and habit. Cultural traditions, rituals, and beliefs are to be located here. The periphery of the semiosphere is less stable. Innovation and change are located at the periphery. New signs emerge here and new structures come into being. In the process of sign development, the periphery may slowly affect the center. Historically speaking, the rules established at the center are always the results of former innovations within the periphery that have gained the status of convention.

Innovation is especially bound to semiotic contact between different semiospheres. In the history of humankind, contact between semiospheres has been a common occurrence. Sign exchange takes place via general communication, trade, or exchange of knowledge, or travel, migration, or even armed conflict. In either case, signs are transported from one semiosphere to another. Sometimes, the sign exchange results in successfully establishing alien signs within another semiosphere. The adoption of Arabic numerals by Western culture may serve as an example. However, more often than not signs that enter another semiosphere may as well be recognized as alien due to the impregnability of the center, and henceforth be rejected or continuously dwell at the periphery labeled with minority status.

The problem rests in the accessibility of the *code*[10] which is necessary to decode and interpret the signs in question. As already mentioned, individual *semiosis* is based on the experience horizon represented in the object of the sign. The rules and conventions for sign interpretations therefore rest on a strong and firm intracultural fundament. Even though signs may evince a minimum of immediate objects that are universally shared by cultures across the world, the multitude and diversity of collateral experience render universally conventionalized interpretation of signs impossible. Each individual culture has a set of codes at its disposal to decode signs it is confronted with, or which it produces itself. These codes are regulated and established within the center of the semiosphere.

Semiotically speaking, the task of foreign correspondents is to gather signs within one semiosphere and transport them to another one, making the sign structures of the first semiosphere transparent to the members of the target sphere. From the application of the semiotic models of Peirce and Lotman, these considerations now illustrate the semiotic problems and mechanics of foreign correspondence, and map the semiotic skills that may be attributed to foreign correspondents.

3.3 Excursus: The Cultural Trap in Foreign Correspondents' Cognition and Communication

Apart from the semiotic skills that a correspondent may be expected to master, there are numerous aspects of the psychological and social 'programming' human beings are exposed to, and which naturally govern their communicational behavior. We should like to add here another short excursus to Hofstede's (2005) ideas on intercultural contact, which may serve to

---

10 In semiotics, the code is seen as a correlational device for interpreting signs. Since signs are not isolated but are always part of sign systems, knowledge of the code of the system is essential for correctly interpreting the sign. For Eco (1976), for example, the code is a "system of rules given by a culture."

illustrate some of the semiotic problems we think foreign correspondents are confronted with.

First, we should like to expand on what Hofstede calls "mental programming." This sort of educational and social disposition of the individual rests on the sheer fact that we are all necessarily immersed in the cultural environment of our families, peers, and social contact partners: "Every person carries within him- or herself patterns of thinking, feeling, and potential acting that were learned throughout their lifetime. Much of it has been acquired in early childhood, because at that time a person is most susceptible to leaning and assimilating. As soon as certain patterns of thinking, feeling, and acting have established themselves within a person's mind, he or she must unlearn these before being able to learn something different, and unlearning is more difficult than learning for the first time. [...] Workers' behavior is an extension of behavior acquired at school and in the family. Managers' behavior is an extension of the managers' school and family experiences, as well as a mirror image of the behavior of the managed" (Hofstede, 2005, pp. 2–3, 364).

Hofstede does not explore journalistic behavior; however, we may assume that the same is valid for the latter profession. Some of the findings of Hofstede's are especially interesting against the background of the cultural text, if we may use a semiotic term here, which every member of a cultural continuum is participating in, as Posner (2003, p. 48) illustrates when defining culture as a mental state of participation and cooperation. In expanding these basic statements on the nature of culture, we might find that Hofstede's empirical studies on what he calls the dimensions of culture are useful for correspondents as a blueprint against which to critically analyze their own behavior.

In Hofstede's analysis of cultural dimensions, he applies a system that identifies a 'culture' as being set somewhere between the absolutes of two poles. This applies to five dimensions altogether mentioned earlier in this chapter. Let us take a look at the fifth dimension, namely long-term orientation. In the numerous surveys that have been employed to collect the data on which Hofstede's assumptions are based, he found that, e.g., East Asian cultures are much more long-term oriented than their Western counterparts. This results in some differences in thinking, and mentally processing cognitive items. The participants in a short-term oriented culture are much more rooted in binary thinking, i.e., they assume that of two opposing ideas, only *one* is supposed to be correct at one given moment. The ownership of *truth*, hence, is imperative, as opposing opinions are assumed not to be correct (Hofstede, 2005, pp. 229–232).

In other words, the analytic, dyadic structure of thinking, which is to be found in Western cultures, may result in shaping the reality to be communicated by correspondents, and distorting it, even unwittingly. The general tendency to pick one side in a conflict as the 'good' one may be one result of this 'mental programming.' Taking a larger perspective, we may find that whatever trend in the discourse we may follow as participants of a short-term oriented culture, we shall always fall victim to the journalistic trait of 'taking sides,' even if that is what we choose to call a 'neutral' one. According to Hofstede's findings, and combining these with our semiotic assumptions, we may demand that the first and foremost duty of the foreign correspondent is to find a meta-discourse that enables him or her to dispose of culturally programmed dyadic thinking.

3.4 Foreign Correspondents as Semiotic Agents

As it can be easily deduced from the short survey of Peircean semiotics, foreign correspondents as interpreters of signs are bound to the rules of *semiosis*. First and foremost, this means that foreign correspondents share the experiential basis of their own semiotic community. This may also be shown by empirical findings, as by employing Hofstede's system of cultural dimensions. Within the Peircean model, the object determines the *representamen*, and the latter in course determines the interpretant. In other words, the previous experience guides the interpreters in their perception of signs, and the way of perceiving governs the sign effects. Nobody can escape the own experience horizon, and this has a double effect on foreign correspondents as semiotic agents, which may also be illustrated by a model of twofold transfer.

First, foreign correspondents are themselves transferred personally from one semiotic sphere to another. They carry with them the semiotic load of their education and lifelong experience, and necessarily perceive the alien semiosphere as if seen through a filter. Second, in their production of signs, foreign correspondents produce those signs of their own semiotic sphere, as this is the target of their activity. They hence transfer and translate signs from one sphere to another, taking them from one coherently coded environment to another in which other codes are valid. Both production and transfer are hence mechanisms of foreign correspondents' sign transfer (fig. 3):

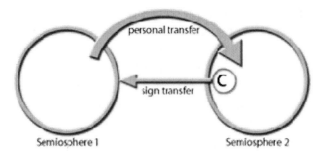

Fig. 3 Sign transfer

The question of translatability of signs has been an issue for semiotics (Gorlée, 1994). The general opinion is that direct translatability is impossible, as no two sign systems share the same code. In terms of the Peircean model, one can define the double problem of translation as follows: a *representamen* may represent two entirely different objects in two cultures, and the concept identified by an object in one culture may not even exist in another culture.

Foreign correspondents as semiotic agents need to be aware of this problem. The competences of foreign correspondents need to include the capability of deconstructing the sign appearances in the alien culture according to the codes valid therein. Furthermore, foreign correspondents need to be aware of the fact that the target audience is also bound to its own experience horizon, and the codes of its semiosphere.

Above, the codes of proxemics have been mentioned. The spatial occurrence of cultural events, for example a crowd assembling in a street, yelling and waving flags, may be interpreted completely different in diverse semiospheres. Whereas one interpretation may sound: 'This is a meeting of solidarity and sharing the spirit of the moment', another may well proceed as: 'This is another mob gathering in a suburb, they are up to no good. I have been presented with this before. Hence, I recognize it as such.'

In order to avoid the semiotic pitfalls of sign transfer, foreign correspondents may apply methods of cross-cultural pragmatics.[11] As Blum-Kulka & Kasper (1989, p. 3) show in reference to Leech (1983, p. 11), the pragmatic

---

11   Pragmatics is a branch of semiotics and a linguistic discipline concerned with investigating the actual sign usage by interpreters, speakers respectively, in specific situations.

performance is governed by situational variables. Linguistic and social behavior is culture-specific (Blum-Kulka & Kasper, 1989, p. 5). Hence, the
problems of sign transfer previously discussed on the basis of the theory of
semiotics, may be resolved by foreign correspondents with sufficient pragmatic knowledge. This involves two areas of expertise, and these considerations do not address the problem of linguistic competence. Firstly, foreign
correspondents need to be intrinsically acquainted to the cultural traits of the
alien semiosphere, as these will govern the behavior as well as speech acts of
the actors of this culture. Without such expertise, foreign correspondents will
not be able to deconstruct their own semiotic molding. The second competence involves the ability to fill in the meaning gaps of translation, and to
correct the misunderstandings of sign transfer, on what semioticians and lin-
guists call the *meta-level* of sign systems. Speakers, for example, resort to the
meta-level of language in explaining the meaning of what they have said before. In a similar manner, foreign correspondents should be capable of making use of the meta-level in order to make the situational setting and cultural
coding of the signs they transfer transparent.

4. Cultural Studies and Foreign Correspondents:
A Culture of Journalism, a Journalism of Culture

The desire to study foreign correspondents means bridging between the
world of scholarship and the world of journalism. Often these worlds have
existed in a state of conflict, even when their interaction was seen to hold
great potential for contributing to society. John Dewey (1927) expressed the
desire that scholars, like journalists, could create newspapers that would provide generally available useful information, like an early version of news you
can use. A few decades later Wilbur Schramm (1964) argued that scholars
were producing information that journalists should use regularly, since they
were 'watchmen, […] participants in the decision process, and […] teachers'.
As practitioners and researchers were brought together in the academy, debates took place between quantitative theorists, or Chi-squares, and professional practitioners, or Green-eye-shades (Cohen, 2005). Both groups were
suspicious of the relative value of the other.

In journalism, the cliché is that academics have some kind of knowledge
and expertise, but knowledge not appropriately grounded in the so-called real
world. This disconnection distances academics from the world constructed in
the news. Scholars are often called for a final paragraph quote, but the solici-

tation from the journalist already has an expected outcome. She or he is looking for support for an article that is for the most part already written.

However, these perspectives are grounded in notions of both journalism
and the academy that are a bit out of date, however. Despite the continuity of
this interaction, much of the scholarship has changed from Schramm's notions of social science to a whole new world of studying culture. Journalism
has had to contend with similar transformations in the world of information,
produced by globalism in cultural and media interaction. One notes friction
between different models of press identity—this is no longer the world of
Four Theories of the Press (Siebert, Peterson & Schramm, 1956)—and the
odd tension between the desire to understand the other (or others) and the
desire to understand one's own culture.

Foreign correspondents occupy a privileged position in such a world,
given their role in translating news, information, and ideas across cultural
boundaries. They live and prosper because of their position in negotiating the
tension between the foreign culture they cover and the home culture they
speak to.

This particular tension has been the focus of the idea of Cultural Studies,
where notions of self and other are used to investigate the conditions of
power, the interactions of social practices, and the development of the notions of individuals and empire. Given its scope, Cultural Studies can seem
overwhelmingly broad, even though much of the work is criticized for being
destructively relativistic, terministically obscure, and faddish (Brantlinger,
2001, pp. 47–67).

We would like to argue that a careful examination of the history that
produced this intellectual movement will certainly offer a defense against
these criticisms; but to a greater degree, understanding the history and development of Cultural Studies will clearly cause it to be found in the conversation about foreign correspondents. The study of this history will lead to a
couple clear conclusions. First, the work of foreign correspondents itself reflects an inclusion of Cultural Studies notions without knowing it. At the
same time scholars who wish to study journalists, particularly foreign correspondents, are already in the midst of kinds of inquiry that can be greatly
informed by Cultural Studies.

By seeing how practices of mediation for both journalists and scholars
find themselves at the same intellectual crossroads, where the possibility for
objectively verifiable observation is cross-cut by a deeper understanding of

the conditions of power, identity, and struggle, Cultural Studies can shed a unique light on foreign correspondents and their work.

4.1 Origins

Several different stories can be the focus for discussing the origins of Cultural Studies. Each different cultural context will produce a different insight grounded n its own perspective.

Most scholars and historians ground their understanding of Cultural Studies in England, during the second half of the twentieth century. Intellectual influences on this movement include elements from French linguistics in the 19-teens (Saussure, 1959), American sociologists of the Chicago School in the 1920s (Park, 1967; Mead, 1934), Italian anti-fascists in the 1930s (Gramsci, 1971), and, most significantly, German émigré Jewish intellectual critics from the 1930s through the 1970s and beyond (Horkheimer & Adorno, 2002). Each of these sources had an extraordinary influence on the intellectual development of Cultural Studies in England. But the ground for these influences to gather was set by the way English society rethought education at the conclusion of World War II.

The end of the war meant the return of a British citizenry that had been away at a crucial point in their lives. They had completed varying levels of basic education, but were now in need of some sort of additional education and training in order to manage the shift from soldiering to participating in a society. It is less historically certain how gender played into this transition, but the end of rationing and the cessation of war manufacturing certainly had a comparable effect on women.

For several of the returnees, the end of the war and the desire for a different kind of social structure coincided with two other sets of ideas. First, turning the page of the war also saw a shift of political power from the Conservatives to the Labour party in the 1945 election. Through 1951 the Labour Government put in place many progressive social programs, including the nationalization of industries, cradle-to-grave welfare, and the National Health program. Against this background, leaders in higher education saw the opportunity to develop a system of adult education that would be able to offer retraining, and offer a more-well rounded liberal education than had previously been available. As the system developed over the 1950s and 1960s, several individuals got involved in teaching this adult population who had political sympathies with the working class they were teaching. Many were sympathetic to the social conditions of the working class, and saw their roles as advocates for self-determination through liberal education. In his history of modern British adult education, Roger Fieldhouse (1996, p. 212) observes: "This post-war generation of university adult educators included a number of exceptionally talented individuals such as E. P. Thompson, Raymond Williams, and Richard Hoggart, who went on to make a major academic and cultural impact. It was a characteristic of their work which sprang from their experience as adult education tutors that it transcended traditional academic boundaries and was frequently both inter-disciplinary and intellectually innovative, challenging traditional conceptions of historical, literary and sociological disciplines."

These teachers became authors who wrote several of the foundational works for what was later to be called Cultural Studies. A brief look at their interdisciplinary contributions and their intellectual innovations should lead to an understanding of how their work can be applied to the study of journalists in general, and foreign correspondents in particular.

4.2 Sources

E. P. Thompson

E. P. Thompson made critical contributions to the direction that one could look to develop these contexts. The study of any particular media formation makes it greatest contribution in linking the production of signs and meanings to some set of contexts that locate it in time and space. Thompson had been teaching literature in the late 1940s, and his courses grounded the study of literature in both the Romantic movement and the industrial revolution. He was, however, gradually evolving these contexts into an understanding of social history (Steele, 1997, p. 21). Thompson's views of education were heavily influenced by his emphasis on the recognition of the relationship between education and social control. His attention to social history, given its greatest expression in his 1963 history *The Making of the English Working Class*, established his understanding of the way social control was a site of struggle for the identity of the working class and the social contexts that gave it shape. Education, in its post-war form, has the potential to extend this notion of social control; Thompson thought that it could alternately be used as a consciousness-raising situation.

Thompson strongly felt that the possibilities for self-determination of any disempowered identity were in a critically tenuous situation. He saw his own work, then, as an attempt to resist the tendency of the ideologically powerful from running a monopoly on the way groups and individuals are defined. In the often-quoted passage from the preface of *The Making of the English Working Class,* Thompson (1963, p. 12) clarified his objective: "I am seeking to rescue the poor stockinger, the Luddite cropper, the 'obsolete' hand-loom weaver, the 'utopian' artisan, and even the deluded follower of Joanna Southcott, from the enormous condescension of posterity."

Thus, Thompson's scholarship emphasized how the historical documentation of whole social and cultural contexts produced an understanding of identity that reached well beyond the standard presentations of political and social history. He was essentially arguing for the extension of 'bottom-up' histories, which worked against the tendency to disenfranchise the majority of the culture in favor of its political and economic victors.

Raymond Williams

Whereas Thompson made critical contributions to the connection between the circulation of signs about people and their self-determination, Raymond Williams offered an understanding of the way materialism and culture were intimately related. Williams worked with these relationships by maintaining a connection to history in two senses of the term. The first sense is connected to his own biography and the desire to maintain the connection to a historically significant personal context. Williams maintained a connection to his own history and his origins in a Welsh working class background. In one of the most important of his essays, he argues for understanding the notion that when we speak of culture, we speak of *whole ways of life* (Williams, 1958). As he puts it, "Culture Is Ordinary." Therefore, one significant frame for this foundation for Cultural Studies was the historical connection to the material of life, in all of its dimensions, simultaneously average and completely unique.

The second sense of history Williams uses connects the notion of history to the notion of communication. We can think of the mediated manifestations of our communication practices as the material out of which our understandings are made. We participate in the flow of material representations in the form of sounds, images, and other arrangements. Williams, in a move that echoes E. P. Thompson, answers the question, 'What does X mean?' through a recount of its history. Speech is seen as a practice made of materials. Each new use materializes new formations, carrying the potential for new meanings.

Specifically, Williams defined the notion of 'culture.' In 1976 the first edition of Williams' book *Keywords* arrived. This book is a kind of selective list of definitions, assembling terms appropriate for a deep historical understanding of culture. Williams (1976, p. 15) writes in the introduction: "It is not a dictionary or a glossary of a particular academic subject. It is not a series of footnotes to dictionary histories or definitions of a number of words. It is, rather, the record of an inquiry into a vocabulary: a shared body of words and meanings in our most general discussion, in English, of the practices and institutions which we group as culture and society."

Williams believes that these words have definitions that transform over time. He presents a chronology of meaning per word, each attending to the political and social over time. Williams (1983, p. xiii) understands these changes as "a special kind of map by which it is possible to look again at those wider changes in life and thought to which the changes in language evidently refer." Therefore, transformations are studied to give an indication of how the society is itself transforming. Since shifts in language are used by groups of people in a context where they react to changes in circumstance, words are ways of identifying meaning required in new language forms.

Williams's project worked this idea through large-scale notions of culture. In *Culture & Society: 1780–1950*, he writes about the transformations over the stated span in art, perspectives on art, and especially the language used in understanding the transformation of the role of art. His later work expands these notions into contemporary (mass) media. When these critical approaches investigate the content of a medium like television, Williams is careful to note how history itself appears as content within the media. On the one hand, one can easily find in its representation of history a sentimentalization of the past (Heath & Skirrow, 1995, pp. 362–363), which must be deconstructed for its historical manipulation of "popular memory." On the other hand, such manipulations are in themselves significant; they carry some notion of the feeling in the society that produced them. In one of Williams' (1977, p. 132) more well-known constructions, we can describe this relationship through the investigation of the "structure of feeling." 'Feeling' replaces such formal notions as world-view or ideology, in an effort to "see meanings and values as they are actually lived and felt."

This represents a profound shift in the place where studies of culture take place. Williams contributes to the dismantling of the traditional split between high culture and popular culture. The traditional view of culture clearly delineated the differences between high and low and between what was considered 'the best of what humanity thought and said' from the popular communication of the people. High culture understood the notion of culture as a process of becoming 'cultured' into understanding this superior set of values. But Williams observed, in his experience as a working class and continuing education teacher from the end of WWII until the early 1960s, high culture was too far separated from the values of the people he taught. The social practice of judging this group by the standards of high culture suggested that they lacked 'culture,' a notion that Williams rejects. Rather than seeing a defect in the popular culture, Williams seeks to understand it as it is lived, based on its own inherent value and legitimacy.

Here is where the impact of Cultural Studies can be seen as either its most profound or its most misguided. Traditional structures of culture are overturned if a sense of relative value coheres in different varieties of experiences. An empowered group, whether through wealth, privilege, politics, or tradition, looses its default power to determine the conditions of absolute value. Such a perspective is profoundly aligned with notions of egalitarian democracy. But it is also considered misguided in its relativism, yet the desire in Williams and in Cultural Studies to value the popular is mischaracterized as an abandonment of standards, giving in to a kind of thorough relativism. There is very little justification for this criticism, however. Rather than the abandonment of values, Williams' work allows a researcher to form an understanding of the variety of value systems as they are experienced, and in particular how they struggle over the way power is distributed in society.

For the study of foreign correspondents, this question of the relationships of power is crucial. In their work these reporters combine the analysis and identification of a different value system from their own with the need to translate that different system for their home culture. The great advantage of a Cultural Studies analysis arises out of its need to focus on the terms of power that shape each side of the meaning making process. Cultural Studies research could use this analysis of power to develop an understanding of the 'structure of feeling' developed in the correspondent's work. In some cases, one would hope that such an analysis would indicate where the 'structure' is shared between the source culture and the audience. It would be equally informative, however, to analyze the cases where that 'structure of feeling' is not shared, and the foreign correspondent must translate not just the details of the story, but enough of the context of the 'structure of feeling' from the source to make the events comprehensible.

Richard Hoggart

The intersection between traditionally educated cultural perspectives and post-WWII adult education arises often in the understanding of the foundations of British Cultural Studies. Richard Hoggart, like Thompson and Williams, became involved in teaching adult education and brought to it his own cultural conflict. Not only did Hoggart grow up in a working class environment, but he also experienced an education aligned with traditional high culture values. Rather than abandoning the former for the latter, Hoggart (1958) brought the two together in *The Uses of Literacy*, a text that laid discussed how Cultural Studies analysis could be applied to the process.

The Uses of Literacy is eclectic. The first half, "An 'Older' Order," offers a nostalgic look at a working-class culture experienced from within. The emphasis is placed on the real conditions of a class as it constructs its experiences, works within its limitations, and expresses its interests. Specific attention falls on family, recognition of 'them' and 'us,' and the characteristics of living in a community of common interests, especially class interests. The picture brings attention to a way of life once ignored. Its values are elevated simply through the profound act of recollection. The second half, "Yielding Place to New," documents the invasion of this way of life through mechanically reproduced attractions of mass culture. Just as Walter Benjamin (1968) noted in his essay "The Work of Art in the Age of Mechanical Reproduction," the replacement of the authentic experiences with the mass produced ones cuts ties to history, to the past. Instead members of this class are conditioned to live in the present and become obsessed with newness, youth in general, and what Hoggart (1958, p. 193) describes as a "kind of shiny barbarism."

These reflections of Hoggart's followed his own education in the traditions of literary theory. Following his education at Leeds and his service in the military, he found work teaching in adult education programs. As with Thompson and Williams, the experience of teaching in adult education emphasized the notion that the study of texts needed to maintain cultural relevance. They could do this, Hoggart realized, if the analysis refrained from jargon, and most significantly if the analysis was applied to the popular culture texts that made up the experiences of the place that was yielded by the 'older' order of working class life.

Here we can see Hoggart's significant contribution to the base of Cultural Studies in the attention paid to popular culture (Steele, 1997, p. 135). Through the analysis of the way these texts operated, adult education students and later students of all types would be able to extend their critical faculties. Rather than limit the eye of analysis to highly praised examples in the tradition of the highest of high culture, that analytic tool could make deeper and richer sense of the experiences in the popular culture, especially in the (mass) media, which had been the chief agent of social transformation.

Birmingham Centre for Contemporary Cultural Studies (BCCCS)

The development of Cultural Studies found its institutional home at the Birmingham Centre for Contemporary Cultural Studies (BCCCS). Started in 1964, Richard Hoggart BCCCS's first director. With this Centre the idea of Cultural Studies found an institutional starting point. Central figures in the development of the Birmingham Centre included Stuart Hall, who developed the encoding/decoding model described earlier in this chapter. The Centre is notable for its contributions to the organizing of Cultural Studies, but its existence also brings up one of its central dilemma. One notes that the contributions made by Thompson, Williams, and Hoggart were outside of mainstream disciplines and from intellectuals outside of the intellectual mainstream, whose teaching was happening in the world of adult education, not in traditional university settings. This context defines both these ideas and the spirit of Cultural Studies as a practice. It resists the institutionalization that recognizes the power of traditions, particularly traditional academic disciplines. It would be a mistake to see Cultural Studies as an outgrowth of any particular established discipline, whether English or Sociology or History.

Cultural Studies, unlike these other areas, was inherently interdisciplinary. Since the center of their concerns was the production of cultural meaning, and since cultural meaning happened in the flow of life, where all sorts of disciplinary concerns interfere with each other, it followed that the practice would be disciplined not by a tradition but by the production of meaning in particular cultural, historical, and social contexts. As Julie Thompson Klein (1990, p. 125) explains in her book on interdisciplinarity: "The most common methods are Marxism, feminism, deconstruction, psychoanalysis, ethnography, race and gender theory, semiotics, and textual analysis. Sometimes methods are combined, meshing survey research with ethnography, information from modern marketing research with more utopian conceptions of empowered consumers, and textual or ethnographic analysis with social, political, and cultural commentary. Methods typically reflect original disciplinary training, amplified by situational borrowings."

The historical conditions that allowed for and encouraged the development of these elements are still debated. At the same time the success of the project is widely recognized, in the expansion of publishing outlets in both journal and book form, in the expansion of conferences that used Cultural Studies as a central theme, and in the acceptance of scholars who self-identify as Cultural Studies researchers.

Much of the BCCCS's work was collaborative as well as interdisciplinary. The influence of the interdisciplinarity, however, outlasted the employment of collaboration as a specific characteristic of Cultural Studies work. Authorship in subsequent years is more typically single-authored.

This reflects the typical author situation of the foreign correspondent, who works, oftentimes, individually rather than in a group. Research might lead, however, to investigate what social communities play a role in the production of their coverage. Many foreign correspondents find themselves in each other's company. To the extent that this forges an identity or contributes to their practices, such relationships are worth study.

4.3 The Critical-Populist Split

The final development to consider is the structure of the cultural understanding developed by Cultural Studies. This structure reflects the influences of both critical Marxist social politics and anthropological methods. In both cases, the focus from dominant mass communication research shifts from the study of empowered creators of culture to the largely disempowered receivers of culture. These so-called masses are not taken for granted, particularly in the way that they make meaning out of the cultural materials that are produced and sold to them.

Cultural Studies research has evidenced a split in the understanding of this meaning making process, and in some ways, this a split brought in the practice of Cultural Studies through its British traditions focuses on class concerns (Brantlinger, 1990, p. 127). The pessimism of Richard Hoggart is perhaps the best representative of one side of this split. In this line of thinking the mass culture media sphere acts to replace the best interests of the individuals that make up the audience with the interests of the capital and institutions that are constructing the media 'spectacle.' Cultural Studies work seeks to pull back the curtain on this effort and reveal the ideologies of those in power as translated through media, in an effort to enable the culture to better understand what is being done to it through the analysis of media messages.

But the limitations of this approach can be seen in how the audience is essentially silenced rather than empowered or how they are seen as victims in an oppressive cultural state. The other side of the split noted this emphasis, and chose instead to focus on the way audiences made meanings out of their cultural experiences for their own ends. Critics like John Fiske (1987) and Janice Radway (1984) focused instead on the way resistance is expressed through the meaning-making processes that audiences employ. Rather than having their own sense of identity and values replaced, these authors argued that the meanings of media experiences were decoded for their own ends. Texts were seen as sites of struggle, where dominant meanings were pushed back by the power of an audience member to reconstruct messages into a resistant ideology. In other words, they pushed back. There are other similar splits that follow from a practice that seeks legitimacy, but wants to critique the power structure on which the legitimacy bases itself. The result is that Cultural Studies continues to build a dynamic understanding of the way meaning is and can be made.

4.4 Cultural Studies: Applications to Foreign Correspondents

Foreign correspondents present an ideal location for the development of Cultural Studies research because of their unique position as a cultural interface. As was discussed earlier, foreign correspondents are positioned as translators from one semiosphere to another. If we connect the history of concerns in Cultural Studies directly with foreign correspondents, a valuable sense of intercultural studies would result.

First, foreign correspondents can be understood to occupy a position that advances the cultural politics of audience empowerment. To the extent that a foreign correspondent includes descriptions and analyses of institutional structures, the knowledge that crosses the cultural border empowers the audience. One clear route of research, therefore, might analyze how a foreign correspondent makes institutional power comprehensible. These institutions and their ideologies will cover a wide range of positions, some familiar to the audience of the reports, some quite alien to the audience. One area of focus, for example, might be the way editors and correspondents negotiate the need to 'background' a specific historical incident to make the issue comprehensible from a different cultural perspective. A Cultural Studies analysis might take note of both where this background is seen as necessary, and also where it is not seen as necessary because of a close collusion between ideological systems (i.e., on ideas about democracy, citizenship, and human rights). Research of this kind needs to see the foreign correspondent as both a producer and an audience member. The reporter is a producer of cultural material in one semiosphere, and at the same time they are in an 'audience' position in the semiosphere on which they report. The use of ethnographic interviewing with these reporters would provide an understanding of the way reporters share the perspective of the audience they write for. The question of empowerment can be addressed directly in such research.

Second, foreign correspondents could be studied for the way they implement some of the founding ideas of Cultural Studies in their individual context. Much in the spirit of the notion of audience empowerment, the work of foreign correspondents could be understood as E. P. Thompson might approach it. Certainly much of the work foreign correspondents produce offers an understanding of foreign events out of a fairly traditional 'news' framework and often reflect the ideology of power. But how are the correspondents using their understanding of their audience to frame their work? The boundary crossing work in which foreign correspondent are engaged require a certain kind of 'bottom-up' notion of their audience. A well-grounded Cultural Studies approach would address the meaning structure of the particular audience as it influences the work of the foreign correspondent, however the category of the 'bottom' is figured as a media audience.

On the other hand, the work of these correspondents might be studied for the way they decide how to focus their reports between the traditional institutional framers of news content and the less empowered sectors of the society they cover. For example, foreign correspondent might decide that the best way to discuss capital punishment in the U.S. to an audience outside the U.S. would focus on the controversy as expressed by individuals who represent different points of view in the U.S. 'audience,' rather than simply the decision makers in the political system that create policy. These audience members would offer a 'bottom-up' sense of the meaning of the issue in focus.

If we take some of the notions from Raymond Williams and use them to approach the work of foreign correspondents, two strong possibilities emerge. First, a Cultural Studies analysis would be able to investigate the transformation of ideas through language over time. The historical work of a particular media outlet or a particular reporter could be examined longitudinally, to find out how terms are transformed. These transformations would offer ways of understanding the change in meaning that happen across the complex border of two different cultures. As Williams suggests, the use of a term offers a window into the value system to which it is connected. The choices made by foreign correspondents could be analyzed for their transformations in two directions; first the changes in the society being reported on, and second the changes in the society who is receiving the reports.

Williams' notion of Cultural Studies would also prove essential in understanding the way high culture and low culture are negotiated. Once again, we have the privilege in such studies of developing an understanding of the flow of high and low culture in two locations at once; the source culture and the audience culture. Consider, for example, the complicated picture of high and low culture that arises from a foreign correspondent's reporting about funding for the arts from private and public sources. Ethnographic interviews with the reporter could be combined with the close analysis of textual evidence (the stories he or she produced) to understand the changing relationship between arts activities and public and private or corporate support. Additionally, audience plays a significant role in the way cultural activities are perceived. How do the reporters understand how their audiences make meaning of the notion of arts funding, as well as the notions of culture value that are attached?

Finally, from Richard Hoggart, we might see an arena of cultural analysis that focuses on the effects of mass culture across national boundaries. Whereas Hoggart described the negative effects of mass culture as it effected the British working class, foreign correspondents are in a position to discuss the way culture are effected from outside of themselves. Much of the critical work in Cultural Studies takes on this notion and uses versions of cultural imperialism as a framework. Media crosses boundaries following the expansion of markets for media. On an individual scale foreign reporting does much of the reflective observation of this process, usually with an eye toward the way cultures talk to each other, and sensitive to the power balances or imbalances as they play out in various media. From Hoggart's lead, Cultural Studies analysis might focus on the way these cross-border media situations change and sometimes replace the ideology structures of the places into which they are imported.

Because of the existing gap in attention paid to this site of analysis, opportunities for the application of Cultural Studies approaches to the study of foreign correspondents abound. Researchers will find many opportunities for developing an understanding of foreign correspondents and their work. Likewise, these opportunities are especially significant because of the tools that Cultural Studies employs to communicate its understanding of the cultural situations under analysis. Researchers are able to reflect on the implications of their methodological choices. They can focus critical attention on the ideological structure that is inherent in research methods, both to fine-tune their observations, and to fairly assess the limitations of such work. That reflexive posture means that meanings are contingent on the choices the researcher makes in defining the limitations of their subject in both time and space. Since we are frequently focusing on correspondents that are moving ideas across linguistic boundaries, which we need to see as cultural boundaries, we are also seeing the changing frontier and the border zones.

References

AIM Research Consortium (ed.) (2007a). *Understanding the Logic of EU Reporting from Brussels: Analysis of Interviews with EU Correspondents and Spokespersons*. Bochum, Freiburg/Brsg.: projekt verlag (= Adequate Information Management in Europe (AIM)—Working Papers, vol. 3).

AIM Research Consortium (ed.) (2007b). *Comparing the Logic of EU Reporting: Transnational Analysis of EU Correspondence from Brussels*. Bochum, Freiburg/Brsg.: projekt verlag (= Adequate Information Management in Europe (AIM)—Working Papers, vol. 4).

AIM Research Consortium (ed.) (2007c). *Reporting and Managing European News: Final Report of the Project "Adequate Information Management in Europe" 2004–2007*. Bochum, Freiburg/Brsg.: projekt verlag.

Bartholy, H. (1992). Barrieren in der interkulturellen Kommunikation. In H. Reimann (ed.). *Transkulturelle Kommunikation und Weltgesellschaft: Zur Theorie und Pragmatik globaler Interaktion*. Opladen, Wiesbaden: Westdeutscher Verlag, pp. 174–191.

Bassnett, S. (2002). *Translation Studies* (3rd ed.). London, New York: Routledge.

Benjamin, W. (1968). The Work of Art in the Age of Mechanical Reproduction. In W. Benjamin. *Illuminations: Essays and Reflections*. New York: Harcourt Brace Jovanovich, pp. 217–251.

Blum-Kulka, S. & Kasper, G. (1989). Investigating Cross-Cultural Pragmatics: An Introductory Overview. In S. Blum-Kulka, J. House & G. Kasper (eds). *Cross-Cultural Pragmatics: Requests and Apologies*. Norwood/NJ: Ablex, pp. 1–34.

Brantlinger, P. (1990). *Crusoe's Footprints: Cultural Studies in Britain and America*. New York: Routledge.

Brantlinger, P. (2001). *Who Killed Shakespeare? What's Happened to English since the Radical Sixties*. London: Routledge.

Chase, S. (1951). *Roads to Agreement*. New York: Phoenix House.

Cohen, B. C. (1963). *The Press and Foreign Policy*. Princeton, NJ: Princeton University Press.

Cohen, J. (2005). Connecting the Dots between Journalism Practice and Communication Scholarship. *Journalism & Mass Communication Educator*, 59(4), pp. 335–338.

Deely, J. (2001). A Sign Is What? *Sign System Studies*, 29, pp. 705–744.

Dewey, J. (1927). *The Public & Its Problems*. New York: Holt & Company.

Eco, U. (1976). *A Theory of Semiotics*. Bloomington, IN: Indiana University Press.

El-Nawawy, M. & Iskandar, A. (2002). *Al-Jazeera: How the Free Arab News Network Scooped the World and Changed the Middle East*. Boulder, CO: Westview Press.

Esser, F. (1998). *Die Kräfte hinter den Schlagzeilen: Englischer und deutscher Journalismus im Vergleich*. Freiburg/Brsg., Munich: Karl Alber.

Fieldhouse, R. (1996). *A History of Modern British Adult Education*. Leicester, UK: National Institute of Adult Continuing Education.

Fiske, J. (1987). *Television Culture*. New York: Methuen.

Gorlée, D. L. (1994). *Semiotics and the Problem of Translation: With Special Reference to the Semiotics of Charles S. Peirce*. Amsterdam: Rodopi.

Gramsci, A. (1971). *Selections from the Prison Notebooks*. New York: International Publishers.

Gudykunst, W. B. & Ting-Toomey, S. (1988). *Culture and Interpersonal Communication*. Newbury Park, CA, Beverly Hills, London, New Delhi: Sage.

Hafez, K. (2002). *Die politische Dimension der Auslandsberichterstattung: Theoretische Grundlagen* (vol. I). Baden-Baden: Nomos.

Hahn, O. (1997a). *ARTE—Der Europäische Kulturkanal: Eine Fernsehsprache in vielen Sprachen*. Munich: Reinhard Fischer.

Hahn, O. (1997b). ARTE an der Kreuzung der Kommunikationskulturen: Interkultureller und multilingualer TV-Nachrichtenjournalismus beim Europäischen Kulturkanal. In M. Machill (ed.). *Journalistische Kultur: Rahmenbedingungen im internationalen Vergleich*. Opladen, Wiesbaden: Westdeutscher Verlag, pp. 137–153.

Hahn, O. (2008). Journalismus an der Kreuzung der Kulturen und Sprachen: Grundlagen der anthropologischen interkulturellen Kommunikationsforschung und Ethnolinguistik. In O. Hahn & R. Schröder (Eds.). *Journalistische Kulturen: Internationale und interdisziplinäre Theoriebausteine—Lehrbuch*. Cologne: Herbert von Halem, pp. 31–55.

Hahn, O. & Lönnendonker, J. (2005). State-of-the-art Report on Foreign Correspondence and Foreign Correspondents in the U.S. and Europe: The Case of Germany, URL: http://www.brost.org/static/transcoop/germany.pdf (11-28-2005).

Hahn, O. & Lönnendonker, J. (2009). Transatlantic Foreign Reporting and Foreign Correspondents after 9/11: Trends in Reporting Europe in the United States. *The International Journal of Press/Politics*, 14(4), pp. 497–515.

Hahn, O., Lönnendonker, J. & Schröder, R. (Eds.) (2008a). *Deutsche Auslandskorrespondenten: Ein Handbuch*. Constance: Universitätsverlag Konstanz (UVK).

Hahn, O., Lönnendonker, J. & Schröder, R. (2008b). Auslandskorrespondenten als Kontextvermittler zwischen den Kulturen: Interdisziplinäres Theoriemodell journalistischen Transfers und translatorischer Äquivalenz. In O. Hahn, J. Lönnendonker & R. Schröder (Eds.). *Deutsche Auslandskorrespondenten: Ein Handbuch.* Constance: Universitätsverlag Konstanz (UVK), pp. 44–63.

Hall, E. T. (1959). *The Silent Language.* New York, London, Toronto, Sydney, Auckland: Anchor Books/ Doubleday.

Hall, E. T. (1960). The Silent Language in Overseas Business. *Harvard Business Review*, 38, pp. 87–96.

Hall, E. T. (1963a). Proxemics—A Study of Man's Spatial Relationships. In I. Galdston (ed.). *Man's Image in Medicine and Anthropology.* New York: International Universities Press, pp. 87–96.

Hall, E. T. (1963b). A System for the Notation of Proxemic Behavior. *American Anthropologist*, 65(5), pp. 1003–1026.

Hall, E. T. (1964). Adumbration as a Feature of Intercultural Communication. In J. J. Gumperz & D. H. Hymes (Eds.). The Ethnography of Communication Issue. *American Anthropologist* (special issue), 66(6), pp. 154–163.

Hall, E. T. (1966). *The Hidden Dimension.* New York, London, Toronto, Sydney, Auckland: Anchor Books/Doubleday.

Hall, E. T. (1976). *Beyond Culture.* New York, London, Toronto, Sydney, Auckland: Anchor Books/Doubleday.

Hall, E. T. (1983). *The Dance of Life: The Other Dimension of Time.* New York, London, Toronto, Sydney, Auckland: Anchor Books/Doubleday.

Hall, E. T. & Reed Hall, M. (1984a). *Les différences cachées : Une étude sur la communication interculturelle entre Français et Allemands.* Hamburg: Stern/Gruner & Jahr.

Hall, E. T. & Reed Hall, M. (1984b). *Verborgene Signale: Studien zur internationalen Kommunikation—Über den Umgang mit Franzosen.* Hamburg: Stern/Gruner & Jahr.

Hall, E. T. & Reed Hall, M. (1987). *Hidden Differences: Doing Business with the Japanese.* New York, London, Toronto, Sydney, Auckland: Anchor Books/Doubleday.

Hall, E. T. & Reed Hall, M. (1990). *Understanding Cultural Differences: Germans, French, and Americans.* Yarmouth, ME: Intercultural Press.

Hall, E. T. & Trager, G. L. (1953). *The Analysis of Culture.* Washington, DC: Foreign Service Institute (FSI)/American Council of Learned Societies.

Hall, E. T. & Whyte, W. F. (1960). Intercultural Communication: A Guide to Men of Action. *Human Organization*, 19(1), pp. 5–12.

Hall, S. (1980). Encoding/Decoding. In S. Hall, D. Hobson, A. Lowe & P. Willis (eds). *Culture, Media, Language: Working Papers in Cultural Studies, 1972–79.* London: Hutchinson, pp. 128–138.

Hall, S. (1996). Who Needs "Identity"? In S. Hall & P. du Gay (Eds.). *Questions of Cultural Identity.* Newbury Park, CA, Beverly Hills, London, New Delhi: Sage, pp. 1–17.

Hallin, D. C. & Mancini, P. (2004). *Comparing Media Systems: Three Models of Media and Politics.* Cambridge, UK: Cambridge University Press.

Heath, S. & Skirrow, G. (1995). Interview with Raymond Williams. In C. Prendergast (Ed.). *Cultural Materialism: On Raymond Williams*. Minneapolis/MN: University of Minnesota Press, pp. 359–376.

Hofstede, G. (1980). *Culture's Consequences: International Differences in Work-related Values*. Newbury Park, CA, Beverly Hills, London, New Delhi: Sage.

Hofstede, G. (2005). *Cultures and Organizations: Software of the Mind* (2nd ed.). London, New York: McGraw-Hill.

Hoggart, R. (1958). *The Uses of Literacy*. London: Penguin.

Horkheimer, M. & Adorno, T. (2002). *Dialectic of Enlightenment: Philosophical Fragments*. Stanford/CA: Stanford University Press.

Huntington, S. P. (1993). The Clash of Civilizations? *Foreign Affairs*, 72(3), pp. 22–49.

Huntington, S. P. (1996). *The Clash of Civilizations*. New York: Simon & Schuster.

Ipsen, G. (2008). Auslandskorrespondenz als Phänomen der Zeichenübertragung: Zur Bedeutung metasemiotischer Kompetenz. In O. Hahn & R. Schröder (Eds.). *Journalistische Kulturen: Internationale und interdisziplinäre Theoriebausteine—Lehrbuch*. Cologne: Herbert von Halem, pp. 235–252.

Klein, J. T. (1990). *Interdisciplinarity: History, Theory, & Practice*. Detroit, MI: Wayne State University Press.

Kleinsteuber, H. J. (1993). Mediensysteme in vergleichender Perspektive: Zur Anwendung komparativer Ansätze in der Medienwissenschaft—Probleme und Beispiele. *Rundfunk und Fernsehen*, 41, pp. 317–338.

Kleinsteuber, H. J. (2003). Der Dialog der Kulturen in der Kommunikationspolitik. In C. Cippitelli & A. Schwanebeck (Eds.). *Nur Krisen, Kriege, Katastrophen? Auslandsberichterstattung im deutschen Fernsehen*. Munich: Reinhard Fischer, pp. 145–192.

Koller, W. (2004). *Einführung in die Übersetzungswissenschaft* (7th ed.). Wiebelsheim: Quelle & Meyer.

Kopper, G. G. (ed.) (2006). *'How are you, Mr. President?' Nachrichtenarbeit, Berufswirklichkeit und Produktionsmanagement an Korrespondentenplätzen deutscher Medien in den USA: Arbeitsbuch für Medienpraxis und Forschung*. Berlin: Vistas (= Informationskultur in Europa, vol. 5).

Koschwitz, H. (1979). Internationale Publizistik und Massenkommunikation. *Publizistik*, 24, pp. 458–483.

Leech, G. (1983). *Principles of Pragmatics*. London: Longman.

Löffelholz, M. (2002). Globalisierung und transkulturelle Krisenkommunikation. In A. Hepp & M. Löffelholz (Eds.). *Grundlagentexte zur transkulturellen Kommunikation*. Constance: Universitätsverlag Konstanz (UVK), pp.186–204.

Lotman, J. M. (1990). *Universe of Mind: A Semiotic Theory of Culture*. Bloomington, IN: Indiana University Press.

Maletzke, G. (1981). Internationale und interkulturelle Kommunikation: Vorschläge für Forschung und Lehre. *Publizistik*, 26, pp. 345–352.

Marx, T. (1970). *Das Problem der Harmonisierung des europäischen Presserechts unter besonderer Berücksichtigung des Rechtes des Auslandskorrespondenten*. Unpublished manuscript of a JD thesis presented to the Faculty of Law, University of Munich, Germany.

McLeod, J. M. & Chaffee, S. R. (1972). The Construction of Social Reality. In J. T. Tedeschi (Ed.). *The Social Influence Processes*. Chicago, IL, New York: Aldine Atherton, pp. 50–99.

Mead, G. H. (1934). *Mind, Self, & Society from the Standpoint of a Social Behaviorist*. Chicago, IL: University of Chicago Press.

Morgenthau, H. J. (1978). *Politics among Nations: The Struggle for Power and Peace* (5th ed.). London, New York: McGraw-Hill.

Park, R. E. (1967). *The City*. Chicago/IL: University of Chicago Press.

Peirce, C. S. (1931–58). *Collected Papers* (vols. I–VI, ed. C. Hartshorne & P. Weiss; vols VII–VIII, ed. A. W. Burks). Cambridge, MA: Harvard University Press.

Posner, R. (2003). Kultursemiotik. In A. Nünning & V. Nünning (Eds.). *Konzepte der Kulturwissenschaften: Theoretische Grundlagen—Ansätze—Perspektiven*. Stuttgart/Weimar: Metzler, pp. 39–72.

Radway, J. (1984). *Reading the Romance: Women, Patriarchy, and Popular Literature*. Chapel Hill/NC: University of North Carolina Press.

Robertson, R. (1992). *Globalization: Social Theory and Global Culture*. Newbury Park/CA, Beverly Hills, London, New Delhi: Sage.

Rosecrance, R. N. (1973). *International Relations: Peace or War?* London, New York: McGraw-Hill.

Said, E. W. (1978). *Orientalism: Western Conceptions of the Orient*. New York: Pantheon.

Said, E. W. (1993). *Culture and Imperialism*. New York: Knopf/Random House.

Said, E. W. (2001). The Clash of Ignorance. *The Nation*, 22 October (prepublished online 4 October), URL: http://www.thenation.com/doc/20011022/said [and /2 and 3] (5-18-2009).

Sange, R. (1989). Japanische Auslandskorrespondenten in der Bundesrepublik Deutschland: Qualifikationsmerkmale, Arbeitsbedingungen und Berufseinstellungen. *Publizistik*, 34, pp. 62–77.

Saussure, F. (1959). *Course in General Linguistics*. New York: Philosophical Library.

Schenk, B. (1987). Die Struktur des internationalen Nachrichtenflusses: Analyse empirischer Studien. *Rundfunk und Fernsehen, 35*, pp. 36–54.

Schramm, W. (1964). *Mass Media and National Development: The Role of Information in the Developing Countries*. Stanford, CA: Stanford University Press.

Schroeder, M. (1993). Frankreich-Deutschland: Zwei unterschiedliche Auffassungen von Kommunikation. France-Allemagne: L'existence de deux logiques de communication. In U. E. Koch, D. Schröter & P. Albert (Eds.). *Deutsch-französische Medienbilder: Journalisten und Forscher im Gespräch. Images médiatiques franco-allemandes: Un dialogue entre journalistes et chercheurs*. Munich: Reinhard Fischer, pp. 21–42.

Schroeder, M. (1994). *Internationale Markt und Managementstrategien für Printmedien*. Munich: Reinhard Fischer.

Siebert, F. S., Peterson, T. & Schramm, W. (1956). *Four Theories of the Press*. Chicago, IL, London: University of Illinois Press (Urbana).

Steele, T. (1997). *The Emergence of Cultural Studies: Adult Education, Cultural Politics and the English Question*. London: Lawrence & Wishart.

Thompson, E. P. (1963). *The Making of the English Working Class*. New York: Vintage.

Trompenaars, F. & Hampden-Turner, C. (1998). *Riding the Waves of Culture: Understanding Diversity in Global Business* (2nd ed.). London, New York: McGraw-Hill.

Watzlawick, P., Beavin, J. H. & Jackson, D. D. (1967). *Pragmatics of Human Communication: A Study of Interactional Patterns, Pathologies, and Paradoxes*. New York: W. W. Norton.

Weber, M. (1982). *Gesammelte Aufsätze zur Wissenschaftslehre* (7th ed.). Tübingen: UTB.

Williams, R. (1958). Culture Is Ordinary. In N. MacKenzie (ed.). *Conviction*. London: MacGibbon & Kee, pp. 74–92.

Williams, R. (1976). *Keywords: A Vocabulary of Culture and Society*. New York: Oxford University Press.

Williams, R. (1983). *Culture & Society: 1780—1950*. New York: Columbia University Press.

CHAPTER 8

Professional Values, Ethics, and Norms of Foreign Correspondents

Katerina Tsetsura, David Craig, and Olivier Baisnée

Introduction

Professional values, ethics, and norms of foreign correspondence are vitally important because they inform the picture of the world audiences take away from the coverage. Foreign correspondents today work in an environment which is rapidly becoming more globalized and connected, but at the same time they face continuing challenges in dealing with local sources in a wide range of cultural settings. The conflict between global professional ethics and local practices highlights the need for careful consideration of universal, regional, and local values and norms in journalism.

Despite the broad attention to professional ethics in recent decades, there has been little focus on the ethics of foreign correspondents specifically. This gap in research needs to be filled because professional values and ethics play a key role in the work of foreign correspondents. How journalists understand and apply ethical principles shapes both the process and the product of their work.

The terms "ethics," "values," and "norms" are often used in media studies in ways that overlap, so it is important to delineate the boundaries of their meaning for the purposes of clarity in research. "Ethics" is taken here to refer to matters of personal, professional, or social responsibility, and benefit or harm. "Values," as Elliott put it, "are beliefs expressed in judgment statements rather than in fact statements. That is, statements about values are normative as distinguished from descriptive statements that express facts." (Elliott, 1997, p. 69) Elliott focuses on judgments "that implicitly express an assumption about harm or benefit" (p. 70), but values are also used in media ethics in reference to "professional values," which may be less clearly linked to matters of benefit or harm. "Norms" are taken as parallel in meaning to values—so they, too, may refer to ethical judgments or to professional judgments that may not be explicitly ethical.

The chapter explores these concepts in relation to globalization of news, the changing nature of sources, the ethical context of foreign correspondence, and the problematics of navigating between local norms and professional standards. The chapter also discusses media bribery as an example of an existing tension between global and local practices. Finally, recommendations for future studies and research methods for approaching them are suggested.

Globalization of News

In the 21st century, a global newsroom has become a norm. Information flow transcends the borders, and international news media are in stiff competition for readers and viewers' attention. The very fact that international news agencies continue to have a strong presence in the media market and that global newspapers, magazines, and broadcasters are popular simultaneously in different parts of the world demonstrates a significant role of truly global news carriers. Newspapers such as *The New York Times, Times* of London, and *The Guardian* which are most valued by opinion leaders have online versions available to readers all over the world. A truly global newspaper, *International Herald Tribune*, is American-owned and based in Paris (Rampal, 2002). However, despite the continued influence of large global media outlets, the ability for readers and viewers to access a news medium online has transformed the traditional understanding of the journalist's role as a deliverer of information and gatekeeper.

The globalization of news and Internet expansion developed a new information model, radically different from the old model of consumers relying on journalists to deliver information (Rampal, 2002). Journalists lost the ability to be the sole gatekeepers of information; in fact, anyone can be a journalist by reporting what is happening in any part of the world, via Internet. Online communication, instantly global and yet very local, becomes essential in information dissemination processes of exchanging news. In addition to publicity-generating materials created and distributed by primary sources through their official websites, weblogs secured their place in information exchange with community members (Singer, 2006), as social networking sites, such as Facebook and Twitter, have more recently. Social media usage in the United States grew from 17 percent in 2006 to 26 percent in 2008 for social networking sites and from 13 percent in 2006 to 24 percent in 2008 for blogs (*Media Myths and Realities: 2008 Media Usage Survey*, 2009). Internet has become one of the major sources of information for many journalists, especially foreign correspondents who rely on the primary sources to access desirable information and contact potential interviewees (Wu & Maxwell, 2004). The *Preliminary Findings from the Middleberg/SNCR Survey of Media in the Wired World* showed that 92 percent of 160 editors and reporters of traditional and online news organizations use companies' websites to gather information for reporting, about 70 percent use blogs, and 41 percent use social networks (McClure, 2008).

The loss of media monopoly encouraged a paradoxical impact on "any sense of journalism ethics on a global scale" (Kruckeberg & Tsetsura, 2004, p. 90). This led to a reconceptualization of the journalist, who is becoming a "socially responsible existentialist," according to Singer (2006). Engaging theories of existential journalism (Merrill, 1996) and social responsibility (Siebert, Peterson, & Schramm, 1956), Singer proposed to reconsider journalistic norms of independence and accountability so the journalist could choose to be a trustworthy source of information that serves public interest. For an average reader or viewer, the source now is no longer just a medium, or just a journalist: it can be a primary source itself or another community member who has access to information dissemination channels, such as Internet Web sites. Moreover, because of the financial and time pressures, modern media heavily rely on primary sources who are actual information providers. For many media outlets the use of publicity materials, often without a direct indication who and under what circumstances had provided information, has become a norm.

Public relations and communication departments of organizations and corporations share media information packages with the media on a regular basis in hopes that journalists will use the company's or organization's name and experts or advocates of their point of view in the finished pieces. Media packages, often called media kits, may include news releases, fact sheets, backgrounders on issues and organizations, photos, video news releases, ready-to-use quotations, ideas for feature stories with names and contact information of potential interviewees, or any combination of those. Public relations practitioners generate thousands of news releases and media kits each day and enjoy multiple opportunities to shape information communicated through the media to different publics about their organizations (Christians, Fackler, McKee, Kreshel, & Woods, 2009). Reporters can take information, analyze, and write about it, still performing their roles as gatekeepers for the audience, but "the information gleaned there has certainly passed through the public relations gate before moving to the reporter and on to various audiences" (Christians et al., p. 199). Today, public relations practitioners engage in discussions with journalists and readers via social networks, write blogs, participate in online forums, or become members of social media and participants in the blogosphere to communicate organizations' viewpoints. The hope is that online readers, including journalists, will adopt key messages public relations practitioners put forward.

Is shaping news about an organization through media relations deceptive? Who is responsible for letting the public know how information was gathered and used? Many believe it is a journalist's ethical responsibility to honestly disclose sources of information to the publics (Kruckeberg & Tsetsura, 2004; Singer, 2006). By the nature of their work, public relations practitioners share and pursue the interest of primary sources of information, organizations and corporations they work for (as employees or as contracted consultants). If someone works for a company X, the public knows that this person would most likely share information that advocates for this company. One *expects a public relations practitioner to be biased.* On the other hand, one *counts on journalist's independence and accountability* when accessing information via mass media. And if a journalist does not disclose how he or she received the information, the public would have no means of knowing whether the information gathering and presentation may potentially be biased. That is why it is desirable that any journalist, especially a foreign correspondent, let the audience know to what extent he or she relied on the primary news sources' information when preparing a news story.

The issue of the nature of journalistic sources in the 21st century is closely related to the issue of independence and accountability. Not only the nature of gatekeeping has changed; the nature of news sources has changed as well. The next part addresses the changing nature of sources specifically for foreign correspondents.

Changing Nature of Sources for Foreign Correspondents

Foreign correspondents encounter numerous challenges when trying to access information overseas (Fleishman, 2004; Hess, 1996; Hoffman, 2004). In addition to direct information access challenges, such as contacting government representatives and getting interviews with public officials (*Economist,* 2004), correspondents often experience other professional problems, such as limited travel budgets (Schoen, 1994), cultural mismatch of norms (Wu &

Maxwell, 2004), gender discrimination (Pedelty, 1997), and even competition against other foreign journalists, including their loved ones (Blumenthal, 1998). In other words, the challenges encompass the issues of gatekeeping, financial constraints, and cultural, professional, and personal conflicts.

Foreign journalists actively look for and often find alternative ways of getting access to information and readily use the help of primary sources, including public relations practitioners, because journalists are "hungry to extend their network of resources and break news" (Hoffman, 2004, N. PAG). It does take time to establish a trusting relationship between a source and a journalist, especially a foreign correspondent. But public relations practitioners worldwide are continuously encouraged to invest time in understanding of foreign correspondents, their news criteria, and "what they deal with and what makes them tick" (Hoffman, N. PAG).

Because of the financial pressures put on the media outlets that utilize foreign correspondence, today's editors, reporters, and specialized journalists become more dependent on sources from other countries to provide accurate, up-to-date, relevant, detailed, and fast information that becomes the basis for news. Much of this information comes for free, and journalists no longer need to hunt for it, but journalists must still perform the gatekeeping role of deciding whether to distribute the information through the media channels and as such set an agenda. It is particularly important if this information is accessed via the Internet sources or comes from social media. And publics rely on journalists to decide which information is the most important, most newsworthy, and most relevant out of the continuous flow of information (Tsetsura, 2006).

As such, the public expects the media to follow several essential information gatekeeping principles: independence of opinion; fair and honest judgment of facts and reporting; and freedom from outside, non-media influences. Most important, the public expects them to separate news content from advertising on the pages of newspapers and magazines and on the air space of radio and TV programming. These actions are important elements in defining the ethical behavior of journalists worldwide.

Globalization forces foreign journalists toward following unified common practices of gathering news and covering events. At the same time, journalists face difficult choices in dealing with local sources on an everyday basis. Journalists are pressured to follow global journalism standards on one hand and use different techniques in collecting information in a wide variety of local settings on the other hand. This tension underlines the importance of examining commonalities and differences in ethical norms worldwide.

The Media Ethics Context: Commonality vs. Difference in Norms

Although little research has explored what the ethics of foreign correspondents are or ought to be, other scholarly work in media ethics has important implications for thinking about ethical norms for foreign correspondents. Some scholars have explored the possibility of universal or common moral values for media practice (e.g., Brislin, 2004; Christians, 1997; Christians & Nordenstreng, 2004; Christians et al., 2009; Herrscher, 2002; Kovačič, 2008; Klaidman, & Beauchamp, 1987; Lambeth, 1992; Patterson, & Wilkins, 2008; Perkins, 2002; Strentz, 2002; Ward, 2005). Others have looked at what values are actually expressed in media ethics codes across the world, finding commonalities there (e.g., Bertrand, 2000; Cooper, 1989, 1990; Hafez, 2002). But differences have emerged in research on codes, as well as in the limited amount of work done on the ethics of foreign correspondents themselves. Both the commonalities and differences in argued-for and actual norms have important implications for research about foreign correspondents.

Much of the substantial body of academic work that has developed in media ethics in the past three decades has implied, or argued outright, that certain ethical values ought to be considered binding widely if not universally. For example, Lambeth (1992) laid out a normative framework that included five principles to guide journalists: truth telling, justice, freedom, humaneness, and stewardship. Klaidman and Beauchamp (1987) presented several ethical values including reaching for truth, avoiding harm, and maintaining trust as part of the life of *The Virtuous Journalist*. Textbooks hold up ethical perspectives such as Kant's categorical imperative and Mill's principle of utility as broadly applicable to the work of journalists, though often discussed in the U.S. context (Christians et al., 2009; Patterson & Wilkins, 2008).

Christians (1997) has argued repeatedly and directly for the universality of values, seeking to retain moral universals while addressing the postmodernist critique of ethical foundations and the variety of cultures worldwide. Building on the work of German philosopher Jonas (1984), Christians (1997) contended that humans have a natural reverence for life and for its preservation, and that this regard represents a "protonorm" that creates oneness in human purpose. Although people value life with or without explicit reflection on ethical principles, Christians said that when people do reflect, "we recognize that it entails such basic ethical principles as human dignity, truth, and nonviolence" (1997, pp. 12–13). Because these are derived from the universal human respect for life, these principles have cross-cultural relevance for the practice of journalism. Christians and Nordenstreng (2004) used the argument from nature again in discussing the worldwide development of notions of social responsibility. They noted that social responsibility as a norm for journalism has emerged in a number of democratic societies since World War II, both in connection with the Hutchins Commission (Commission on Freedom of the Press, 1947) and in the context of professional codes and practice. But they argued that social responsibility needs to be grounded in universal values based on common humanness, not on the particular obligations of professionals in journalism. More recently, Christians (2005, 2008) has called for further development of models of moral universals in media ethics. However, he has stressed that universals must be situated in history and cultures, not presented as abstractions insensitive to these particulars worldwide. Similarly, Wasserman (2006) and Rao and Wasserman (2007) provided an important qualifier in the quest for universal values in media ethics. Using postcolonial theory, they argued that such efforts should be sensitive to local contexts and issues such as power imbalances. Rao and Wasserman (2007) used two ethical theories, *ubuntu* from South Africa and *ahimsa* from India, to show how indigenous perspectives shape particular understandings of ethics.

Other scholars have also argued that journalists ought to consider certain ethical standards as universal for the field, though they have differed on exactly which standards. Strentz (2002) proposed an eclectically grounded set of four standards: use of restraint (avoiding violence), knowledge of oneself (avoiding self-deception), respect for others (not abusing "one's authority or stewardship"), and accountability (bearing "responsibility for the consequences of one's actions") (p. 267). Herrscher (2002) proposed issues for a universal code of ethics including truth, completeness, conflict of interest, freedom, honesty, respect for privacy, and treatment of diverse groups of people. Perkins (2002) used international human rights law to argue for three universal principles: truth-telling, independence, and freedom with responsibility. Using a contractualist approach, Ward (2005) argued for the principles of credibility, justifiable consequence, and humanity. Brislin (2004) focused on empowerment of citizenry as a universal value. Kovačič (2008) argued that journalists across the European Union should not adhere to a formal code but should embrace responsibility, tolerance, and empathy.

In addition to academic discussions of what the common values of journalists ought to be, journalists themselves have debated possible common ground. The international interest in delineating principles of journalism ethics was evident in consultative meetings from 1978 to 1983 under the auspices of UNESCO. The meetings included international organizations of journalists as well as regional organizations from Latin America, the Arab world, Africa and Asia. The meetings culminated in a statement of "International Principles of Professional Ethics in Journalism" (1988). The statement was aimed at expressing common ground and inspiring the development of national and regional ethics codes. Among the 10 principles were social responsibility, professional integrity, public access and participation, respect for universal values and cultural diversity, and—more controversially—promotion of a new world information order.

Descriptive studies of common values in media ethics, particularly values expressed in codes, have shed additional light on what journalists may regard as shared notions of ethics—at least in the ideal. Bertrand (2000) has argued:

> Media values are largely the same in all regions of the globe where the regime is democratic. Media ethics is founded on universal values, like the refusal of hatred, of violence, of the contempt for human beings (fascism) or just some types of them (racism). (p. 36)

However, he also said that different cultures have different hierarchies of values. Based on study of journalistic codes of ethics, he concluded that the same fundamental rules are found in most ethics codes both because of the influence of cultures where the first codes emerged and because of several decades of international dialogue. Common fundamental values are respect for life and promotion of solidarity among humans. Fundamental prohibitions are not lying, appropriating property, or hurting people needlessly. Journalistic principles include competence, independence, accuracy, and improvement of society.

Cooper's (1989, 1990) studies of international research on ethics codes found that the theme of truth and truthfulness was most dominant, followed by responsibility. Freedom of expression was common but not as dominant as either truth or responsibility. Hafez (2002), who studied codes in Europe, North Africa, the Middle East, and Muslim Asia, found that truth, accuracy, and objectivity were almost universal in professional codes. Most codes studied addressed protection of privacy. Taken together these studies of codes suggest that the values formally expressed by journalists and journalistic organizations do have common ground, particularly around issues of truth.

Both the normative arguments for common or universal values and the descriptions of values commonly expressed in codes have implications for the study of foreign correspondence even though this research has dealt more broadly with journalism. If it is ethically important to seek universal ethical ground (while being sensitive to cultural distinctions), then it is important to research whether foreign correspondents indeed have common ethical values and, if so, to what extent. Surveys, in-depth interviews, and focus groups could all shed light on these questions. It is also critical to examine the actual ethical practices of foreign correspondents and to determine what common values and choices are reflected in those practices. The same methods could also help address these questions, but ethnographic observation—though logistically difficult—would provide important confirmation of what they do in practice versus how they describe their practices. In addition, given the overall commonalities in codes of ethics, it is important to explore through content analysis what commonalities exist with specific relevance to foreign correspondents.

However, it is evident from research already done that while there are commonalities across ethics codes, important differences exist as well. Hafez (2002) found substantial differences in how codes address freedom. Some treated it as a central value limited only if it impinges on other fundamental rights; others treated it as a central value limited because of "political, national, religious, and cultural considerations" (p. 233); still others did not mention freedom at all. France was the only European nation with a code that did not mention freedom. The other European nations with codes that were studied, Finland, Germany, Italy, Norway, Spain, and the United Kingdom, were all in the first category (Hafez).

Differences have also been evident in studies of journalists themselves. Rao and Lee (2005) found that political journalists in Asia and the Middle East agreed on some core values, but they placed less emphasis on truth-telling than one might expect from codes and put priority on respect and the maintenance of community. Willnat and Weaver (2003) did a study that also points to differences in ethical norms. They carried out a survey of foreign correspondents, many of them from Europe, in the United States. Among the issues they examined were the correspondents' perspectives on the acceptability of controversial reporting practices such as getting hired in an organization to get inside information, badgering unwilling sources to get stories, paying for confidential information, and breaking a promise of confidentiality. The study found that foreign correspondents held substantially different views on some of these issues than U.S. journalists and that Europeans sometimes differed from other foreign correspondents. Willnat and Weaver said the findings "suggest that there are few universal roles or norms of journalism at this time" (p. 419). That finding seems at odds with the commonalities expressed in codes and argued philosophically by some normative theorists. But much more research needs to be done to explore these differences and the reasons for them through in-depth interviews with correspondents about their ethical values and decisions.

The next section of this chapter looks in depth at the tension among and between local norms in foreign correspondence, journalists' own sense of ethics, and expectations of journalists' news organizations. It specifically addresses the nature of local norms and problematics associated with such norms. In addition, it looks at the first period of cultural assimilation any foreign correspondent goes through and analyzes steps of ethical and professional judgment a foreign correspondent engages into when he or she starts working abroad.

Making Sense of "Local Norms" Applying to Foreign Correspondents

The main question that should be addressed here is the local character of many norms foreign correspondents have to deal with. But what exactly does "local" mean? In the very particular situation of foreign correspondents, local might be very far away from home and, sometimes, rather exotic. One should recall that "exotic" might encompass not only countries and areas located near the tropics, but also ones in another cultural area. The United States might appear very far away from the cultural landmarks of a European journalist. On the other hand, many European customs and "a way of doing things" (including professional standards and specific arrangements between political sources and journalists) might surprise a U.S. journalist when she or he arrives in Paris, London, or Berlin. Even within European borders there are examples of local systems of news production that barely fit with national journalistic traditions. One example of this is the European Union press corps located in Brussels. It is in charge of covering the EU institutions and proposes a very specific set of rules and norms (from very formal to very informal ones) that, because of the multinational-multicultural environment, do not resemble to any national tradition.

These specific local arrangements (foreign press corps or postings) can be, in theoretical terms, considered as social institutions providing journalists with specific sets of rules and norms deeply embedded in daily practices (Baisnée, 2003). They provide individuals with expected social behaviors (social "roles" in the wording of Berger and Luckman, 1989; see also Lagroye, 1997). They offer a set of norms, rules, and beliefs with which newly arrived correspondents will have to deal. Their individual characteristics and their journalistic position (with respect to the media they belong to) might fit or, on the contrary, misfit with the role as it is locally institutionalized. This might provoke moral, professional, and even ethical dilemmas.

Then "local norms" are specific local (in the sense that they are specific to a country, place, or area) arrangements that foreign correspondents discover when they are sent to a foreign country. Several levels of norms and rules might be distinguished. They would occupy a wide spectrum of arrangements from *local journalistic norms* to *local traditions of source-journalist relationships.*

Local journalistic norms can be very institutionalized (such as conditions to obtain an official accreditation or the obligation to join a professional foreign correspondents' association) or very loose and unclear at first (what is the internal and often "silent" hierarchy between correspondents, who are the "examples to be followed," who is the "right person" to ask for some help when you are a complete layman).

Local traditions of source-journalist relationships might use the whole spectrum of norms from the most formal (how to get an accreditation to enter official institutions) to the most informal (what kind of tone is appropriate when directing a question to a prime minister or a head of state). The degree of institutionalization of these norms has to be studied.

From a methodological point this implies that particular attention must be paid to the structure of the working environment of correspondents. Elements such as the degree of institutionalization (press corps, legal accreditation, professional associations, and foreign press clubs) and hierarchies between correspondents (depending on the country or area they come from, including geographical, cultural, and political particularities, proximity, etc.) might give an idea of the context in which foreign correspondents from a specific country or area find themselves when they arrive. This can be investigated through the study of legal documents that regulate the local system of news production for foreign correspondents, observation of interactions between officials and foreign correspondents, and through in-depth interviews with foreign correspondents and with representatives of professional associations, people in charge of accreditation, etc.

Another problem that has to be addressed is the constraints linked with the foreign correspondents' media. The latter might have specific needs and expectations that do not fit with the working environment of journalists (some areas, institutions, individuals might be out of reach) and the "reality" the correspondents discover (which differs heavily from what editors in chief and desk editors think is happening).

This might in some cases provoke in correspondents a deep moral dilemma and real moral suffering. Sometimes, correspondents might decide to give up their own judgments and beliefs just to adapt production to what is awaited "back home." In other situations, they might resist pressures and, thus, be accused of misbehaving and having an unfriendly and egotistical attitude. They might even be accused of not being a "good professional" when articles and news reports they send differ heavily from what is expected. Newsroom expectations might indeed heavily rely on misperceptions or biased understandings based on readings of what peers and competitors are producing about the area, and contacts with national sources. This might end in asking foreign correspondents to report about aspects that appear to them as of minor importance, odd, or even false. In his highly autobiographical novel, Chaillou (2002), former foreign correspondent for TF1, commercial French TV, recalled how he was obliged by his newsroom to report about a so-called "road of fear" in Thailand (a name found by a reporter of a French national daily who wrote about it without being a correspondent in Asia). This road was said to be pretty dangerous because of rebels, and the newsroom thought it would give a very good news report. When Chaillou, doubtful from the beginning, went to report about this road, it appeared to be rather quiet. However, he had to prepare the whole news report in a way so that it fit his news organization's expectations.

Obviously, foreign correspondents do not always end up in these tricky situations where they must give up their ethics and professional judgment. Their ability to escape the tension between the local situation they are involved in and the constraints due to their belonging to a national news organization heavily rely on several factors:

1) The journalist's background and reputation. (Is she or he someone the newsroom acknowledges to be reliable?);
2) His or her newsroom's general attitude toward foreign news. (E.g., is there a permanent and consistent coverage of the area or does coverage rely on a "hot news" definition of foreign news newsworthiness?);
3) The correspondent's professional status. Being a stringer for different media is indeed very different from being a staff correspondent of *The New York Times*, *Le Monde* or the BBC.

The decline of the quality of foreign news has been documented in several countries (Marchetti, 2005). Describing the situation with the U.S. foreign correspondence in Stephen Hess's book (Hess, 1996), Dan Rather shared this insight he heard from one editor:

> "Don't kid yourself; the tendency in American journalism is away from, not toward, increased foreign coverage. Foreign coverage is the most expensive. It requires the most space and the most time because you're dealing with complicated situations which you have to explain a lot. And then there is always somebody around you who says people really don't give a damn about this stuff anyway.... If you have to do something foreign, Dan, for heaven's sake, keep it short, will you?" (p. 6)

The professional status, especially in harsh environments, influences heavily the journalistic daily work as Pedelty (1995) pointed out by distinguishing what he called the "A team" from the "B team" of U.S. correspondents in Panama. Depending on whether U.S. correspondents were stringer or staff journalists and which media they were working, their work and relationships with the local environment and people heavily differed. The "B team" members (stringers) have been much more involved in local life, whereas the "A team" members have been much closer to the diplomats and expatriates' milieu.

In short, foreign correspondents have to be studied both as members of a local community (they have local peers, local interlocutors, local friends and enemies) and as representatives of the media that have a peculiar place within their national media system.

This place does not depend on the type of media. At least, it does not depend solely on the type of media they work for. It has much more to do with the standards and reputation of the media among journalists. Professional references can be found in each and every type of media depending on the national context. Foreign correspondents are the projection in a foreign territory of a national reality both in terms of what is expected from them "at home" and of what is expected of them "here." Depending on what media they represent and in what context they have to work, reciprocal influences of the personal status and of the local working environment might heavily vary. In some places, representing a major U.S. television network might be a real asset. In other situations, it can make correspondents' days harder. In other words, being a French correspondent in London might mean something to British officials while being a French correspondent in Washington might not mean much as In-depth interviews with former French Washington correspondents showed: "Even if you're from *Le Monde*, they [U.S. officials] won't even call you back" (Baisnée, 2003, p. 429).

The next section discusses the phenomenon of media bribery and its relevance to foreign correspondence. Media bribery can be regarded as an illustration of different local norms in journalist-source relationships. This section builds on previous discussions on ethics and professional norms and practices and analyzes these issues from the perspective of global media transparency.

Media Bribery: An International Problem

The issue of deliberate use of primary sources' information for journalistic purposes becomes a real problem when a journalist or an editor receives compensation for usage or direct publication of publicity-generating materials. A special case of media bribery has been at the center of debates on the nature of publicity materials and media relations practices for a long time (Kruckeberg & Tsetsura, 2003). Offering and paying cash for publishing publicity materials, such as news releases, often becomes a standard practice in many countries, including China (Tsetsura & Lin, 2009), Poland (Tsetsura, 2005), Romania (Tsetsura, 2009), Russia (Tsetsura & Klyueva, in press), and Ukraine (Tsetsura & Grynko, 2009). McGraw (2003) provided examples of how media professionals can discredit themselves by accepting bribes from the information sources. He demonstrated that media bribery has become one of the most difficult problems to overcome.

Media bribery is a truly international problem. Examples of media bribery include publishing fake news releases in Russia (Sutherland, 2001), bribing journalists to put doctors on a popular show in Egypt (Tsetsura, 2006), and putting advertisers' pressures to newsrooms in Ukraine (Tsetsura & Grynko, 2009). A scandal in the United States featured the well-known public relations agency Ketchum and President George W. Bush's administration, when a famous TV commentator Armstrong Williams was paid to actively promote the No Child Left Behind campaign's benefits and advantages (Toppo, 2005). Non-transparent social media practices and unethical blogging are rapidly growing areas of concern. From the infamous scandal with Wal-Mart paid bloggers (Craig, 2007) to the latest efforts of the U.S. Federal Trade Commission to regulate blogger endorsements and product placement in social media (Felten, 2009), research related to new media bribery focuses on examining ethical challenges and concerns in regard to electronic and online media, including social networks and blogosphere.

The first global index of media bribery was published in 2003 by the Institute for Public Relations in the United States. Its authors, Kruckeberg and Tsetsura, decided to focus on a small part of the phenomenon by studying the offerings or demands of cash payments for publishing materials of public relations nature in the ten largest daily newspapers in 66 countries. The objective of the study was to find a way to compare the media bribery phenomenon practiced in different countries and track progress of minimizing this phenomenon over time. After the extensive literature critique and a survey of experts, eight final factors that influence the likelihood of cash for news coverage in a given country were identified:

1) Long-time tradition of self-determination by citizens.
2) Comprehensive corruption laws with effective enforcement.
3) Accountability of government to citizens at all levels.
4) High adult literacy.
5) High liberal and professional education of practicing journalists.
6) Well-established, publicized and enforceable journalism codes of professional ethics.
7) Free press, free speech and free flow of information.
8) High media competition (multiple and competing media).

One more factor, journalists are paid at a professional level, was not in the final list of factors because it was impossible to acquire objective secondary data for this factor. However, the factor was evaluated as important and should be included in the future studies of cash for news coverage and media bribery as soon as the data become available.

The study found a wide range in the likelihood of bribery for news coverage in different countries. Bribery was most likely to occur in China, Saudi

Arabia, Vietnam, Bangladesh, and Pakistan; it was least likely to happen in Finland, Denmark, New Zealand, and Switzerland (Kruckeberg, Tsetsura, & Ovaitt, 2005). Follow-up studies collected primary data on media bribery and media non-transparency in Eastern European countries. Findings indicated that media bribery happened at three levels, interpersonal, intra-organizational, and inter-organizational (Tsetsura & Grynko, 2009). However, no study distinguished how media bribery pressures and challenges can be different for local and foreign correspondents. As of today, none of the studies investigated whether media bribery is perceived differently by foreign correspondents and in what ways foreign correspondents can be influenced by non-transparent media practices, forced to engage in media bribery, or avoid and prevent such practices. Further research, through surveys and in-depth interviewing, is needed to determine just how and why media practices, specifically source-reporter relations, differ from country to country, with a particular emphasis on foreign correspondents.

Recommendations for Future Research

Issues discussed in this chapter are essential for understanding the nature of foreign correspondence. Unfortunately, today many of these issues are understudied and underdeveloped in the mass communication research. Research on ethics in foreign correspondence, assimilation to local norms and practices, the changing nature of news and primary information sources, as well as the role of globalization and the Internet in covering news worldwide has been practically non-existent in the past. Future studies of foreign correspondents should first and foremost employ qualitative methods of data gathering, such as participant observation, in-depth interviews, and focus groups, to describe, understand, and explore the issues and questions of concern for foreign correspondents.

One area of future research should address the issue of foreign correspondents' interaction with public relations practitioners and other information providers. Generators of news, including companies and organizations in the United States, have a long, rich tradition of media relations, which involves relationship building with the media in order to generate publicity. Media relations practitioners have developed tips and recommendations how to communicate not only with local and national media representatives, but also with foreign correspondents (Schoen, 1994). They emphasize the importance of having strong relationships with foreign correspondents and sharing relevant materials with them because it is an opportunity for an organization to get international attention, to build relations with the other country's publics, and "generate visibility throughout the world" (Hoffman, 2004, N. PAG). These media relations practitioners realize that foreign correspondents might have different points of view from local journalists. They also acknowledge that foreign correspondents often rely on assistance of local governments and company representatives to gather news and look for relevant news to present a different angle in their country. It creates a real opportunity for media relations practitioners to share their organizations' points of view because these journalists are "a great source of information about local markets" (Schoen, 1994, p. 14).

But foreign correspondents are still journalists, so the primary sources are very aware that these journalists look for relevant and accurate information that "will interest readers in their home countries" (Schoen, 1994, p. 14). The process of pitching stories to a foreign correspondent happens the same way as it does in relation to any U.S. journalist: public relations practitioners are recommended to know "as much about their [foreign correspondents'] publications or news station as any U.S. media outlet" (Schoen, p. 15).

However, there is little, if anything, written about how foreign correspondents can use publicity-generating materials and interact with media relations practitioners, and what obstacles and potential issues they might encounter as they utilize information from these sources. Future studies of foreign correspondents should specifically address issues of usage of media relations source materials, information access, and the changing nature of gatekeeping in relation to Internet information dissemination. One important area for future study is the relationship between bloggers who write about issues in particular countries and foreign correspondents (MacKinnon, 2008).

Further research, through surveys and in-depth interviewing, is also needed to determine just how and why ethical practices differ from country to country, with a particular emphasis on foreign correspondents. One important area for further research is the place of truth-telling and objectivity in the work of foreign correspondents. The importance of ethical norms in the life of correspondents is perhaps most evident in how they view their role in relation to these ideas. Truth-telling has been widely discussed in scholarly work in the U.S. context (e.g., Christians, 1997; Christians et al., 2009; Klaidman & Beauchamp, 1987; Lambeth, 1992; Patterson & Wilkins, 2008), in addition to being a near-universal feature internationally in ethics codes. However, in practice, truth plays out differently in the different media systems. In a study of the culture of foreign correspondents in El Salvador, Pedelty (1995) stated that the dominance of the notion of objective reporting in U.S. journalism distinguished the American press from what he called the "pluralist presses" of Europe, Latin America, and many other places. "Most of the world's press are comprised of news organs either openly affiliated with political parties or otherwise identified with overt ideological positions," Pedelty argued (p. 169).

Thus, journalists, including foreign correspondents who work out of the U.S. media context versus those who work out of a "pluralist" context from many other countries are likely to apply the principle of truth-telling differently. A foreign correspondent from the United States may seek to tell all sides of a story without overt comment, while a foreign correspondent from France may report more from the standpoint of one political point of view.

Each of these applications of truth-telling has limitations. Pedelty (1995) argued that "objective" reporting by foreign correspondents supported a centrist perspective in which capitalism was a neutral condition, not an ideology. It could also be argued that foreign correspondents reporting in an advocacy mode might obscure understanding of the sides of the story with which they do not agree. Regardless of what view of truth foreign correspondents take, however, it will shape their views of the affairs being reported. Therefore, it is important to explore more broadly how the work of foreign correspondents is specifically informed by their views of truth.

Future research should also address the impact of the acceleration of the news cycle on journalists' ability to report in an ethical manner. A study of Australian war correspondents suggested that the ability to report in real time 24 hours a day, thanks to changes in technology, has actually had a negative impact on accuracy, depth, and context (Anderson, 2009). Accuracy, depth, and context are all important dimensions of truth-telling and therefore central to ethical foreign correspondence. Given the ethical significance of these aspects of journalism, study of the impact of new technology and shifting news practices has important implications for future public understanding of events worldwide.

References

Anderson, F. (2009). "Mosquitoes dancing on the surface of the pond." *Journalism Practice, 3*, 404–420.

Baisnée O. (2003), La production de l'actualité communautaire (Production of actual communication). Unpublished doctoral dissertation. University of Rennes.

Berger, P., & Luckmann, T. (1989). *La construction sociale de la réalité.* Méridiens-Klincksiek.

Bertrand, C.-J. (2000). *Media ethics and accountability systems.* New Brunswick, NJ: Transaction Publishers.

Blumenthal, R. G. (1998). Foreign affairs, family affairs. *Columbia Journalism Review, 36,* 62–64.

Brislin, T. (2004). Empowerment as a universal ethic in global journalism. *Journal of Mass Media Ethics, 19*(2), 130–137.

Chaillou, A. (2002). *La lésion étrangère.* Paris: Alias Etc.

Christians, C. G. (1997).The ethics of being in a communications context. In In C. Christians & M. Traber (Eds.), *Communication ethics and universal values* (pp. 3–23). Thousand Oaks, CA: Sage.

Christians, C. G. (2005). Ethical theory in communications research. *Journalism Studies, 6*(1), 3–14.

Christians, C. G. (2008). Media ethics in education. *Journalism & Communication Monographs, 9*(4), 178–221.

Christians, C. G., Fackler, M., McKee, K. B., Kreshel, P. J., & Woods, R. H., Jr. (2009). *Media ethics: Cases and moral reasoning,* 8th ed. Boston: Allyn & Bacon.

Christians, C. G., & Nordenstreng, K. (2004). Social responsibility worldwide. *Journal of Mass Media Ethics, 19,* 3–28.

Commission on Freedom of the Press (1947). *A Free and Responsible Press.* Chicago: University of Chicago.

Cooper, T. (1989). Global universals: In search of common ground. In T. Cooper (Gen. Ed.), *Communication ethics and global change* (pp. 20–39). White Plains, NY: Longman.

Cooper, T. (1990). Comparative international media ethics. *Journal of Mass Media Ethics, 5,* 3–14.

Craig, D. A. (2007). The case: Wal-Mart public relations in the blogosphere. *Journal of Mass Media Ethics, 22,* 215–128.

Economist (2004, January 24). Members only. *The Economist, 370*(8359), 38–39.

Elliott, D. (1997). Universal values and moral development theories. In C. Christians & M. Traber (Eds.), *Communication ethics and universal values* (pp. 68–83). Thousand Oaks, CA: Sage.

Felten, E. (2009, October 9). Taste—de gustibus: Save us from the swag-takers. *The Wall Street Journal.* W13.

Fleishman, J. (2004, Summer). Developing word pictures to inform a complex story. *Nieman Reports,* 52–53.

Hafez, K. (2002). Journalism ethics revisited: A comparison of ethics codes in Europe, North Africa, the Middle East, and Muslim Asia. *Political Communication, 19,* 225–250.

Hess, S. (1996). *International news and foreign correspondents.* Washington, DC: Brookings.

Herrscher, R. (2002). A universal code of journalism ethics: Problems, limitations, and proposals. *Journal of Mass Media Ethics, 17,* 277–289.

Hoffman, L. (2004, March). International PR. *Adweek Magazines' Technology Marketing,* N. PAG.

Jonas, H. (1984). *The Imperative of Responsibility* [Macht oder Ohnmacht der Subjektivitat? Das Lieb-Seele Problem im Vorfeld des Prinzips Verantwortung]. Chicago: University of Chicago Press.

International principles of professional ethics in journalism, with comments by Kaarle Nordenstreng. (1988) (4th ed.). Prague: International Organization of Journalists.

Klaidman, S., & Beauchamp, T. L. (1987). *The virtuous journalist*. New York: Oxford University Press.

Kovačič, M. P. (2008). Journalism ethics in multinational family: "When in the EU, should one do as the EU journalists do?" *Journal of Mass Media Ethics*, 23, 141–157.

Kruckeberg, D., & Tsetsura, K. (2003). International index of bribery for news coverage: A composite index by country of variables related to the likelihood of the existence of "cash for news coverage." Published report. Institute for Public Relations. Last accessed on March 22, 2006, at: http://www.instituteforpr.com/international.phtml?article_id=bribery_index

Kruckeberg, D., & Tsetsura, K. (2004). International journalism ethics. In A. S. de Beer and J. C. Merrill (Eds.), *Global Journalism* (4th ed., pp. 84–92). Boston: Pearson A & B.

Kruckeberg, D., Tsetsura, K., & Ovaitt, F. (2005). International index of media bribery. In *The Global Corruption Report 2005: Transparency International* (pp. 258–261). London: Pluto Press.

Lagroye, J. (1997). "On ne subit pas son rôle," entretien avec Brigitte Gaïti et Frédéric Sawicki, *Politix, 38*, 7–17.

Lambeth, E. B. (1992). *Committed journalism: An ethic for the profession* (2nd ed.). Bloomington, IN: Indiana University Press.

MacKinnon, R. (2008). Blogs and China correspondence: Lessons about global information flows. *Chinese Journal of Communication 1*(2), 242–257.

Marchetti D. (2005). La fin d'un Monde ? Les transformations du traitement de la "politique étrangère" dans les chaînes de télévision françaises grand public (The end of the Monde? The transformation of a concept of "foreign politics" through French television channels to public). In L. Arnaud & C. Guionnet (Eds.), *Les frontières du politique* (Frontiers of Politics) (pp. 49–77). Rennes, France: Presses Universitaires de Rennes.

McClure, J. (2008). Preliminary findings from the Middleberg/SNCR survey of media in the wired world. *Proceedings from the 2008 Society for New Communication Research Research Symposium*. Last accessed on January 3, 2010 at: http://sncr.org/2008/11/18/symposium-proceedings-2008/

McGraw, M. (2003). Money vs. ethics: A balancing act. IPI Global Journalist, 1st quarter. Last accessed on October 30, 2005 at:http://www.globaljournalist.org/archive/Magazine/money031q.htm

Media myths and realities: 2008 media usage survey (2009). Ketchum and USC Annenberg Strategic Communication and Public Relations Center. Last accessed on January 3, 2010 at: http://annenberg.usc.edu/CentersandPrograms/ResearchCenters/SCPRC/MediaMyths.aspx

Merrill, J. C. (1996). *Existential journalism*. Ames, IA: Iowa State University Press.

Patterson, P., & Wilkins, L. (2008). *Media ethics: Issues and cases*, 6th ed. New York: McGraw-Hill.

Pedelty, M. (1995). *War stories: The culture of foreign correspondents*. New York: Routledge.

Pedelty, M. (1997). The marginal majority: Women war correspondents in the Salvadorian Press Corps Association (SPCA). *Critical Studies in Mass Communication, 14*, 49–76.

Perkins, M. (2002). International law and the search for universal principles in ethics. *Journal of Mass Media Ethics, 17*(3), 193–208.

Rampal, K. R. (2002). Global news and information flow. In Y. R. Kamalipour (Ed.), *Global communication* (pp. 97–119). Belmont, CA: Wadsworth.

Rao, S., & Lee, S. T. (2005). Globalizing media ethics? An assessment of universal ethics among international political journalists. *Journal of Mass Media Ethics, 20*(2&3), 99–120.

Rao, S., & Wasserman, H. (2007). Global media ethics revisited: A postcolonial critique. *Global Media and Communication, 3*(1), 29–50.

Schoen, L. (1994). News coverage overseas begins at home. *Public Relations Tactics, 1,* 14–15.

Siebert, F. S., Peterson, T., & Schramm, W. (1956). *Four theories of the press.* Chicago: University of Illinois Press.

Singer, J. (2006). The socially responsible existentialist. *Journalism Studies, 7*, 2–18.

Strentz, H. (2002). Universal ethical standards? *Journal of Mass Media Ethics, 17*, 263–276.

Toppo, G. (2005, January 31). Spellings: "Errors of judgment" made in paying Williams. *USA Today*, 4A.

Tsetsura, K. (2005). International media transparency experiences. In J. Olędzki (Ed.), *Media, reklama i public relations w Polsce: Research Annual* (pp. 83–99). Warsaw, Poland: University of Warsaw.

Tsetsura, K. (2006, April). *International media experiences.* Paper presented at the Public Relations Division of the Central States Communication Association Convention, Indianapolis, IN.

Tsetsura, K. (2009, October). *Media transparency in Romania.* Paper presented at the Romanian Public Relations Week organized by the Romanian PR Association, Bucharest, Romania.

Tsetsura, K., & Grynko, A. (2009). An exploratory study of the media transparency in Ukraine. *Public Relations Journal, 3*(2). Last accessed on December 18, 2009 at: http://www.prsa.org/prjournal/Vol3No2/6D-030205.pdf

Tsetsura, K., & Klyueva, A. (in press). Media relations in the Urals Federal District of Russia: Examination of the non-transparent media practices. *Russian Journal of Communication.*

Ward, S. J. A. (2005). Philosophical foundations for global journalism ethics. *Journal of Mass Media Ethics, 20*(1), 3–21.

Wasserman, H. (2006). Globalized values and postcolonial responses: South African perspectives on normative media ethics. *The International Communication Gazette, 68*(1), 71–91.

Willnat, L., & Weaver, D. (2003). Through their eyes: The work of foreign correspondents in the United States. *Journalism, 4,* 403–422.

Wu, H. D., & Maxwell, H. D. (2004). U.S. foreign correspondents: Changes and continuity at the turn of the century. *Gazette: International Journal for Communication Studies, 66,* 517–532.

CHAPTER 9

The Impact of the Internet on Foreign Correspondents' Work Routines

Rolland Schroeder and Jim Stovall

The Internet and the application of information technologies have caused far-reaching changes within work processes and routines in most industries around the world. The digitalization of value chains and content has created a demand for a strategic change in perspectives within the media and communication industries (Zerdick, A., Picot A., Schrape, K. et al., 2001:18). Procurement, supply, sales, payments and even delivery are increasingly managed online. The higher the Internet penetration in a country, the higher is the number of potential customers using online technologies. In 2006 most European countries accounted for a penetration rate of more than 50 percent of the population (Internet World Stats, 2006). Aside from drastic effects on the economy and business organizations these developments result in radical changes for the employees and their work processes and routines.

Customer Relationship Management (CRM) Systems have automated work routines to a noticeable extent: the customer calling, e.g., an insurance company will be identified by the systems through his caller ID and directly transferred to the responsible associate. Before the contact is established the associate has the necessary files and information on his screen in order to respond to customer needs without a waiting period or a telephone run-around. For all involved parties, customer, business, and employee, modern CRM systems facilitate, speed up and cheapen business processes. It is evident, though, that these systems need much smaller staff then conventional systems. The media and content rich industries are also strongly affected by these developments as content production and publication increasingly turn digital: a journalist for instance will create digital text, photos, audio, or video files. Modern newsroom technology will allow the content publication through content management systems (CMS) via the Internet from practically every place equipped with an Internet access. Idealistically, the production follows the strategy *One Source, all Media*, which means that the journalist creates the content once and then publishes it in a newspaper, for broadcast or online without alterations. Once again, less personal seems to be the logical consequence. The technological progress in the media industry goes along with increasing media convergence activities that challenge journalists and their work routines.

Already in 1999, Carl Shapiro and Hal R. Varian have raised the issue of digital information and the problem that it can be copied at almost no additional costs. The first copy is relatively expensive to produce but copies

Also Shapiro and Varian mention the term *Economics of Attention* (1999:6), stating that information is available ubiquitously and at low prices which created an information overload. In order to keep the information exclusive media worldwide have tried to develop revenue models to lock-in their customers. So far only a few models work effectively, mostly within special interest groups or target audiences such as business journals (e.g. *Financial Times*, www.ft.com; *Wall Street Journal*, www.wsj.com). These journals offer some content free of charge but require a subscription for full access[1]. Therefore journalist are increasingly in demand of exclusive content which should put an emphasis on investigative journalism. As no surveys have been conducted on this topic there is a clear research need to state if the information overload has led to an augmentation of investigative journalistic products.

How can these sometimes radical changes be described? Which effects have they had on content production or research behaviors? Manuel Castells (2000) referred to the new economy as "informational, global and networked" (77) and underlined that a crucial determinant for productivity and competitiveness would be the efficient application of knowledge-based information (77). Aside from describing the effects on a global economy Castells also focused on how the factor *work* is affected by a network economy. He classified employees by their access to networked information and simultaneously attributed them their capacity within decision-making processes:

- the *networkers*, who set up connections on their initiative (for example, joint engineering with order departments or companies), and navigate the routes of the network enterprise;
- the *networked*, worker who are on-line but without deciding when, how, why, or with whom;

---

1   For versioning stategies, see Shapiro and Varian (1999). pp. 53–83

- the *switched-off* workers, tied to their own specific tasks, defined by non-interactive, one-way instructions (260)

Applying these categories to the example of the CRM system of an insurance would determine the employee as networked. The work processes of journalists, however, can include two levels of decision-making processes: (a) *networked*: the production routines are defined and predetermined by the structures of the content management system not allowing the journalist to apply individual methods and (b) *networker*: in order to research, communicate, write, and select a news story the journalist clearly connects to his network on his own initiative. Having stated this the journalist's role within the decision making process of his company must be declared as crucial and decisive and must be therefore subject to detailed research. Some studies have been conducted in the past years and all come to the conclusion that the Internet and online communication has drastically changed the journalist's work routines. Most recently, Keel and Bernet (2005) analyzed the Swiss-German journalist community from all media genres. An interesting result was that journalists create a hierarchy of credibility: most importantly, they trust websites of public administration units, universities, news portals and NGOs. In 2002, a follow-up study conducted by *news aktuell* in Germany from a first study in 2000 stated as an advantage that information and research opportunities are available 24 hours a day, but the evaluation of credibility and trust of online information still represents the biggest deficiency. On the other hand, the usage of internet tools has remarkably increased between 2000 and 2002 (7). The Harvard Business School published in 2000 the study "USA Today: Pursuing the Network Strategy" and revised it in 2005. The authors focused more on organizational and convergence issues than on work processes. The Dutch scholar Mark Deuze presented several articles in the field: "Journalism and the Web" in 1999, "Understanding the Impact of the Internet (2001), "What Is Multimedia Journalism?" (2004) and "Liquid Journalism" (2006). Combined, these articles offer an interesting timeline of the development of online media and the consequences for online journalism as an organizational issue. The challenges that journalists are exposed are mentioned but not in the focus of these articles. In 2003, Alan Knight published the article "Globalised Journalism in the Internet Age," presenting a selection of articles, books and studies about how the Internet influences information flows through new technologies. John Herbert observed the emergence of digital journalism in the 2000 in his book *Journal-*

ism in the Digital Age and built categories of work tasks for print and broadcast journalists concerning the online publication of content with a focus on Computer Assisted Reporting (CAR). He also refers to media convergence at this early stage as a driving force in the media industry that changes work routines for journalists (14–15). Finally, one of the first scholars structurally researching the interface between journalism and new media technologies was John Pavlik in 2000. In his article "The Impact of Technology on Journalism" he described recent developments and proposed

> "that technological change influences journalists in at least four ways. Technological change affects: (1) the way journalists do their job; (2) the nature of news content; (3) the structure and organization of the newsroom; and (4) the nature of the relationship between and among news organizations." (230)

Pavlik concludes with a research agenda (236–237), including the usage of feedback in the online arena, how e-mails transform the relationship between reporters and their audience, the question if the blurring from journalistic content and advertisements jeopardizes the credibility, if news narratives on the Internet differ from those in conventional media, if the globalization of content and its availability worldwide changes media reception habits in cultures where international news play a marginal role (such as the US), which business models will be developed to support online journalism and the role of journalists in a media system where citizens can gather information directly from original sources online.

In order to structure the above mentioned material from the view-point of journalistic work routine we propose this classification that needs further investigation:

1) The Internet as a mean of Information and Transaction
2) The Internet as a mean of Communication
3) The Internet as a mean of Production

Foreign Correspondents

This research agenda has only partly been addressed within the international research community as the above listed results show. The focus has clearly been set on organizational and content levels rather than the employees within these organizations. Therefore, the research need in the field of the internet and the direct influence on journalists can be stated. As a first step, an empirical study has been conducted at the Erich Brost Institute for International Journalism[2] in 2006 with an explorative outlook on German correspondents in the United States to define their work environment, their work agendas, their relations and communication towards their home news rooms and the availability of sources. Fifteen correspondents from major German media (Public Service and Commercial Television and Radio, Newspapers, Magazines) have been personally interviewed with semi-structured qualitative interviews at their offices in Washington, D.C. Each interview took about 45 to 60 minutes. One question was directly related to the influence of the Internet on their journalistic work. All respondents stated that the Internet had become the predominant communication medium, such as e-mail or VoIP phoning.

Most of the correspondents read at least one national US daily newspaper but use either turn to the websites of other media at least once or twice a day or have subscribed to special news services. In another question the journalists had been asked about the source availability in Washington especially information from the government or other official bodies. Almost all respondents indicated that they use the Internet in this respect quite frequently and often do not bother to participate in a press conference because they will not be able to ask questions. Following the press conference on the Internet provides them with sufficient news. The correspondents also find it helpful that governmental reports are accessible directly on the Internet without any delay so that they do not use printed copies of these documents anymore. As an advantage most respondents claim that a digital version of a report allows easy search features to find relevant parts of the document quicker.

The correspondents also use websites to find new topics for their work and use them as an inspiration. A few of them even turn to weblogs, communities and forums to find out what is being discussed in the Internet community and where news might develop. As a disadvantage they complain about the opacity in this field and the credibility of these sources.

Another problem for correspondents is that the editors at home also have access to most Internet sources and increasingly request topics they found on the news agenda without being part of the American news culture. Especially those correspondents who have spent more that ten years in Washington

---

2   A special thanks to Sonja Stamm who conducted and transcribed the interviews in Washington, D.C.

claim that this recent development demands more justification for their work than ten years ago. They also mention the time difference as problem: When the correspondents in Washington get to their offices in the morning the German colleagues are already six hours ahead and sometimes better informed about news developments in the US than the correspondent corps. The selection criteria have changed through the Internet: Correspondents in foreign news cultures used to have the function of translating news developments from one culture to the other. The global accessibility of news on the Internet have created the demand of finding news niches and more detailed research for foreign correspondents.

In conclusion, the empirical study proves a significant influence of the Internet on journalistic work routines within the segment of foreign correspondence. There is a clear research need to further investigate this phenomenon for a broader view on journalism including topics such as citizen journalism, participatory journalism, user-generated content and related fields. Also media convergence as a part of new media journalism will change journalistic work routines at a decisive extent. As the process is still in motion research will have to gradually start within well-defined segments.

References

Castels, M. (2000). *The Rise of the Network Society, 2nd edition.* Malden, MA: Blackwell Publishing.

Deuze, M. (2006). Liquid Journalism. *International Communication Association & American Political Science Association*, Vol. 16, Nr. 1.

Deuze, M. (2004). What Is Multimedia Journalism? *Journalism Studies*, Vol. 5, Nr. 2, 139–152

Deuze, M. (2001). Understanding the Impact of the Internet: On New Media Professionalism, Mindsets and Buzzwords. *e-journalist,* 01-01, 1–20.

Deuze, Mark (1999). Journalism and the Web. An Analysis of Skills and Standards in an Online Environment. *Gazette*, Vol. 6, Nr. 5, 373–390.

Herbert, J. (2000). *Journalism in the Digital Age: Theory and Practice for Broadcast, Print and On-line Media.* Oxford: Focal Press.

Internet World Stats (2006). Top 32 Countries with the Highest Internet Penetration Rate. Retrieved October 14, 2006 from http://www.internetworldstats.com/top25.htm

Keel, G. & Bernet, M. (2005). *Journalisten im Internet 2005. Eine Befragung von Deutschschweizer Medienschaffenden zum beruflichen Umgang mit dem Internet.* Retrieved October 14, 2006 from http://www.iam.zhwin.ch/download/Studie_2005.pdf# search=%22journalisten%20im%20internet%202005%22

Knight, A. (2003). Globalised Journalism in the Internet Age. *e-journalist*, 03-02, 2003, 1–15.

news aktuell (2002). *media studie 2002 Journalisten online—die Folgestudie*. Retrieved October 14, 2006 from http://www.newsaktuell.de/de/download/ms2002-d.pdf#search=%22media%20studie%202002%22

Pavlik, J. (2000). The Impact of Technology on Journalism. *Journalism Studies*, Vol. 1, Nr. 2, 229–237.

Shapiro, Carl & Varian, Hal R. (1999). *Information Rules. A Strategic Guide to the Network Economy*. Boston, MA: Harvard Business School Press.

Tushman, M. & Roberts, M.J. (2005). *USA TODAY: Pursuing the Network Strategy*. Boston, MA: Harvard Business School Press.

Zerdick, Axel, Picot, Arnold, Schrape, K., et al. (2001). *Die Internet-Ökonomie. Strategien für die digitale Wirtschaft* (Rev. ed.). Berlin: Springer.

Major Turning Points in the Field of Foreign Correspondence Based on Technological Development

Communication Technology
Postal Service
Signal Telegraphy
Electromagnetic Telegraphy (Morse)
News Agency Organization
Telephone Land-Based
Telephone Overseas
Radio Transmission
Picture Electromagnetic Transmission
Telex
Film Distribution News Reels
TV-Introduction
TV News Agency Organization
International News Pool Organizations (e.g., Eurovision)
Satellite Telephony
Transportable Satellite Uplink Technology
Mobile Telephony GSM
Mobile Multiband Telephony
Internet Distribution
Digital Compression Technology
Video Broadband Internet-Based Distribution

Changes in Media Organizations and Media Structures

Economic & Cultural Highlights of Change
International Stock Exchange Trading
Military Conflicts
World War I
International Entertainment Industry (Star System)
Illustrated Weeklies (*Berliner Illustrirte Zeitung, Münchener Illustrierte Presse, Saturday Evening Post, Life*)
International Sport Events (Olympics, Championships)
Branding of International Consumer Products
International Automobile Industry (Racing Formulae)
International Air Traffic
World War II
International "Branded" Personalities (International Dedicated Press Offices)
TV Entertainment
International Comics Culture

NOTES ON CONTRIBUTORS

Benjamin J. Bates, Ph.D., is a Professor at the School of Journalism & Electronic Media of the University of Tennessee. He was the inaugural Sir David Beattie/Ericsson Professorial Research Fellow at Victoria University of Wellington (NZ), and has served as visiting faculty at the University of Salzburg (AT), University of Tampere (FI), the University of Helsinki (FI), and the Chinese University of Hong Kong. His research focuses on media and information economics and policy, and their application to studying the evolution of media and information systems. Bates earned his Ph.D. from the University of Michigan (1986), and has degrees from the University of Wisconsin, Stevens Point (M.A., Communication, 1981), the University of Wisconsin, Madison (M.S. Statistics, 1978), and Pomona College (B.A, Economics and Mathematics). He has authored over forty book chapters and journal articles. E-mail: bjbates@utk.edu

Olivier Baisnée, Ph.D., is Associate Professor of political science at the Institut d'Etudes politiques of Toulouse, France. He is a member of the LaSSP (Laboratoire des sciences sociales du politique) and responsible for a Master program in journalism. His researches focus on political communication, journalism and EU, and international news. He recently published in *Ethnography* and the *European Journal of Communication,* and in various edited book collections. obaisnee@club-internet.fr

Ralph Beliveau, PhD, is an Assistant Professor at the Gaylord College of Journalism and Mass Communication, the University of Oklahoma, USA. E-mail: beliveau@ou.edu

Meta G. Carstarphen, Ph.D., APR, is Associate Professor and the first Gaylord Family Professor at the University of Oklahoma. A former Poynter research fellow and Gaylord College associate dean, her scholarly writing focuses on topics exploring race, rhetoric, gender, diversity and the intersection of culture with media. Her publications comprise numerous journal articles, chapters and books, including *Sexual Rhetoric: Media Perspectives on Sexuality, Gender and Identity*, and *Writing PR: A Multimedia Approach.* Her current research explores the influence of American Indian and African American newspapers on Oklahoma's cultural history. E-mail: mcarstarphen@ou.edu

Mihai Coman is the Founding Dean of the School of Journalism and Communication Sciences at the University of Bucharest, Romania. He is the author/co-author of thirteen books and countless scholarly and journalistic articles published in Romania and throughout the world. He has lectured and presented papers in Europe, Asia, North Africa and the U.S.A., won numerous awards, was twice a Fulbright Scholar. His research interests are in media anthropology; cultural anthropology (myth, ritual, religion, anthropology of modernity); media studies (sociology of the journalists, reception studies); and media and post-communist transition. E-mail: mcoman53@yahoo.com

David Craig, Ph.D., is Associate Professor and Associate Dean for academic affairs in the Gaylord College of Journalism and Mass Communication at the University of Oklahoma. He teaches journalism ethics, editing and graduate research courses. He is the author of *The Ethics of the Story: Using Narrative Techniques Responsibly in Journalism* (2006) and is completing a book about standards of excellence in online journalism. His research interests include the ethics of journalistic language, excellence in journalistic practice, coverage of ethics in professions and values for ethical decision-making. Craig worked for nine years as a news copy editor at the *Lexington* (Ky.) *Herald-Leader*. He earned a B.S. in journalism from Northwestern University, an M.A. in communication from Wheaton College and a Ph.D. in journalism from the University of Missouri-Columbia. He taught editing courses at Northwestern and Missouri. He has been a professor at Oklahoma since 1996. E-mail: dcraig@ou.edu

Dave Ferman is a Ph.D. student at the Gaylord College of Journalism and Mass Communication at the University of Oklahoma. He received his master's in journalism at Texas Christian University in 2007. He is the author of *Journalism in Ireland—How Two Irish Newspapers Covered the 1960 Presidential Election of John F. Kennedy*, which was published in 2007; his work has also appeared in the *Southwestern Mass Communication Journal* and *Journalism Studies*. He has worked as a reporter, feature writer and music critic for several Texas newspapers, including *The Dallas Morning News* and the *Fort Worth Star-Telegram*.

Peter Gade, is the journalism area head and a Gaylord Family Endowed Professor in the College of Journalism and Mass Communication at the University of Oklahoma. Before entering the academy, he worked for midsize newspapers in New York state in a variety of news-editorial tasks (bureau chief, assignment editor, reporter). His Ph.D. is from the University of Missouri School of Journalism. Gade's research explores the normative values of journalism and their relation to organizational change and management in the newspaper industry. He is a co-author of *Twilight of Press Freedom*, a philosophical and historical analysis of public journalism in relation to Enlightenment liberalism, published in 2001. His research has appeared in *Journalism & Communication Monographs, Journalism & Mass Communication Quarterly* and *Newspaper Research Journal.* He has won research awards from the Media Management & Economics and the Newspaper divisions of the Association for Education in Journalism and Mass Communication. He has also worked as a newsroom organizational consultant for the *St. Louis Post-Dispatch* and several newspapers in Oklahoma. E-mail: pgade@ou.edu

Peter Gross, Ph.D., is Director of the School of Journalism and Electronic Media at the University of Tennessee and a Professor specializing in international communication, with a particular focus on East-Central Europe. The author/co-author of eight books and dozens of scholarly articles published in the U.S.A. and Europe, he was instrumental in establishing a new journalism program at the University of Timisoara West, Romania, and was the workshop leader and administrator of training programs for foreign journalists in the U.S. and in East-Central Europe for the last 20 years at California State University-Chico, The University of Oklahoma, and The University of Tennessee, including for the U.S. State Department's Edward R. Murrow program. He was a Research Fellow at the Woodrow Wilson Center for International Scholars and has won numerous research grants and other awards, including one from the Joan Shorenstein Center for Press and Politics, Harvard University. He taught at universities in China, Hungary, Romania and Spain. E-mail: pgross@utk.edu

Oliver Hahn, PhD, is a Professor of Journalism and a Vice-Dean in the Department of Communication and Media Studies at the Business and Information Technology School (BiTS), University of Applied Sciences, Iserlohn, Germany. E-mail: oliver.hahn@udo.edu

Guido Ipsen, PhD, is a Lecturer for Communication, Linguistics, and Semiotics at the Universities of Wuppertal and Südwestfalen, Germany, and a Guest Professor for Semiotics of the Finnish Network University for Semiotics Imatra, Helsinki, Finland. E-mail: guido.ipsen@uni-dortmund.de

Gerd G. Kopper, Ph.D., is a fellow of the Japan Society for the Promotion of Science (JSPS) and served as Visiting Scholar of Waseda University, Tokyo, Japan. From 1978 to 2006 he had been chair for policy, economics and the law of mass media at the Journalism Institute of the University of Dortmund. He initiated and directed the first Centre for Advanced Study in International Journalism (CAS) in Europe at Dortmund, sponsored by the nonprofit Erich-Brost-Institute in 1991. He served as chairman of a number of large-scale international research projects in communication science. Kopper graduated from Indiana University, Bloomington, Ind. (M.A. 1965) and took a degree of Dr.phil. of the Free University of Berlin (1967). He worked as a journalist, editor, foreign correspondent (Japan), permanent consultant (OECD, Paris), and had been head of R&D of one leading German media company before entering a university career. He is author and editor of more than twenty-five books and numerous articles in fields of his expertise and served as counselor on a number of government committees in his country and in Europe. gerd.kopper@udo.edu

Julia Lönnendonker is research fellow at the Center for Advanced Study in International Journalism (Erich Brost Institute) and lecturer at the Department of Journalism at the University of Dortmund, Germany. E-mail: julia.loennendonker@udo.edu

Roland Schroeder, Ph.D., is Professor for media management at BiTS University of Applied Science in Iserlohn, Germany. He has worked on several international research projects investigating international communication processes. Together with Julia Lönnendonker and Oliver Hahn he has edited a book on *German Foreign Correspondents*. He is also Dean of the Media & Communication School at BiTS. E-mail: roland.schroeder@udo.ed

Charles C. Self, Ph.D., is Edward L and Thelma Gaylord Chair of Journalism and Mass Communication and Professor at The University of Oklahoma and Director of the Institute for Research and Training. He has been President of the Association for Education in Journalism and Mass Communication, the Council of Communication Associations, the Association of Schools of Journalism and Mass Communication, and the Southwest Education Council for Journalism and Mass Communication. Research interests include International Communication, Communication and Democracy, Journalism Skills, Media Technology and Society, and Communication Theory and Philosophy. He was Founding Dean of the Gaylord College at OU, Associate Dean of the College of Liberal Arts and Head of Journalism at Texas A&M University, and Chair of Journalism at the University of Alabama. He also taught journalism at the University of Iowa and the University of Missouri. He was Founding Editor of *The Journal of Communication Inquiry* and has authored dozens of articles and book reviews. He has conducted research about journalism and communication policy around the world and is currently completing the first-ever census of journalism education programs worldwide for the World Journalism Education Council under a grant from the Knight Foundation. E-mail: cself@ou.edu

James Stovall, Ph.D., is Edward J. Meeman Distinguished Professor in the School of Journalism and Electronic Media at the University of Tennessee. He has previously taught at the University of Alabama and Emory & Henry College and is the author of several books in journalism including *Writing for the Mass Media* and *Web Journalism: Practice and Promise of a New Medium*. He was instrumental in launching the student news website, tnjn.com, at the University of Tennessee and the initiator of the Intercollegiate Online News Network (ICONN), which has dozens of American university news networks as members. E-mail: stovall@out.edu

Katerina Tsetsura, Ph.D., is a Senior Assistant Professor of strategic communication/public relations in the Gaylord College of Journalism and Mass Communication at the University of Oklahoma (USA). Her interests include international and global strategic communication, global media and public relations ethics, and public affairs, and issues management in countries with transitional economies. Her research appeared in internationally recognized books (such as the *Handbook of Global Public Relations* and Merrill's *Global Journalism*), annuals (e.g., *The Global Corruption Report 2005: Transparency International* and *Public Relations across Borders: Research Annual*), journals (e.g., *Journal of Public Relations Research, Public Relations Journal, Public Relations Review, Asian Communication Research,* and *Russian Journal of Communication*), and online research centers (e.g., Institute for Public Relations) published on three continents. Dr. Tsetsura also presented papers at the numerous research and professional communication conferences around the world, including Germany, Mexico, Poland, Russia, U.A.E., the U.K., Ukraine, and the U.S.A. As one of the two leading researchers of the landmark Global Media Transparency project, supported by the Institute for Public Relations (USA), the International Public Relations Association, the International Federation of Journalists, and the International Press Institute, Dr. Tsetsura is currently collecting the data on media practices in the USA and around the world for a forthcoming book, *Truth and*

Global Media Transparency (together with Dr. Dean Kruckeberg, University of North Carolina-Charlotte). An active public relations professional, Dr. Tsetsura continues to provide strategic counseling to agencies, companies, and organizations in North American and Eastern European countries in the areas of strategic planning, environmental and public scanning, issue monitoring, and crisis management. E-mail: tsetsura@ou.edu

Index